Cuba As Never Before
Cuba Como Nunca
2016

CUBA
AS NEVER BEFORE

Cuba Como Nunca

2016

The Absolutely, Positively Up-to-the-Minute Indispensable Guide to Cuba

Edited by Louis E.V. Nevaer

Cuba As Never Before / Cuba Como Nunca

Although the author and publisher have made every good faith effort to ensure the accuracy and completeness of information contained in this book, we assume no responsibility for errors, inaccuracies, omissions, or inconsistencies herein.

This book is published by Hispanic Economics, Inc., and is strictly intended for educational and informational purposes. It expresses the personal opinions, conclusions, and recommendations of the author and contributors and does not necessarily reflect the opinions, conclusions, or recommendations of the publisher. No liability is assumed for damages resulting from the use of information contained herein.

This book will be updated annually, and subsequent editions will reflect corrections, updates, and changes in the opinions, conclusions, and recommendations for firms offering goods and services to the public. The book is also available as an electronic book at Amazon.com.

Publication date: October 2015.

Published by Ediciones del Mayab
Calle 59 #572 x 72 & 74
Mérida, Yucatán, México
edicionesdelmayab@gmail.com

ISBN: 978-1-939879-05-9

Cover and Interior Design by John Clifton
john@johnclifton.net

COMPLETE QUICK FIND

Granma Province..71
Guantánamo...71
Matanzas Province...71
Santiago de Cuba...71
Havanautos Car Rental Locations...72
Havana Airport..72
Old Havana..72
Vedado..73
Havana Centro...73
Miramar...73
East Beaches and Varadero...74
Jibacoa...75
Jardines del Rey/Cayo Coco...75
Holguín..75
Villa Clara Province...76
Sancti Spíritus/Trinidad..76
Camaguey Province...76
Cienfuegos...77
Las Tunas...77
Pinar del Río..77
Viñales...78
Granma Province...78
Guantánamo...78
Matanzas Province...78
Santiago de Cuba...78
Rex Car Rental Locations...79
Havana Airport..79
Old Havana..79
Vedado..80
Miramar...80
East Beaches and Varadero...80
Jardines del Rey/Cayo Coco...80
Holguín..81
Villa Clara Province...81
Camaguey Province...81
Cienfuegos...81
Pinar del Río..81
Ciego de Ávila Province...82
Santiago de Cuba...82
Vía Car Rental Locations...82
Havana Airport..82

EDITOR'S NOTE

On July 20, 2015, Cuba and the United States resumed diplomatic relations.

This ended more than fifty-four years of a diplomatic impasse that created a conflict between the two neighbors. The opening of embassies in Havana and Washington, D.C., however, does not mean things are back to normal.

The U.S. embargo still stands. Travel restrictions, although more accommodating, are still in effect. There is a long way to go.

Diplomatic negotiations are now under way that will lead to reconciliation as the Cuban, American, and Cuban Diaspora come to terms with the unanticipated consequences of revolution.

I am delighted that this is a "go-to" guide to Cuba—one that strives to provide much useful information to a visitor to Cuba. This is its first edition. In subsequent years, as our network of contributors expands, the guide will include comprehensive information on the entire island-nation.

Remember, Cuba is in a state of transition. Private enterprise—"Creeping Capitalism"—is making its way. Every day, a business opens its doors. Every day, another venture closes for good. The establishments listed here have been verified. But there is no guarantee that a room listed in a private home or a favorite *paladar* recommended is still in business. That's the nature of the beginnings of a market economy and economic "ownership."

Consider this an invitation. If you have any information, whether it is a correction or a recommendation, to improve this guide, please send me an e-mail and let me know about it. I want to know about it! And remember, there are hundreds of businesses that were not included. That said, an omission is not to be construed as a negative recommendation!

With that caveat, enjoy this guidebook. May you find it instructive, illuminating, and useful.

Louis E.V. Nevaer

E-mail: *CubaComoNunca@gmail.com*

ACKNOWLEDGMENTS

~~~~~~

This book represents the collaboration, contributions, and opinions of many people. The 2015 edition includes what readers have requested, including a broad guide to AirBNB listings and a Cuban political primer. As Editor, I would like to thank the following for contributing, making suggestions, offering information, or providing material quoted about Havana, which makes this the most comprehensive guide to the new Cuba.

My thanks go to the many contributors, writers, reviewers, and advisers who have enriched this book: Olga Michel, José Martínez Varo, Luis R. Varela, Uva de Aragón, Jacqueline Cervera, Luminito Fernández, Estela Keim, and fourteen Cubans living in Havana who wish to remain anonymous.

The author also wishes to express his debt of gratitude to Christine Valentine for her sage advice every step of the way in this endeavor.

As 2015 drew to a close, Cuba had an estimated 485,000 *cuentapropistas*, or entrepreneurs. These nongovernment workers are quickly transforming Cuba into a nation of cottage industries and shopkeepers. It is the beginning of capitalism and a market economy that have the potential to revive the island's mordant economy.

A New Beginning

INTRODUCTION: THE PROMISE OF A NEW DAY

In July 2015, when Cuba and the United States were preparing to reopen embassies in each other's capitals, the Editor of this guide was asked to report on the state of Havana at this momentous time. Here is the report published July 20, 2015.

In Cuba, "Creeping Capitalism" Arrives

HAVANA—When the U.S. embassy reopened in Havana on Monday after more than 54 years, it signaled what Cubans have now accepted: creeping capitalism is the future.

A stroll through Old Havana is enough to convince anyone that the entrepreneurial spirit that is fast-transforming this city into a nation of shopkeepers is in full swing. This isn't to say that corporate America is about to descend on this island nation of 12 million people. Raúl Castro's reforms place sharp restrictions on capitalism: one can work for one's self, but only the state can hire more than two employees.

For now, this is enough. Capitalism has arrived: families are running small restaurants called *paladares*; people are renting out rooms in their homes to foreign tourists; artists are inviting buyers into their studios and homes; and entrepreneurs are providing goods and services as best they can to all manner of buyers.

Capitalism is creeping in—and there is nothing that the communist regime can do to prevent it. Not that the government wants to stop the changes.

"Our task is to provide assistance to those who are working to make things better," Eusebio Leal, who runs the Office of the City Historian, said as he discussed the restoration of Old Havana—declared a World Heritage Site by UNESCO in 1982 and being restored with funds provided by the international community, primarily the European Union. Along with Patricia Rodríguez, who is in charge of the Master Plan for the Integral Restoration of Old Havana, officials have encouraged entrepreneurs to forge ahead.

They are—ever since the December 2014 announcement by the White House that it would normalize diplomatic relations—opening restaurants, gift shops, tattoo parlors, and spa centers. "Right now there is a boom in the private initiative in the area [of Old Havana], and it is good that it's like this," Rodríguez told Spain's *El País*.

As of July, there are almost 100 independent restaurants and bars in Havana—and almost 2,000 listings on AirBNB.

The excitement of the promise of being in on the ground floor is something that is attracting foreigners as well, particularly Spaniards and Mexicans.

Andrés Buenfil, a Mexican living in Havana, opened the first Mexican restaurant—El Chile Habanero—in a district that caters primarily to Cubans, not tourists.

"We Mexicans are very attached to our cuisine and, wherever we travel to in the world, we always try and seek out places that serve our favorite dishes," he told *Havana Times*.

When asked how it's going, he expressed delight: "Business is better than I had anticipated—and government officials have been only encouraging."

The nature of creeping capitalism, however, is different in Cuba. Unlike Mexico, which, after the implementation of NAFTA in 1994, quickly became a nation obsessed with American franchises, the lack of capital in Cuba makes that possibility less likely.

In Mexico, McDonald's, Starbucks, Walmart, and Costo seem to be everywhere.

In Cuba, on the other hand, by keeping multinationals out, there could be an opportunity for an organic, sustainable capitalism that may be healthier for the local economy.

Within the next years there will be a dozen or so new coffee shops throughout Old Havana joining the ones now open—making Starbucks unnecessary.

This possibility is not wishful thinking, but very likely because of the nature of U.S.–Cuba relations: While full diplomatic relations have been reestablished, only the U.S. Congress can lift the embargo, and currency controls remain in place. And Republicans are vowing to keep the punitive embargo in place.

That's why neither McDonald's nor Starbucks will be able to set up business in Havana in the near future.

The good news? The absence of multinationals allows individual entrepreneurs the opportunity to set up shop and flourish. Buenfil, who runs the Mexican restaurant, laughs at the prospect that Taco Bell could be competition anytime soon. "I'm going to spoil Cubans into knowing what good Mexican food is, so if Taco Bell ever shows up, the only ones interested in them would be American tourists," he said.

If what is happening in Havana is a "softer, kinder" form of capitalism, then it is in keeping with current thinking.

Pope Francis, two years ago, began to speak out against "savage capitalism," a message he reinforced on his recent pilgrimage to South America where he called for a new world order.

But whether this kind of "humanistic" capitalism can be sustainable remains to be seen.

—New America Media, News Analysis

2 THE CUBANS

~~~~~~

About the Cubans you will meet . . .

Cuban Cubans versus Exile Cubans

Cuban Cubans

Cuba is a closed society. Cubans have little opportunity to travel, and they have limited access to the outside world. When you visit Cuba you will encounter people who are oddities in the world today.

Consider what this means. The Cubans have never bought anything on Amazon. They have never seen a McDonald's. They have never shopped at well-stocked department stores. They have never taken their children shopping for pastimes at a toy store. They cannot reasonably expect to take their kids to Disney World. Yes, they can read and write, but they can neither go to a library to read any book they want, nor can they write a letter to the editor and openly declare an opinion that runs counter to the government's position on an issue.

The Cubans are also a people who live lives of material deprivation. They, in a very real sense, punished for no reason; they are denied the fundamental right to take ownership of their own lives and their futures.

It's easy for visitors to forget how isolated Cubans are from the modern world.

It's important to sympathize and show empathy for their situation. It's also important to be open to engaging the Cubans you encounter.

Consider this example. A friend asked me to hand deliver, on a trip to Havana, an envelope with a cash donation to the synagogue in the Vedado district. Cuban Jews have suffered terribly under the Revolution and have relied on assistance from Mexican Jews over the decades. Once in a while, American Jews send aid.

As I walked toward Víctor Hugo Park, I noticed an older woman filling two buckets of water in the small yard in front of her building. When I greeted her, she said, "Good morning." I asked her why she was filling the blue pails with water. She told me that she lived in a third floor walk-up and that her plumbing had broken sometime in 1998. This was in 2012. Her morning ritual consisted of taking two buckets of water each morning to her apartment. One she used to flush the toilet at the end of the day. The other she used for cooking and drinking.

I offered to help her. She accepted. After we walked up to her apartment, we sat down and talked. She was embarrassed by her circumstances, but proud.

"This is my country," she told me. "And this is my destiny. Besides, I have no family overseas."

We talked and at the end of the visit, I told her I wanted to help her out. She shook her head, but when I handed her some money, she grasped the bills in her fist.

I opened my backpack and offered to give her some things I had. I had two Bic disposable razors and two lollipops. She told me the razors were worth their weight in gold; she could barter them for something she could really use. With the money she would buy whatever protein she could. And the lollipops, well, those were a treat.

She thanked me for my kindness. I went on my way. The Jews in need a few blocks away awaited my friend's donation. But the encounter with this woman was the highlight of my day.

These are the realities of Cubans' lives today.

As a visitor, it is important to remember that Cubans are proud, but they are also in need. They are people for whom a disposable razor is worth its weight in gold and who have long been deprived of something as simple as a piece of candy.

Remember, you have the choice of moving through Cuba as a spectator—from one orchestrated tour to another micromanaged guide—or you can engage the Cubans.

The end of deprivation is, I hope, at hand; as a visitor to Cuba in 2016 you are a witness to history as much in the making as in the unmaking.

Exiled Cubans

In addition to the Cubans who live in Cuba, you may encounter Cubans who are exiled but are visiting Cuba. These can be, generally, divided into two categories: Pre-Mariel Cuban exiles and Post-Mariel Cuban exiles.

Pre-Mariel Cuban exiles are, for the most part, those who lost everything to the Revolution, the ones whose businesses, homes, bank accounts, and personal belongings were seized by the Revolution. These are the Cubans who arrived in the U.S., Mexico, Spain, and other host countries with nothing but their education and drive.

They are back in Cuba to visit relatives, to make peace with the past, and to see for themselves what has become of their homeland. It's a bittersweet journey, one that breaks hearts when they see the ruin Havana has become and when they reflect on their interrupted lives. What might weigh on their minds?

I have seen these Cubans cover their mouths and gasp at the sight of their former homes. I have seen them cry when they see the ruins of their old neighborhoods.

Post-Mariel Cuban exiles, by comparison, have tougher skins. They were born into this regime, lived under this system, and are not sentimental about Cuba. They left after 1980 and are back because they have family, friends—and now perhaps an opportunity.

These Cuban exiles are young enough and savvy enough about how Cuba works, and doesn't work, to have aspirations of making it big and making a fortune as Cuba changes.

It's astounding to see the interactions of these three types of Cubans: those on the island, those on visits of nostalgia, and those who are desperate to start doing business. Add to this mix the Cubans who are part of the government, who are unsure what the future holds and of their place in a Cuba that anticipates the passing of both Fidel and Raúl Castro.

There are many kinds of Cubans—and many opportunities to engage them, which will make your visit that much richer.

The Ethics of "Authentic" Tourism

The explosion in interest of travel to Cuba stems in part from fear: Americans are afraid that Cuba will change and that they will miss out on seeing Cuba in its "authentic" state of being. This is presumably before Starbucks, McDonald's, Coca-Cola, and the rest of corporate America descends on the island.

Rest assured that it will be years and years before these American companies set up shop in Cuba.

The quest for "authenticity," however, raises the question of the ethics of taking a trip to see people who are suffering.

Cuba's people are in need, living in the ruins of what remains of their country. They try to make the best they can of being stuck in a day-to-day struggle for survival. Tens of thousands of Cubans flee their country each year; Cuba has the largest percentage of people over sixty in Latin America and the lowest birthrate. The young risk their lives to escape; the old are resigned to lives of deprivation.

There is authentic suffering, and visitors to Cuba must not cross the line and become voyeurs witnessing the humiliation of this once-great country as mere entertainment—a photo op to upload to Facebook once you return home.

Consider the frustration Cuban teenagers expressed to a reporter for the *New York Times* last summer when asked if he thought that the reestablishment of relations between the U.S. and Cuba meant they would have a better future: "Change? My life won't change," Yunior Rodríguez Soto, 17, told the reporter as he and his friends played basketball at an improvised basketball court, the basket hoop assembled from a piece of bent rebar. "I mean, look how we're living, look how we are playing?"

The reporter wrote: "The ball zipped out of bounds and a friend raced to retrieve it. Change, in his mind, would come in spite of the government, not because of it. 'They won't let it happen,' he said, referring to the Cuban government. 'It's just how they are.'"

For the people you will meet, as the *New York Times* reported, there was "an air of cynicism among the Cuban youth who see the ideals of Fidel Castro's revolution as dated as the battered cars that traverse Havana's streets. Once so integral to life on the island, they are relics of a bygone era, removed from the economic imperatives that are driving the young to flee in record numbers. As much as the young welcome political opening and economic reform, such changes are unlikely to filter down to their lives anytime soon. Measurable change will come slowly, stalled between the leadership's desire for prosperity and its determination to maintain control."*

It is that desire to keep political control that continues to keep Cubans living lives of authentic need and deprivation.

In Cuba, people speak about the despair they feel at their economic misery with irony: "They pretend to pay us and we pretend to work."

Americans romanticize Cuba as a place frozen in time. The truth is that Cubans live in poverty. There is nothing romantic about poverty. Be respectful of the Cuban people's suffering and remember that their diminished circumstances do not exist for your voyeuristic entertainment and amusement.

After all, you get to leave Cuba and go home. The Cubans don't get to leave.

(Excerpted from "Cuban Youth See New Embassy, but Same Old Drab Life," Azam Ahmed, *New York Times*, August 6, 2015.)

Overview of Cuba, Getting There, Hotels, Restaurants, and Car Rentals

3 GENERAL INFORMATION ON CUBA

Do you know the way to Havana? Of course!

What to Pack

When traveling to Cuba, pack as if you were going to Miami or Cancún. In addition, be sure to take everything you will need — from toothpaste and shampoo to over-the-counter medicines and clothing. Many things are difficult to find in Havana. This isn't Miami or Cancún where lobby shops have everything you need and where there are shopping centers a few blocks from your hotel.

In addition, *I strongly recommend taking things to give away to Cubans as gifts*. The Editor of this guide always packs a small suitcase with travel-size toothpaste, toothbrushes, a hundred Bic disposable razors, boxes of Tampax, travel-size bottles of aspirin, antacid medications, bags of hard candy, and travel-size bottles of shampoo, soaps, and deodorants. These things are worth more than money, and waiters, waitresses, tour guides, cabdrivers, hotel staff, and people you encounter on the streets appreciate such items.

In addition, take one hundred $1 bills to tip and give away to folks.

Currency

Four currencies are used in Cuba.

Cuban Peso. This currency is for Cuban citizens. The black market exchange rate is around 24 Cuban pesos for $1 USD. *It is illegal for foreigners to have Cuban pesos in their possession.*

Convertible Peso (CUC). This currency acts as a voucher for the U.S. dollar. One Convertible Peso, or *peso convertible*, known as the CUC, is exchangeable for $1 USD. *It is illegal for foreigners to take Convertible Pesos out of the country; they must all be exchanged for U.S. dollars at the point of departure.*

U.S. Dollar. The U.S. dollar should, technically, be exchanged for the Convertible Peso, but it is the currency of choice among Cubans.

European Euro. The Cuban government officially encourages the euro as the hard currency of choice, and it is widely accepted, but people still prefer the U.S. dollar.

At the airport and throughout Havana look for Cadeca Foreign Exchange offices. This is the official place for all foreign transactions for most visitors. Please note that there is often a long line at the Cadeca Foreign Exchange office at the airport. If you have prepaid transfers to your hotel, it might be best to wait until you get to your hotel. (This is one of the reasons you are advised to have one hundred $1 bills with you — to tip the driver.) Exchange rates are standardized across Cuba; you can change your U.S. dollars or, preferably, euros, at your hotel at the same exchange rate as at a bank or Cadeca Foreign Exchange office.

The Banco Financiero Internacional in Havana's Vedado district will also exchange other foreign currencies—from the Mexican peso to the Japanese yen—but their manner is brusque, and they do not like to deal with the public at large.

U.S. Dollar versus the Euro

Diplomatic relations may have been established, but the Cuban government still taxes exchange rates using U.S. dollars.

How?

The exchange is $1 USD = $1 CUC, but there is 13% tax on the exchange rate. When you hand in $100 USD, you get $87 CUC. You can spend these convertible pesos as you please, and when you leave the country you can trade your leftover CUCs for an equal amount of American dollars, but the tax has already been taken into account.

There is no tax on the euro, however. So, if, for instance, €1 = $1.20 USD, then €100 = $120 USD. Exchange €100 and you will get $120 CUC!

Consider this advice: Take euros with you to Cuba, along with one hundred $1 bills to give as tips to people you will encounter. By taking euros, you avoid the 13% tax on the USD-CUC exchange rate.

Depending on where you live in the United States, you might also consider trading your U.S. dollars for Canadian dollars or Mexican pesos. Neither the Canadian dollar nor the Mexican peso is subject to the 13% tax when exchanged for CUCs.

Travelers Cheques

Most traveler's checks are accepted in Cuba, regardless of the bank that issued them. American Express Travelers Cheques are also accepted.

Bear in mind, however, that:

1. There is a 3% fee for using traveler's checks.
2. If lost or stolen they cannot be replaced in Cuba.
3. You must keep all purchase receipts because there are random checks at the airport when leaving Cuba.
4. Traveler's checks may not be accepted outside Havana.

Wire Transfers

If you run out of cash, one option is to have money wired to you in Havana. There are Western Union offices throughout Cuba. Another option is Caribbean Transfers, which operates out of Canada.

For more information:

Western Union: *www.westernunion.com*
Caribbean Transfers: *www.caribbeantransfers.com*

A Note on Paper Money and Coins

Cuba, like most countries, is firm about mutilated or defaced currency. That means that before you travel to Cuba, make sure that the cash bills you bring are neither stained nor have marks. They must also be free of rips or tears. Paper money that is not clean, crisp, and free of markings will not be accepted.

DO NOT BRING COINS! Coins are worthless, even the $1 dollar coins.

Credit Cards

Credit and debit cards issued by U.S. banks cannot be used in Cuba. Visa and MasterCard credit and debit cards issued by banks in Europe, Canada, Latin America, and Asia can be used.

As the rules are changing, it might be possible to use your MasterCard or Visa in a few places. If you can do so, it would be at the Banco Financiero Internacional, the Banco Metropolitano, the Cadeca Foreign Exchange, and some ATM machines. There is a 3% processing fee on every credit card transaction for cash advances in addition to whatever fee your own bank imposes.

That said, most bank cards issued by U.S. banks will not work. Neither will a bank card issued by a European or Mexican bank if that bank is owned by a U.S. holding company. Be aware that outside Havana there may not be reliable communication links for processing your credit card purchases.

There is also the unexplained phenomenon that many ATM machines swallow Visa cards issued by banks in the U.S. Talk about "lost or stolen" bank cards!

For some reason, *the most reliable ATM machines in Havana are the ones at the Mirarmar Trade Center and the Panorama Hotel*. Use the machines there—and see how lucky you are.

The final recommendation: To be on the safe side, U.S. visitors are advised to bring enough cash to pay for their expenses while in Cuba.

Medicines and Over-the-Counter Medications

Do not plan on being able to buy any toiletries or over-the-counter medications while in Cuba. This includes toothbrushes, toothpaste, dental floss; feminine hygiene products; razors or razor blades; aspirin; insect repellant; suntan lotion; lighters; antidiarrheal medicines, including Pepto-Bismol or Imodium; antacids, including Rolaids or Tums; vitamins; or anything else you regularly purchase at a pharmacy.

Clothing

Pack as if you were going to Miami. Tropical wear should include comfortable shoes, shirts, blouses, and shorts. Women should wear sleeveless cotton dresses and men should pack a couple of long-sleeved shirts. A blazer for men and an evening dress for women are in order. Bring walking pants. Khaki trousers will do just fine. Remember that Havana is a city and, unlike the U.S., in Latin America it is not seen as correct for men to walk around a city in shorts or wear sandals. Do not bring camouflage trousers, since this remains a police state and will draw unwarranted attention. If your plans include nightclubs or fancy restaurants, such as the Tropicana or La Guarida, bring something nice to wear.

Here's one thing you may want to consider: Bring clothes you can give away to Cubans. They need gently-used clothing, and you could use the space in your luggage for souvenirs. Hotel chambermaids are well versed in making sure that whatever article of clothing you donate to them will find someone who is happy to have it.

Weather

Cuba has a subtropical climate. Its location produces a Northern Hemisphere weather pattern. This means the winters are cool and dry. Summers are hot and wet. December through February may be too cold for you to lie on the beach, as is the case in south Florida. During these winter months you may also need a sweater in the evenings. Hurricane season runs June 1 through November 31. Cuba is seldom subject to major hurricanes, but given the erratic weather patterns of recent years, no one knows with certainty.

Below are the average temperatures for Havana throughout the year.

Average Sea Temperature

Jan	Feb	Mar	Apr	May	Jun	Jul	Aug	Sep	Oct	Nov	Dec
23°C	23°C	24°C	26°C	27°C	28°C	28°C	28°C	28°C	27°C	26°C	24°C
73°F	73 °F	75°F	79°F	81°F	82°F	82°F	82°F	82°F	81°F	79°F	75°F

Books and Reading Material

Unless you're interested in a Spanish-language edition of *The Communist Manifesto* in Braille—which I found at a flea market once—there's probably no book or magazine you would want to buy in Cuba. Bring all your reading material with you. You might want to consider bringing books and magazines that you can give away to the Cubans you meet. This is a country desperate for anything that tells them about the outside world. Whether it's an issue of *National Geographic, Cosmopolitan,* or *People Magazine,* it will be very much appreciated.

Where Will I Be Staying, Comrade Immigration Officer?

Only recently have the visa forms changed; the government no longer requires you to write down the name of the hotel where you will be staying. That doesn't mean, however, that upon entry the immigration official will resist asking you where you are staying. Please know the name of the hotel or

AirBNB that you have booked. Immigration officials reserve the right to ask for a booking confirmation to prove your accommodations while in Cuba.

Voltage in Cuba

One of the benefits of the U.S. taking possession of Cuba after the Spanish America War ended? Cuban electricity is 110V, just as it is in the United States, since an American company set up electricity throughout the island. Whether you're charging a cell phone or iPad or planning to use a hair dryer or electric toothbrush, you shouldn't have a problem. Do note that some hotels have 220V and the round sockets. Most hotels have adapters that they will make available to you.

Sports and Miscellaneous

As a general rule, bring anything you will need. This includes batteries, sandals, hats, or nutritional supplements. If you plan on doing any sports, whether it is rock climbing, cycling, surfing, or fishing, bring all your equipment and supplies. If you are generous, you might want to bring equipment you can give or donate, a considerate gesture given the scarcity in Cuba.

Tipping in Cuba

Tipping at restaurants is addressed in the chapter listing where to eat. If a tip is not already included in the bill, it is customary to add 10% to 12% to the bill.

For other instances where tipping is called for, here are general guidelines:

Tour Guides

Tour guides expect to be tipped 2 CUCs per person for groups of five or more. That means if you're taking a tour that consists of 10 people, the guide should be tipped 20 CUCs. For a large group that requires a bus driver, the group should decide how much to tip. Bear in mind that tour guides tend to tell sob stories to American groups, hoping for a handout. If you want to be played, then be aware that you are being played. Do remember, however, that to be a professional tour guide, that person must be a member in good standing with the government authorities; they report back to the government, so watch what you say. NO FIDEL JOKES in mixed Cuban company (Communist Cubans and non-Communist Cubans).

Staff at All-Inclusive Resorts

All-inclusive resorts have a variety of staff tending to visitors' needs. A general guideline is to tip 20–25 CUCs per week. This would be divided among all the staff members that waited on you. If there is a staff person who goes out of his or her way to accommodate a special request—a round of mojitos at 2 AM, for instance—then reach out to that person before departure. Depending on how gracious they

13

were, tips to individual staff members should range from 2 to 5 CUCs. All-inclusive resorts are ideal places for distributing gifts you brought along with you—a bag of lollipops, toiletries, aspirin, boxes of Tampax.

Parking Lot Attendants

Estacionamientos or *parqueos*—parking lots—are vexing. The prices are usually listed in Cuban pesos, which tourists are prohibited from possessing. Chances are the parking lot attendant will do what they often do: charge you 1 CUC, exchange them for Cuban pesos, put the Cuban pesos in the register, and pocket the rest.

Tip the attendant 1 CUC and you can rest assured that nothing will happen to your car under his or her watchful eye.

Toilet Attendants

How much to pay someone to hand you a towel to dry your hands? A few coins in the jar will do, but no more than 50 cents CUC.

Musicians

If you stop to listen to a performance, whether on the street or in a club, the musicians would very much appreciate a tip. On the street, tip 1 CUC per member. This is, after all, the land of egalitarianism. At a nightclub, you may want to tip 2 CUC per member. If the band plays requests for you and your table, hand the leader an extra 1 or 2 CUCs.

Panhandlers

Remember those bags of lollipops I suggested you pack? Walking around Havana, where just about everyone needs something and will come up to you with a hand outstretched, be prepared to hand out a coin here or a coin there. *"Lo siento,"* Spanish for "I'm sorry," is a Spanish phrase you will master during your visit.

The solution?

Hand beggars a small coin and a lollipop (or some other kind of gift). Exercise subtley. On occasion, other kids realized this Editor had a bag of lollipops in my backpack, and I was mobbed by schoolchildren—running out of candy for all the kids who mobbed me.

Online Tourist Resources

What's the best way to find out what's happening? Check out these websites before you go, just to find out about things that are happening in Havana during your stay.

Here are five recommended online resources to check right before you go—and while you're in Cuba.

www.OnCubaMagazine.com
www.CubaAbsolutely.com
www.LaHabana.com
www.Havana-Cultura.com
www.HavanaTimes.org

For information on politics and society, this is a great resource:
www.CubaNet.org

Cuba Junky App

What's the best app for information on Cuba?

Cuba Junky!

Started by Anja Verlaan in the Netherlands, this resource has a tremendous collection of information about Cuba—and it even has an app you can download to book places to stay in private homes, or *particulares*, throughout the island nation.

www.cuba-junky.com

Gay and Lesbians in Cuba

Cuba's government maintains that sexual deviancy of any kind is a capitalist decadence. During the 1980 Mariel Boat Lift gays and lesbians were rounded up and deported as antisocial elements detrimental to the building of socialism.

With this caveat, Calle 23 in the Vedado district is the center of Havana's gay scene. The area between Cinema Yara and the Coppelia ice cream parlor are the hangouts for LGBTQ Cubans and visitors alike. At the foot of Calle 23 and the Malecón, visitors will find numerous gay entertainment places, including the Las Vegas nightclub and the Bim Bom bar.

Although Cuba remains hostile to the LGBTQ community, in recent years, under pressure from international activists, the police usually do not bother gay or lesbian tourists.

Exercise caution, however, especially when meeting new people; prostitution is rampant.

The English Language in Cuba Returns

Cuban schools, since the early 1960s, have taught Russian as a mandatory foreign language requirement.

That changed with the school year that began September 2015; English is now the mandatory foreign language taught throughout the island. Russian is now an elective once the English language requirement has been met.

The future unfolds.

Before You Go

If you want to get in the right frame of mind to understand what Cuba was and what Cuba has become, you have to watch two films before you go. One tells the story of the upheaval occasioned by the Revolution. The other, a sci-fi allegory, mocks what Cuba has become. Many American reviewers have failed to understand the cultural nuances of the second film, often missing the jokes that only Cubans understand.

The Cuba you'll be visiting, after all, is not the Cuba of the first film. And how Cuba went from the first movie to the second one is Cuba's history over the past half century!

The Lost City (2005)

Summary: In Havana of the late 1950s, a wealthy family, one of whose sons is a prominent night-club owner, is caught in the violent transition from the oppressive regime of Batista to the government of Fidel Castro. Castro's regime ultimately leads the nightclub owner to flee to New York.

Director: Andy García
Starring: Andy García

Juan de los Muertos (Juan of the Dead) (2011)

Summary: A group of Cuban slackers faces an army of zombies. The Cuban government and media claim the living dead are dissidents revolting against the government.

Director: Alejandro Brugués
Starring: Alexis Díaz de Villegas

If you see these movies back to back, the impact is undeniable.

16

SEX TOURISM AND HUSTLING

Sex and hustling predominate. The darker side of a visit to Cuba—and a serious problem.

The Cuban Revolution had, as an ideal, the creation of an egalitarian society based on socialist principles. Critics point out that it succeeded in making everyone equally miserable.

What can be said is that, as reforms are implemented, the once-classless Cuban society is no more. Today there are two kinds of Cubans: those with U.S. dollars and those without U.S. dollars.

As a general rule, Cubans with access to hard currency—the U.S. dollar or European euro—have family overseas who send them remittances or work in the tourist-related establishments where they get tips from tourists. Now there are entrepreneurs as Havana becomes a place with small-business people, cottage industries, and shopkeepers.

Human nature being what it is, here's the rub about the darker side of visiting Cuba: No Cuban wants to be left without U.S. dollars.

In consequence, sex tourism and hustling are on the rise.

Sex Tourism

Most male visitors to Cuba will, almost invariably, be approached by a prostitute or a pimp.

DO NOT ENGAGE IN SEX TOURISM. YOU CAN LAND IN JAIL.

Pedophiles and Sex Crimes Against Children

The level of desperation for money continues to lead some families to turn a blind eye to the sexual exploitation of their children or to participate actively in these sex crimes. The Editor of this guide, while walking from the Japanese Embassy to the Capri Hotel in the Vedado, was approached by a man who offered to give him his daughter for $50 USD; his daughter looked like she was 13 or 14.

A father who has to pimp his own teenage daughter is a tragedy. During the rest of my walk from the Japanese embassy to the Capri Hotel, I thought about this family. As a father, one has to wonder what it takes to feel so desperate that one would offer a stranger one's teenage daughter. And what of the girl? Two decades from now, when she's in her mid-30s, what will she remember? That there was a time when, to put food on the table, she was forced to have sex with strangers, with her father's approval? How will she be traumatized? Will she resent her country for creating such desperation?

These are questions that, as a visitor, you will contemplate, since, if you venture forth and stroll the streets of Havana, you will inevitably be solicited in one form or another.

When it comes to child pornography and sex crimes against children, be aware that it is taking place all around you in Cuba. In one spectacular case, James McTurk, a Canadian tourist, was arrested

17

and prosecuted in Toronto for sex crimes he committed against children while in Cuba. Child prostitution, child molestation, and child pornography are a measure of the desperation many Cubans feel now that their world has changed.

If you suspect the sexual exploitation of children, please report it to the front desk at your hotel. If you have information on sex trafficking with minors involving U.S. citizens, you are encouraged to report it to the following:

George L. Piro
Special Agent in Charge
Federal Bureau of Investigation
2030 SW 145th Avenue
Miramar, FL 33027
Phone: (754) 703-2000
E-mail: *Miami@ic.fbi.gov*

Carol Smolenski
Executive Director
End Child Prostitution and Trafficking USA (ECPAT-USA)
30 Third Avenue
Suite 800A
Brooklyn, NY 11217
www.ecpatusa.org

Hustling, Scams, and *"Jineteros"*

Street hustlers are known as *"jineteros"* in Cuba. A *jintero* is a jockey, and the implication is that a *jintero* or *jintera* will take you for a ride the way a jockey takes a horse under his or her command.

Jineteros are primarily found in Old Havana, along the Malecón, or in the Vedado district near the principal hotels. They are primarily young men, often of color, and they will approach you in a friendly manner to strike up a conversation.

"Do you like Cuba?" he'll ask, with a smile. "Where are from?" he may inquire. "Can you buy me some candy for my children at the lobby shop?" he might ask.

The goal is to engage you in conversation. In this conversation, the *jinetero* will offer to take you to a great *paladar*, or know where you can stay for a great rate, offer to get you cigars at a fantastic price, or the best rum at an unbeatable price. He may also offer to get you a girl, or a boy.

Offering sex for pay to travelers is illegal and can get both you and the *jinetero* in trouble. In all likelihood, the police, both uniformed and plain clothes, know all the *jineteros* and their haunts. Chances are they have been arrested before.

It's important to remember that these are, almost universally, good and decent people who happen to find themselves in difficult situations.

18

It breaks your heart, especially when you see young women act in degrading ways to get by in the world, or when you see young men offer to sell boxes of cigar or bottles of rum that were pilfered from state-owned companies.

"Watch out for hustlers near the Parque Central," Beth Harpaz of the Associated Press warned in June 2015. "Resist all invitations from overly friendly strangers who invite you to a bar or to buy cigars."

The most common complaint travelers to Cuba have about their visit is having been interrupted by *jineteros*.

The good news, of course, is that only a small percentage of people in Cuba are *jineteros*—and they are a source of shame for the majority of their compatriots. This is the situation the world over, where most people are honest and generous.

Police and Tourists

A message from TripAdvisor:

"It is against the law in Cuba to take photographs of military, police, airport or other transportation facilities, although enforcement of this law is understandably erratic. If you do not wish to draw unpleasant government attention to yourself, avoid taking photographs in any of these locations!

Cuba generally has the reputation as a safe location for tourists and there are usually police on every block. Be aware of crowds as violence can erupt very quickly and the police may respond immediately or they may not—motives in Cuba vary situation to situation.

Increased sanctions and a campaign against prostitution have contributed to greater vigilance from police for Cubans fraternizing with tourists. Police will often detain or even arrest Cubans who are consorting with tourists on the street or in cafes especially around Malecón. If you care about the fate of the people you meet:

- Be aware of the police—in uniform and undercover
- Avoid photographing Cubans when police are nearby
- Don't speak to your companions when police are within earshot
- Dress in a manner that does not clearly indicate that you are a tourist, (i.e. khaki shorts, polo shirt, baseball hat, backpack and fanny pack)
- Have an agreed upon story for how you met other than "on the street"
- Avoid sitting or dancing with the girls in the cafes who police will assume are prostitutes
- Avoid public discussions of political or social issue
- Be aware of who has a license to receive tourism money and who does not."

GETTING TO CUBA

Cuba is no longer the forbidden island.

It has never been forbidden to most of the world, just American citizens and U.S. permanent residents. Times are changing, however.

Who Can Travel to Cuba?

Because it's possible to travel to Cuba without violating U.S. law, do it the right way. Never, ever break the law.

Here's who can travel to Cuba.

The Treasury Department's Office of Foreign Assets Control (OFAC) authorizes travel to Cuba without a license for the following categories of travelers:

1 Family visits
2 Official business of the U.S. government, foreign governments, certain international agencies, and some intergovernmental organizations
3 Journalists and reporters
4 Research and professional meetings
5 Educational activities and purposes
6 Religious activities
7 Cultural exchanges including public performances and workshops, including sports, athletics, and other competitions, meets, and exhibitions
8 Activities in nonpolitical support for the Cuban people
9 Humanitarian projects and programs
10 Activities of private foundations or research or educational institutions
11 Exportation, importation, or transmission of information or information materials
12 Certain authorized export transactions

More detailed information for U.S. citizens and permanent residents is provided in Chapter 25.

Need a License?

If you would like to secure a "license" to travel to Cuba, the U.S./Cuba's People-to-People Partnership makes it easy.

The application is available online at *http://form.jotform.us/form/51693819046160*.

Flying to Cuba

Americans wishing to travel to Cuba can find the best rates and more options by flying through Mexico.

Flights out of Mexico

Mexico offers the greatest number of flights to Cuba. There are six regularly scheduled flights from Cancún on AeroMéxico, Interjet, and Cubana airlines alone.

AeroMéxico has the most extensive flights to Havana from Mexico City and Cancún:

- *Aeromexico #451* daily Mexico City (MEX)–Havana (HAV), departing midmorning, arriving mid-afternoon
- *Aeromexico #452* daily Havana (HAV)–Mexico City (MEX), late afternoon flight
- *Aeromexico #453*, Sun-Mon-Wed-Sat Mexico City–Havana, early evening flight
- *Aeromexico #454*, Sun-Mon-Wed-Sat Havana–Mexico City, late evening flight
- *Aeromexico #447* daily Cancún (CUN)–Havana (HAV), midmorning
- *Aeromexico #448* daily Havana–Cancún, afternoon

Interjet has flights from Mexico City to Havana and from Cancún to Havana. Some of the fares are great deals. Round-trip between Cancún and Havana can be as low as $225.

Cubana flies to Cancún and Mexico City from Havana. Round-trip between Havana and Cancún can be as low as $275. The only consideration is that Cubana's fleet consists of older, Soviet-era aircraft that are not as comfortable as the planes flown by AeroMéxico or Interjet.

More information on flights to Cuba from Mexico is available at:

AeroMéxico: *www.aeromexico.com*

Interjet: *www.interjet.com*

Cubana de Aviación: *www.cubana.cu*

In addition, AeroMéxico has information on how U.S. residents can purchase tickets to Cuba and vacation packages, known as Gran Plan Vacaciones, on its Mexican website.

For more information, visit:

www.aeromexico.com/en/travel-with-aeromexico/destinations/central-america/havana/?site=us

Charter Flights Out of the U.S.

If you wish to travel from the U.S., book your flight on CheapoAir.com. At present, these are the cities and routes they serve:

Miami to Camaguey: Sunday and Friday

Miami to Cienfuegos: Wednesday and Friday

Miami to Havana: Daily

Miami to Holguín: Thursday

Miami to Santa Clara: Monday, Thursday, and Saturday

Miami to Santiago de Cuba: Saturday

New York to Havana: Tuesday
Tampa to Havana: Sunday and Thursday
To book a flight, visit *www.CheapoAir.com*.

Charter Flights Through Cuba Jet

Cuba Jet offers charter service from many cities in Latin America.
For more information, contact *www.cubajet.com*.

Scheduled Flights through Kayak

Neither Orbtiz nor Expedia nor Travelocity offers flights to Cuba. Only Kayak shows flights to Havana that connect through a third country.

Kayak currently offers flights to Cuba through connections, primarily Mexico City, Cancún, and the Cayman Islands. If you live close to eastern Canada, you may want to consider booking from Toronto or Montreal.

For more information, visit *www.kayak.com*.

JetBlue

It's only a matter a time before U.S. carriers begin to offer regularly scheduled service to Cuba. At present, only JetBlue offers flights to Havana.

As this goes to press, JetBlue offers flights to Cuba (Havana and Santa Clara) through public chartered services originating in Tampa (TPA) and Fort Lauderdale (FLL). It also offers service from New York (JFK) to Havana.

To book a flight from Tampa or Fort Lauderdale, contact:

Xael Charters, Inc.
Toll Free: 1 (877) 923-5359
E-mail: *mercycasals@xaelcharters.com*

To make arrangements to fly JetBlue out of New York, contact:
Cuba Travel Services at *www.cubatravelservices.com*.

Travel Packages from Mexico

The best tour packages are out of Mexico and are provided by Havanatur and Divermex. Each has offices in Cancún and Mérida, Mexico.
For more information:

Havanatur: *www.havanatur.com*
Divermex: *www.divermex.com.mx*

Travel Packages from the U.S.

Cuba Travel Services offers a wide selection of packages from the U.S.
For more information, visit *www.cubatravelservices.com*.

Tour Operators

There are many organizations in the U.S. organizing tours to Cuba. The advantage, of course, is that these tours operate under an umbrella license and have all the details planned out. Most of these organizations offer cultural tours that are excellent.

Here is a list of recommended tours for visitors not ready to venture forth on their own.

Cuba Educational Travel

Website: *www.cubaeducationaltravel.com*
Tel: 215-704-4637

Smithsonian Journeys

Website: *www.smithsonianjourneys.org*
Tel: 855-330-1542

Abercrombie & Kent

Website: *www.abercrombiekent.com*
Tel: 800-544-7016

Grand Circle Foundation

Website: *www.grandcirclefoundation.org*
Tel: 855-423-3443

Insight Cuba

Website: *www.insightcuba.com*
Tel: 800-450-2822

Globus Journeys

Website: *www.globusjourneys.com*

Tel: 866-755-8581

Coda Tours

Website: *www.coda-tours.com*
Tel: 888-677-2632

National Geographic

Website: *www.nationalgeographicexpeditions.com*
Tel: 888-966-8687

Classic Journeys

Website: *www.classicjourneys.com*
Tel: 800-200-3887

Tauck

Website: *www.tauck.com*
Tel: 800-788-7885

Canadian Art Tours to Cuba

Website: *www.cubaarttours.net*
Tel: 877-280-2054

A note on these travel packages: They are expensive. Most run between $2,250 to $5,500 per person. Considering that Havanatur and Divermex offer packages that include airfare, transfers, visa, hotel, city tour, and breakfasts for six days, five nights for about $600 USD out of Cancún, it is more reasonable to book a tour on your own from Cancún.

Recommended Tours

These two trips, scheduled to take place several times in 2016, are highly recommended.

Art Tour to Havana

François Valcke, who had a stellar career at Sotheby's in London, will conduct two tours to Havana in 2016. These tours will offer participants visits to Cuban artists in their studios, the opportunity to learn about the history of Cuban art, personalized recommendations, and professional guidance on how to best build a solid portfolio of contemporary Cuban art. For information about the itinerary and travel dates, please contact:

Galería Tataya

Attn: François Valcke
Calle 72 #468, between Calle 53 and Calle 55
Barrio Santiago
Mérida, Yucatán, Mexico
Tel.: (011) 52 999-928-2962
Website: *www.tataya.com.mx*
E-mail: *francois@tataya.com.mx*

Jewish Outreach to Cuba

Cuban Jews have relied on charitable contributions and material support primarily from Mexican Jews for more than half a century. Only now are U.S. Jewish organizations reaching out to Cuba's Jewish Diaspora in any meaningful and sustainable way. Two trips for American and Canadian Jews interested in learning about Cuba's Jewish history—and helping Cuban Jews—will take place in 2016. For information about the itinerary and travel dates, please contact:

Casa Catherwood

Attn: Luis Salazar
Calle 59 #572, between Calle 72 and Calle 74
Barrio Santiago
Mérida, Yucatán, Mexico
Website: *www.casa-catherwood.com*
E-mail: *info@casa-catherwood.com*

Traveling to Cuba from Other Countries

If you don't live in the United States, traveling to Cuba is easy. Despite the U.S. embargo, Havana is well connected to cities around the world. Here is a list of all airlines providing regularly scheduled service to and from José Martí International Airport. Check out each carrier's website for more information on their flights and rates to Cuba.

Airlines and Destinations from Havana

Aerocaribbean

Baracoa, Cayo Coco, Holguín, Managua, San Pedro Sula, Santiago de Cuba
Website: *www.cubajet.com*

Aeroflot

Moscow
Website: *www.aeroflot.com*

Aerogaviota
Cayo Coco, Cayo Largo del Sur, Cayo Santa María, Holguín, Kingston, Montego Bay, Nassau, Port of Spain, Santiago de Cuba
Website: *www.aerogaviota.com*

Aerolíneas Argentinas
Buenos Aires
Website: *www.aerolinas.com.ar*

Aeroméxico
Cancún, Mexico City
Website: *www.aeromexico.com*

Air Canada
Toronto
Website: *www.aircanada.com*

Air Caraïbes
Pointe-à-Pitre
Website: *www.aerocaraibes.com*

Air Europa
Madrid
Website: *www.aireuropa.com*

Air France
Paris
Website: *www.airfrance.us*

Air Transat
Montréal
Website: *www.airtransat.com*

Avianca
Bogotá
Website: *www.avianca.com*

Avianca El Salvador
San Salvador
Website: *www.avianca.com*

Avianca Perú
Lima
Website: *www.avianca.com*

Bahamasair
Nassau
Website: *www.bahamasair.com*

Blue Panorama Airlines
Milan, Rome
Website: *www.blue-panorama.com*

Cayman Airways
Grand Cayman
Website: *www.caymanairways.com*

Condor
Frankfurt, Munich
Website: *www.condor.com*

Conviasa
Caracas
Website: *www.conviasa.aero*

Copa Airlines
Panama City, Bogotá
Website: *www.copa.com*

Cubana de Aviación
Baracoa, Bayamo, Bogotá, Buenos Aires–Ezeiza, Camagüey, Cancún, Caracas, Cayo Coco, Cayo Largo del Sur, Ciego de Ávila, Guantánamo, Holguín, Madrid, Manzanillo, Mexico City, Montréal–Trudeau, Nueva Gerona, Paris–Orly, San José, Santa Clara, Santiago de Cuba, Santo Domingo–Las Américas, Toronto–Pearson, Victoria de las Tunas
Website: *www.cubana.cu*

Edelweiss Air
Zürich
Website: *www.flyedelweiss.com*

Iberia
Madrid
Website: *www.iberia.com*

Insel Air
Curaçao
Website: *www.fly-inselair.com*

Insel Air Aruba
Aruba
Website: *www.fly-inselair.com*

Interjet
Cancún, Mexico City
Website: *www.interjet.com*

JetBlue
New York—JFK
Website: *www.jetblue.com*

KLM
Amsterdam
Website: *www.klm.com*

LAN Perú
Lima
Website: *www.lan.com*

Neos
Milan
Website: *www.neosair.it*

TAAG Angola Airlines
Luanda
Website: *www.taag.com*

TAME
Quito
Website: *www.tame.com.ec*

Transaero Airlines
Moscow
Website: *www.transaero.ru*

Virgin Atlantic
London—Gatwick
Website: *www.virginatlantic.com*

Cruises to Cuba

Havana's harbor may have been adequate for the Soviet navy during the Cuban Missile Crisis, but the modern cruise industry finds port facilities inadequate for today's luxury cruise ships. As a result, most American cruise companies operate vessels that are too large to berth in Havana's harbor. This, however, does not mean that cruises do not make ports of call in Cuba.

There is tremendous interest in the industry to open Cuba to American cruise lines. This is how Cruise Critic summed up the industry excitement:

"So how long will it take before you see a mainstream cruise ship sail into Havana?

The answer: it depends. With infrastructure issues limiting the size of ships that could berth in Havana and a travel embargo that still needs to be overturned by Congress, a speedy timeline seems impossible. Yet with interest among cruise lines and their passengers already high, Cuba cruising could come quickly for smaller cruise ships, once barriers are removed—and one is already going.

Cruise line CEOs have spoken publicly about their desire to visit Cuba as soon as possible. In a TV interview, *Norwegian Cruise Line CEO Frank Del Rio said he has itineraries locked in his 'upper right hand drawer ready to go.' 'My unfulfilled dream is to be on the bridge of one of my ships coming into Havana harbor,' he said.*

'There's no question if the legislative embargo is lifted, Cuba is a tremendous opportunity,' Carnival Corp & plc CEO Arnold Donald told investors in December. 'There's a lot of pent-up demand to visit Cuba. It would allow us some very fuel-efficient itineraries. Also, it would provide new itineraries for those who love to go to the Caribbean.'"

—*CruiseCritic.com*

29

If you would like to take a cruise to Cuba, consider these resources:

Your Cuba Cruise

Your Cuba Cruise has numerous cruises to Cuba.
For more information, visit: *www.yourcubacruise.com*

Fred Olsen Cruises

This U.K. line has comprehensive cruises to Cuba that continue to receive critical acclaim.
For more information, visit: *www.fredolsencruises.com*

Cruise Ships to Cuba

This operator has small, intimate cruises that visit various ports of call around the island of Cuba.
For more information, visit: *www.cruiseshipstocuba.com*

WHERE TO STAY: OFFICIAL HOTELS & PRIVATE ACCOMMODATIONS

Welcome to the new Cuba.

Two government agencies are responsible for operating hotels in Cuba. Cubanacán and Habaguanex are in charge of tourist accommodations. Cubanacán focuses on most mass-market hotels throughout the nation. Habaguanex focuses on the newer luxury category hotel, principally found in Havana and Varadero.

Part of the reforms Raúl Castro has implemented since taking power in 2008 has been to improve the quality of hotel choices for foreign tourists. This remains an elusive goal, particularly where amenities and room service are concerned. In other words, be sure to bring everything you might need: disposable razor blades, feminine hygiene products, toiletries, over-the-counter medications, and so on.

There are two kinds of places to stay in Cuba: government-regulated hotels and accommodations in private homes. All hotels are government-managed or operated under government auspices. Even the hotels run by foreign hoteliers are restricted in how they manage these properties. Private accommodations, like private restaurants, are the beginning of free enterprise.

Hotel prices are divided into high, medium, and slow seasons. The prices are set by the government and they don't vary greatly.

Most hotel plans include breakfast. This consists of a buffet of fruit, bread, eggs, breakfast meat (often ham), coffee, tea, milk, and juices. Food at most hotels is disappointing, especially for travelers accustomed to the spreads provided at other Caribbean resorts, such as Cancún.

The food is not the only thing that strikes visitors as odd. Internet service is difficult and unreliable. There are security guards posted in the lobbies to prevent Cubans from accessing guest rooms. The towels, blankets, and bedding are not luxurious. Electricity and air-conditioning are not consistent. Ice may not be available. There may not be adequate television reception.

One annoying fact of Cuban hotels is that major hotels have security guards posted in the lobby. They are there to monitor Cuban citizens. (Please note that, as part of a campaign to prevent prostitution, guards monitor the elevator banks and generally do not allow Cubans to accompany hotel guests to their hotel rooms.) Surveillance of everyone everywhere is part of the experience as Cuba goes from a Soviet bloc-style standard of accommodations to those expected in the twenty-first century.

That said, there are some wonderful hotels in Havana. The architecture of some of these vintage establishments—the Capri and Hotel Nacional, for example—take you back to a different era.

For travelers with high standards or who are demanding, think hard about making the trip. Cuba is definitely not a destination for those high-drama individuals; Miami Beach or Cancún can better meet the demands of the discerning traveler. But "drama" is part of the experience, being part of a

31

country and society in the throes of transition. It's an adventure—and the adventure begins with the hotels.

Hotels

Hotel NH Capri

Calle 21, between Calle N and Calle O
Vedado
Tel: (53) 7 839-7200
Website: *http://www.nh-hotels.com/hotel/nh-capri-la-habana*

Without a doubt this hotel has undergone a world-class renovation. It is Havana's newest luxury hotel and sets the standards for Cuba. With its midcentury modern look, the hotel evokes the 1950s. One fully expects Audrey Hepburn and Gregory Peck to stroll through the lobby, followed by Marilyn Monroe and Frank Sinatra. The hotel boasts 220 rooms, with breathtaking views of the city or sea. The rooftop pool offers panoramic views; sunset is stunning. The hotel restaurant, La Florentina, is said to be among the city's best. Surprisingly, it is very good. And "Blue Bar," which is a retro masterpiece, is exquisite.

If this is Havana's future, then come say "Hola," a mojito in one hand and a cigar in another. This is an Editor's Choice selection.

Hotel Saratoga

Paseo del Prado #603, on the corner of Dragones
Old Havana
Tel: (53) 7 868-1000
Website: *www.hotel-saratoga.com*
E-mail: *info@saratoga.co.cu*

This 96-room hotel is on a busy square. The rooftop terrace and pool offer a great view of the Capitolio, modeled after the Capitol building in Washington, D.C. Its decor evokes Ernest Hemingway and the era of colonialism. The hotel restaurant offers breakfast, lunch, and dinner. The mezzanine-level bar is ideal for a drink and smoking a cigar. This is an Editor's Choice selection.

Hotel Meliá Cohiba

Av. Paseo, between Calle 1 and Calle 3
Vedado
Tel: (53) 7 833-3636
Website: *www.meliacuba.com*
E-mail: melia.*cohiba@meliacuba.com*

What the Hotel Nacional once was, today the Meliá Cohiba is: a world-class hotel for business travelers and diplomats. This 462-room high-rise hotel compares favorably to the class of hotels found in most capitals around the world. The amenities are above average by Cuban standards. The Casa del Habano, the chain of government-run cigar stores,, on the second, floor, is a great place to pick up cigars; its selection is excellent. There is a decent gym, a rarity in Havana. The Nacional offers a business office, which is a good thing since Internet service is not reliable in guest rooms.

The Havana Café nightclub, which is favored by the Cuban elite and well-heeled visitors alike, is under the same roof. The hotel is managed by the Spanish company Sol Meliá, and its services are comparable to other properties, most notably Cancún's Sol Meliá. This is an Editor's Choice selection.

Hotel Nacional

Calle 21 and Calle O
Vedado
Tel: (53) 7 836-3564
Web: *www.hotelnacionaldecuba.com*
E-mail: *reserva@hotelnacionaldecuba.com*

This hotel evokes the same era as the Biltmore Hotel in Coral Gables and The Breakers in Palm Beach. The Hotel Nacional, the grand dame of Havana, hosted the Duke and Duchess of Windsor. It is where Fidel Castro and Che Guevara set up headquarters to defend Havana from an aerial attack during the Cuban Missile Crisis. In between the Duke and Duchess and Fidel and Che, in December 1946, the hotel was the site of an infamous mob summit run by Lucky Luciano and Meyer Lansky.

Its 457 rooms offer sweeping views of the Malecón, the seaside promenade, and the Vedado and the district between Old Havana and Central Havana. The lobby has soaring ceilings and formidable arches. The hotel was renovated in the 1990s and now is used primarily by tour groups from Europe and Canada. The food is not the best, but many are enthralled by the Nacional's history and overlook the deficiencies in amenities.

Hotel Conde de Villanueva

Mercaderes #1201, on the corner of Lamparilla
Old Havana
Tel: (53) 7 833-3636

A boutique hotel with only nine rooms, each entered from on an interior courtyard that is open to the sky. This old mansion's staircases are marble, its rooms are generous in size, and the charm is colonial. The Casa del Habano, the chain of government-run cigar stores, on the mezzanine level is well appointed. The decor is a bit fussy and outdated, and guests may feel that they are stepping back in time.

Hotel Meliá Habana

Av. 3, between Calle 76 and Calle 80
Playa, Habana
Tel: (53) 7 204-8500
Website: *www.meliacuba.com*
E-mail: *melia.habana@meliacuba.com*

This is a favorite beach-district hotel in the midcentury modern district of Miramar. The hotel, a modern high-rise with a world-class swimming pool, is not located on the beach itself, however. There are 397 rooms and Executive Floors, which have "Servicio Real." The concierge services are quite good.

33

There is a well-appointed Casa del Habano, the chain of government-run cigar stores. Its restaurants are not exceptional.

Hotel Ambos Mundos

Calle Obispo 153, on the corner of Mercaderes
Old Havana
Tel: (53) 7 860-9530
Website: *www.habaguanexhotels.com*

An explosion of vibrant color is the first thing a visitor sees. This hotel—which looks as if Frida Kahlo had been in charge of painting it—stands out in Old Havana. Located across from the Palacio de Capitanes Generales, the current venue for the Museum of the City of Havana, the hotel was favored by writers and drinkers (and writers who were drinkers, such as alcoholic Ernest Hemingway) before the Revolution. The hotel is conveniently located near Plaza de Armas, the Plaza Cathedral, and La Bodeguita del Medio. It has only 52 rooms—which could use an update—but the lobby is a splendid place to soak up the aura of a bygone era.

Hotel Parque Central

Neptuno between Prado and Zulueta
Old Havana
Tel: (53) 7 860-6627
Website: *www.hotelparquecentral-cuba.com*

Located steps from the Capitol building, the Parque Central, which has 427 rooms, is housed in an old colonial building. What can best be said about this hotel is that it s close to the Prado and the National Theater. The rooftop pool and terrace offer great views of the Capitol. The hotel caters primarily to European and Latin American tour groups.

Hotel Santa Isabel

Calle Baratillo 9, between Obispo and Narciso López
Old Havana
Tel: (53) 7 860-8201
Website: *www.hotelsantaisabel.com*
E-mail: *comercial@habaguanexhsisabel.co.cu*

Located on the Plaza de Armas, this hotel is one of the prettiest places to hang out in Old Havana. It is opposite the Museum of the City of Havana and steps from the Castillo de la Real Fuerza, or Castle of the Royal Force, which was originally built to defend against pirate attacks.

The rooms themselves are spacious, boasting high ceilings; the top floor has terraces. The amenities are adequate, although not the best currently available in Havana.

Palacio del Marqués de San Felipe y Santiago de Bejucal

Calle Oficios #152, on the corner of Amargura
Plaza de San Francisco
Old Havana
Tel: (53) 7 864-9191

This hotel opened in 2010. It was twenty-seven rooms, some of which overlook Plaza San Francisco. There is a lovely rooftop terrace with sweeping views of the city. This hotel aspires to European-style luxury but doesn't quite make it. In the five years it has been open, service has declined. Breakfast service is provided by waiters and is not a buffet. The bar and dining area feature diffused light from a beautiful skylight. The staff is attentive.

Hotel Telégrafo

Prado #408, on the corner of Neptuno
Old Havana
Tel: (53) 7 861-1010
Website: *www.hoteltelegrafo-cuba.com*
E-mail: *subgerente@telegrafo.co.cu*

This hotel, with 63 rooms, is located near the Parque Central. It boasts a splendid atrium bar. The best that can be said of this adequate, no-frills hotel is that it has modern bathrooms and its decor is innocuous.

Hotel Raquel

Calle Amargura #103, on the corner of San Ignacio
Old Havana
Tel: (53) 7 860-8280
Website: *www.hotelraquel-cuba.com*
E-mail: *reservas@hotelraquel.co.cu*

This hotel, with 25 rooms, is a fine example of Art Nouveau. It also alludes to the strong influence Jews have played in Cuban history; there is a stone engraving of the Star of David in the reception area. Fidel Castro ordered it removed, but this is one case where his command was not followed. It's a good thing. The hotel has decent Internet service in the lobby, and meal service, while not kosher, is more than decent.

Hotel Park View

Calle Colón, on the corner of Morro
Old Havana
Tel: (53) 7 861-3293

Considering its location in Old Havana, this is, perhaps, the best value for the price-conscious. Located near the Fine Arts Museum and the Museum of the Revolution, the 55-room hotel offers all the amenities provided in any other hotel run by Habaguanex. The only drawback? It's as mundane in its decor and as charmless as a run-of-the-mill Holiday Inn.

Hotel Comodoro

Avenida 3 and Calle 84
Havana
Tel: (53) 7 204-5551

This no-frills hotel has one of the more interesting pools in Havana. The pool winds and is flanked by bungalows. Again, it is an acceptable hotel, one that provides all of the amenities offered by Habaguanex, although Internet service is unreliable.

Hotel Barceló

Avenida 5, between Calle 76 and Calle 80
Havana
Tel: (53) 7 214-1470
Website: *www.barcelo.com*
E-mail: *comercial@barcelohabana.co.cu*

The Spanish hotel group Barceló manages the hotel. A luxurious high-rise tower that overlooks Fifth Avenue, or La Quinta Avenida, it offers world-class services. The pool is one of the larger ones in Havana and the rooms are adequate. The decor is more contemporary Europe than colonial Havana. Services are good and meals are better than in other hotels. The only drawback is that it is removed from city center. Guests have to rent a car or contract with a driver to taxi them around.

Hotel Occidental Miramar

Quinta Avenida, between Calle 72 and Cale 76
Havana
Tel: (53) 7 204-3584

The Spanish hotel group Occidental manages this hotel, which repeat may visitors may remember as the former Novotel. The hotel offers adequate European-style services and amenities and caters primarily to tour groups from Latin America and Europe.

Hotel Habana Libre

Calle L, between Calle 23 and Calle 25
Havana
Tel: (53) 7 834-6100
Website: *www.meliacuba.com*
E-mail: *tryp.habana.libre@meliacuba.com*

Before the Revolution, this was the Hilton. During the Revolution, it served as Fidel Castro's headquarters. After the Revolution it was nationalized. Today, it is in disrepair. The history of the Cuban Revolution told in one building. The 569-room property was recently (modestly) renovated and is now managed by the Spanish Sol Meliá hotel group. Its services, however, continue to disappoint.

The best things that can be said are that it has one of the largest Casa del Habano, the chain of government-run cigar stores, in the city and a convenient location.

Hotel del Tejadillo

Tejadillo #12, corner of San Ignacio
Old Havana
Tel: (53) 7 863-7283

This is a great value-oriented hotel. Operated by Habaguanex, rooms can be had for under $70 USD. It is clean, functional, and safe. If you are reluctance to try staying at a *particular*, then you should consider this option.

Hotel Terral
On the corner of the Malecón and Lealtad
Havana
Tel: (53) 7 860-2100

This two-year-old hotel only has fourteen rooms. Its charm lies in the junior suites, which are gracious and accommodating. If you are thinking about this hotel, it is because you want unobstructed views of the Malecón and sea. The amenities are minimal, but then again, you will wake up in the middle of Havana.

Tropicana Penthouse
Calle Galiano
Centro
Tel: (53) 7 254-5240

Located behind the Deauville Hotel, the Tropicana's rooftop terrace has sweeping views of Havana landmarks and El Morro. It has recently reopened and features 1950s décor. It is well worth considering for the small, intimate appeal it offers.

Casa Pedro-María
Calle Chacón #209
Old Havana
Tel: (53) 7 861-4641

This small colonial house is located in front of the Museo de la Revolución and has an open courtyard and roof terraces. Its attentive hosts are splendid, and the place is a fantastic spot from which to embark on adventures.

Hotel Rates in Cuba

The rates of official hotels are set by the government. Rooms are priced as single or double occupancy. Junior suites, single or double, are a category apart. Following are the rates visitors can expect. Bear in mind that tour packages, which include airfare, visas, transfers, hotels (breakfasts included), and selected tours are available. The best packages are available from Mexico through Havantur or Divermex or one of the Mexican airline flying to Cuba.

High season is December through March. Median seasons are April, October, and November. Low season is May and June. Discounted-Low is July and August. As a general rule, summers are very hot, and winter is when there is the most demand for travel to Cuba.

Room	High Season	Median Season	Low	Discounted-Low
Single	$140–$175	$125–$165	$ 95–$145	$ 85
Double	$240–$350	$200–$275	$150–$225	$135
Junior Suite Single	$165–$255	$145–$235	$125–$210	$115
Junior Suite Double	$285–$475	$250–$400	$200–$350	$185

Private Accommodations

In addition to hotels, the government now allows private citizens to rent rooms and other accommodations.

The good news? This is a great way to live in the homes of ordinary Cubans. It is a great way to understand the people, make friendships, and get an up-close view of the challenges the Cuban people encounter as they transition to a new era. It's also more economical than staying at a hotel.

The bad news? Not everything may be provided as promised. The air conditioner may work, but not have Freon. There may be a blackout. The power may go out in an entire neighborhood. The neighbors may be noisy.

These possibilities should not discourage you from embarking on an adventure. Power has gone out at the Hotel Nacional for an entire day. The Capri has been without ice more than once. Internet service has proved unreliable at the Hotel Saratoga, arguably one of the best hotels in the city.

That said, following are recommended *particulares*—private accommodations. Prices may vary, depending on the season. Some may no longer be in operation. (One proprietor was renting rooms to make money to purchase a ticket to leave Cuba for Mexico City, from where she planned to take a bus to the U.S. border and seek political asylum.) Reservations at all of these places can be found—along with reviews by previous guests—on AirBNB.

Accommodations Below $50 USD a Day

La Terraza de 23, Calle 23 #307, Apt. 3, Vedado: $14 USD
Port View Apartment, Merced on the corner of Alameda de Paula, Old Havana: $17 USD
Casa Marlene, Calle 45 #1112, between 26 and 36, Nuevo Vedado: $24 USD
Casa Alicia, Calle 36 #122, between Calle 1 and Calle 3, Miramar: $25 USD
Hostal Terraza, Escobar #161, between Ánimas and Virtudes: $25 USD
Silvia and Evelio's House, Calle 470 Apt#305, between Calle 3 and Calle 5: $26 USD
Casa David, Gloria #157, between Cienfuegos and Cardenas: $27 USD
Casa en Renta Centro, Neptuno #462, between Manrique and Campanario: $29 USD
Casa Universidad, Ronda #17, between Neptuno and San Miguel: $29 USD
D Vip, Amistad #159 A (ground level), between Virtudes and Neptuno: $29 USD
Apartamento Karmín, Infanta #53, between Humboldt and Espada: $30 USD
La Casazul, Neptuno #1218, between Mazón and Basarrate: $30 USD
Old Havana Apt., Calle Galiano, between Calle Anima and Calle Vistudes: $30 USD
Colonia 18th Century House, Lamparilla #324, between Aguacate and Compostela: $33 USD

Candy House, Santa Rita #9807, between Real and Pezuela: $35 USD
Casa Havana, Room 5, Calle Habana #209, between Empedrado and Tejadillo: $35 USD
Las Mercedes, Sol #212, Apt. 11, between Cuba and Aguiar, Old Havana: $36 USD
Casa Candida, San Rafael #403, between Manrique and Campanario: $39 USD
Colonial Room in Vedado, Calle F #104, between Calle 5 and Calzada: $39 USD
Villa Costa Habanera, Calle 27 #4, between Calle O and Infanta: $40 USD
Casa Bonia, Línea 112, between Calle L and Vedado Plaza: $40 USD
Maylen's Rental, Calle 46-A #712, between Calle 7ma-A and Calle 7ma-B: $43 USD
La Mulata Cárcel, Capdevila # 59,between Morro and Zulueta: $46 USD
Marta's B&B Guest House, Avenida de los Presidentes, El Vedado: $42 USD
Colonial Carusa, Acosta #412, between Egido and Curazao: $46 USD

Accommodations Between $50 and $100 USD a Day

Casa Malecón Mayra, Malecón #252, fifth floor: $51 USD
La Cochería, Calle Morro #5, between Cárcel and Genios: $51 USD
Urquiza's Room, Prado #20, between Carcel and San Lazaro: $52 USD
My Proud Havana, Calle P #120, Apt. 405, between Infanta and Humboldt: $52 USD
Casa Miriam y Sinai, Neptuno #521, between Lealtad and Campanario: $55 USD
La Rosa de Ortega, Patrocinio #252, corner of Juan Bruno Zayas and Diez de Octubre: $60 USD
Casa Gabriel & Mary Apartment, Calle 470 #303, between Avenida 3 and Avenida 5: $60 USD
Casa Sara, Malecón #155, Apt. 5, between Calle 25 and Principe: $60 USD
Marina House, Marina House, Calle 21 #7812, between K and Lindero: $60 USD
Casa Vitrales Boutique, Calle Habana #106, between Chacón and Cuarteles: $62 USD
Casa Vitrales Room 1, Calle Habana #106, between Chacón and Cuarteles: $62 USD
Casa Vitrales Room 3, Calle Habana #106, between Chacón and Cuarteles: $62 USD
Casa Santy, Calle Cuarteles #120, between Habana and Avenida de las Misiones: $65 USD
Casa Doña Luisa, Aguacate #13, between Chacón and Tejadillo: $68 USD
Casa Yojans, Concordia #953, corner of Infanta: $69 USD
Casa Amada Seaview, Calzada #55: $70 USD
Villa Susana, Apt. 1, Calle 36 #254, between Calle 38 and Avenida Zoologico: $70 USD
Casa Habanera, Industria #58-A, between Colón and Refugios: $75 USD
Lux Apartment, Calle H #360, between Calle 15 and Calle 17: $80 USD
Casa Rosa de Ortega, Patrocinio #252, corner of Juan Bruno Zayas and Diez de Octubre: $80 USD
Modern Flat, San Juan de Dios #108, between Aguacate and Compostela: $80 USD
Casa Vitrales Boutique, Habana #106, second floor, between Chacón and Cuarteles: $83 USD
Casa Nostra, Calle 27 #813, between Paseo and Calle 2: $85 USD
Casa Particular Almiya, Teniente Rey #10, suite 302, between Oficio and Mercaderes: $87 USD
Old Havana Apt. Cristo #34, between Teniente Rey and Muralla: $90 USD

Accommodations More than $100 USD a Day

Nice House, Avenida 49 #3431, Reparto Kohly: $101 USD

Casa Independiente, Calle C #106, between Calzada and Avenida 5: $102 USD

Ocean View Apartment, San Nicolás #54 and San Lázaro: $110 USD

Park Suite 7, corner of Calle 11 and Calle 64: $117 USD

Casa Azul, Calle 54 #3308, between Calle 33 and Calle 35: $120 USD

Casa Yola, Calle 38 #141, between Avenidas Zoologico and Nueva: $120 USD

Cozy House, Calle 6 #302, corner of Calle 3: $120 USD

Luxury White Suite, corner of Calle 11 and Calle 64: $123 USD

Park Suite 6, corner of Calle 11 and Calle 64: $125 USD

Cañaveral House Suite, Calle 39-A #402, between Calle 44 and Habana: $130 USD

Miramar Grand Terrace 3-Bedroom, Calle 4 #103, between Avenida 1 and Avenida 3: $137 USD

Villa Ruíz, Calle 78 #1704, between Calle 17 and Calle 19: $140 USD

Teresa's House, Escobar #161, between Calle Ánimas and Calle Virtudes: $145 USD

Hostal La Serenita, Calle F #515, between Calle 21 and 23: $148 USD

La Rosa de Ortega Master Suite, Patrocinio #252, corner of Juan Bruno Zayas and Diez de Octubre: $150 USD

Casablanca, Morro-Cabaña Park, House 29: $160 USD

Miramar Grand Terrace 8, Calle 4 #103, between Avenida 1 and Avenida 3 1ra: $171 USD

Miramar Grand Terrace, Calle 4 #103, between Avenida 1 and Avenida 3 1ra: $182 USD

Departamento Habana, Calle 18, between Avenida 1 and Avenida 3, $197 USD

Arian's House, Angeles #7, between Reina and Estrella: $200 USD

Independent's Apartments, Galiano #257, between Neptuno and Concordia: $200 USD

Vivian's Apartment, corner of Calle 38 and Avenida 1: $200 USD

Aparthotel Luis & Ada, Corner of Calle 23 and D: $210 USD

Mercy's House, San Rafael #870, between Aramburu and Soledad: $210 USD

Best View Apartment, San Lázaro #464, between Perseverancia and Campanario: $223 USD

Roland's Siboney House, Calle 202 #1908, between Calle 19 and Calle 21, Reparto Siboney: $245 USD

Casa Malecón, San Lazaro #464, 6th floor, between Perseverancia and Campanario: $300 USD

Ocean View House, Ampliación de Calle Marbella: $300 USD

Super Colonial House, Calle 9-NA #458, between Calle E and Calle F: $350 USD

Villa Lauren, Avenida Kolhy, between Calle 39 and Calle 41: $400 USD

AirBNB Safety

Accommodations in private homes are not licensed the way hotels, motels, and resorts are licensed. As a consequence, guests have to be responsible for their personal safety. Cuba is a police state where people are executed by firing squad, a fact of life that instills fear among the Cuban people.

Accordingly, Cubans know there are severe consequences for crimes against foreign tourists. Nevertheless, Cuba is country of very, very poor people.

Following are AirBNB's official recommendations for guest safety:

I'm a guest. What are some safety tips I can follow?

- Look at the profiles and reviews of potential hosts.

- Check for verified phone numbers, connected social networks, and references, and be sure to read any reviews left by other AirBNB guests. If you'd like to see more, you can always ask them to complete profile verifications before booking with them, or look for hosts who already have a strong reputation on Airbnb.

- Read listing descriptions closely.

- It's a good idea to read everything hosts have posted about their listing in the description, the amenities, and the house rules so there won't be any surprises. Make sure you understand the host's cancellation policy before submitting a reservation request, too.

- Pay and communicate on AirBNB.

- Paying or communicating outside AirBNB makes it harder for us to protect your information and puts you at greater risk of fraud and other security issues. That's why we prohibit paying for a reservation outside our website in our Terms of Service and strongly encourage you to communicate using our messaging system.

- Use our messaging system before a booking to confirm details about specific amenities, ask whether other people share the same space, discuss house rules, and talk about the neighborhood. After booking, use it to discuss check-in details.

- Talk to your host.

  After learning more about your host's Airbnb history, start a conversation with them about your plans and what you can expect. Your host will likely know all the great (and not so great) spots. Trust your intuition: if you don't feel right about a reservation, don't book it! If a message makes you feel uncomfortable or you need help during your reservation, let us know.

  - Sign up for traveler's insurance.

41

- Airbnb does not offer traveler's insurance for guests. However, traveler's insurance is a relatively affordable option that can protect you in case of an injury or emergency on a trip. Some policies even cover lost baggage and travel delays. Check with your local insurance provider for details on your options.

- Make copies of documents and keep them safe.

- Make copies of all major documents like passports, visas, and insurance cards. Having a paper or digital copy will help if you lose your ID while traveling. Keep your documents and currency in different places, and don't carry too much cash all at once.

- Be a considerate guest.

- Whether you're still looking for the perfect listing or are already on your way, being a considerate guest matters.

- Remember: if you ever find yourself in an emergency or feel that your personal safety is threatened, always contact local police and emergency services first.

WHERE TO EAT: RESTAURANTS & PALADARES

Where to dine and where to eat.

Restaurants

Fine dining is making a comeback in Cuba. After years of deprivation—the "Special Period" after Soviet subsidies ended were brutal to the food scene—there is a promising future for restaurant dining and the culinary scene.

Following is a list of restaurants and established *paladares* that are popular among foreign tourists. Current ratings and reviews for each establishment listed are available at TripAdvisor. Final note: the Editor's Choice restaurants and *paladares* require reservations.

La Guarida
Concordia #418, between Gervasio and Escobar
Central Havana
Tel: (53) 7 866-9047

This is a must-stop for any tourist. What began as a *paladar* is now one of the city's favorite bonafide restaurants. Under the direction of its chef and owner Enrique Núñez, Havana has a world-class establishment. Caesar salads are prepared tableside, and the sensational papaya lasagna is very popular among Cuba's elite, international business travelers, and the diplomatic community. This is an Editor's Choice selection.

La Terraza
Prado #309, on the corner of Virtudes
Old Havana
Tel: (53) 7 862-3626

This building is owned by the Sociedad Cultural Asturiana, a Spanish organization. The restaurant is located on the rooftop terrace. A specialty is the grilled octopus with pesto and the leg of lamb right off the grill. This is an Editor's Choice selection.

La Moraleja
Calle 25 #454, between Calle J and Calle I
Vedado
Tel: (53) 7 832-0963

The Hemingway shrimp (*Camarones Hemingway*) and the ceviche are exquisite. The service is most attentive, and it is a convenient stroll to nearby attractions. This is an Editor's Choice selection.

La Corte del Principe
> Calle 74, on the corner of Avenida 9
> Miramar
> Tel: (53) 7 255-9091

The beef carpaccio and warm octopus salads are extraordinary. Very popular among the Italian expat community in Havana. This is an Editor's Choice selection.

Santy Pescador
> Calle 240-A, between Calle 3 and Río
> Jaimanitas
> Tel: (53) 7 271-4925

What's on the menu? The catch of the day. This place is a sensation, an experience that cannot be missed—whether you're going to or coming back from Hemingway Marina. This is an Editor's Choice selection.

Doctor Café
> Calle 28 #111, between Avenida 1 and Avenida 3
> Miramar
> Tel: (53) 7 203-4718

Renowned for its shredded crab, this place is around the back of a home in the midcentury modern section of Miramar. This is an Editor's Choice selection.

Casa Grande
> Pezuela #85, on the corner of Foxa
> Cojimar, La Habana del Este
> Tel: (53) 5 316-6295

Under the direction of Chef Jorge Falcón, here you'll find the best grilled dishes in Havana. Whether it is seafood, pork ribs, or lobster, it all goes well, especially if you start the meal with one of the ceviche dishes. This is an Editor's Choice selection.

Hurón Azul
> Humbolt #153 and Calle P
> Vedado
> Tel: (53) 7 879-1691

Under the direction of José "Pepe" Hernández, this place serves sensational octopus with onions, shredded crab with polenta, and shrimp in *malanga* (a tuber) batter. This is an Editor's Choice selection.

El Aljibe

Avenida 7 and Calle 24
Miramar
Tel: (53) 7 204-4233

A great place for comfort food Cuban style—roast chicken, black beans, rice, French fries, it has a solid wine collection, great to accompany the robust food. This is an Editor's Choice selection.

EL Cocinero

Calle 26, between Calle 11 and Calle 13
Vedado
Tel: (53) 7 832-2356

Has the feel of a restaurant in Los Angeles or Condesa in Mexico City. The lobster bisque is exceptional. The octopus and red snapper are also impressive. This is an Editor's Choice selection.

Le Chansonnier

Calle J #257, between Calle 15 and Línea
Vedado
(53) 7 832-1576

The seafood—grilled octopus and red grouper (*cherna*)—are specialties and are perfectly prepared. The caper and anchovy vinaigrette is exceptional. This is an Editor's Choice selection.

VIP Havana

Calle 9 #454, between Calle E and Calle F
Vedado
Tel: (53) 7 832-0178

This is the first Catalan-influenced restaurant and serves excellent dishes from the Mediterranean—to be expected since Jordi, the owner, is from Barcelona. This is an Editor's Choice selection.

Café Laurent

Calle M, between Calle 19 and Calle 21, Penthouse 257
Vedado
Tel: (53) 7 832-6890

One of the better seafood restaurants in Havana and is a short stroll from attractions in Vedado. Try the squid in ink sauce, which is remarkable.

La Cocina de Lilliam

Calle 48 #1311, between Calle 13 and Calle 15
Miramar
Tel: (53) 7 209-6514

Under the direction of Lilliam Domínguez, the casserole shines on the menu of what is one of the oldest *paladares* in Havana. If you have never had *malanga* (a tuber similar to the potato) fries, then this is the place to try them for the first time.

La Fontana

Calle 46, on the corner of Avenida 3
Miramar
Tel: (53) 7 202-8337

This former *paladar* is now a restaurant and renowned among the foreign community in Havana. The chicken with rice (*arroz con pollo*) is terrific. It also features three kinds of sausage (*chorizos*) on the menu. In the evenings there is often live music, adding to the sense of place.

Atelier

Calle 5 #511, between Calle 2 and Paseo
Vedado
Tel: (527) 836-2025

This rootop terrace restaurant has some of the best duck and rabbit in Havana. The octopus is also very good. Enjoy a cocktail in this restaurant that boasts Moorish design.

El Chelo at Club Habana

Avenida 5, between Calle 188 and Calle 192
Miramar
Tel: (53) 7 204-5700

This restaurant, located in what once was the Biltmore Yacht Club, actually has a great ocean view. Seafood is the specialty, and regular patrons rave about the shrimp. There is a decent wine selection.

El Templete

Avenida Carlos Manuel Céspedes and Avenida del Puerto
Old Havana
Tel: (53) 7 204-0624

Renowned for its seafood, especially grilled red snapper and fried calamari.

Iván Justo

Aguacate 9, on the corner of A Chacón
Old Havana
Tel: (53) 7 863-9697

The chef's claim to fame? Chef Iván Justo used to cook for Fidel Castro. The seafood is phenomenal, so are the roast pork and lamb.

La Imprenta

Calle Mercaderes #208, between Amargura and Lamparilla
Old Havana
Tel: (53) 7 864-9581

Another restaurant in that is garnering rave reviews for its seafood.

Café del Oriente

Oficios #112, on the corner of Amargura
Old Havana
Tel: (53) 7 860-6686

Located across from the Marqués de San Felipe Hotel. Go for a great drink and light fare. The food is not exceptional, but the setting is something to behold.

La Campana

alle 212 #2904, between Calle 29 and Calle 31
La Lisa
Tel: (53) 7 271-1073

One of the more popular—if out of the way—places for a sunset dinner poolside. The food is above average and service is attentive.

El Palenque

Calle 17 and Calle 190
Siboney, Playa
Tel: (53) 7 271-8167

This is the place in Havana for pork: roasted or grilled. The only complaint is that service is hit or miss, so hope you get a good server.

Vistamar

Avenida 1, between Calle 22 and Calle 24
Miramar
Tel: (53) 7 203-8328

What began as a *paladar* is now a restaurant located on the second floor of a former residence. Specialties include specializes in lobster, grilled fish, and shrimp.

Paladares

Paladar is the name for restaurants run privately by individuals. Most are family-run businesses. *Paladares* are not only the beginning of capitalism, but also are on the cutting edge of culinary adventure in Havana. They are the antithesis of the state-run restaurants and bars. They also offer a more intimate experience of the emerging Cuba. Most offer traditional Cuban cuisine, *comida criolla*, and, by the nature of the closed economy, they showcase locally procured ingredients.

The following is a list of exceptional entrepreneurial culinary choices in Havana. Be advised that new ones are opening just about every week (and some are closing, given the nature of free enterprise). Accordingly, please check on TripAdvisor for current reviews.

These *paladares* are relatively new to the Havana culinary scene and well worth a try. *¡Buen provecho!*

Havana Centro

San Cristóbal
Address: Calle San Rafael #469, between Lealtad and Campanario
Phone: (53) 7 867-9109
Cuisines: Cuban and International
Average price: $8.00 to $14.00 CUC
Hours of operation: Monday through Saturday, noon to midnight
Payment options: Cuban Peso, Cuban Convertible Peso, U.S. Dollar, and Euro

Mimosa
Address: Calle Salud #317, between Gervasio and Escobar
Phone: (53) 7 867-1790
Cuisine: Italian
Average price: $7.00 CUC and under
Hours of operation: Daily from noon to midnight
Payment options: Cuban Peso and Cuban Convertible Peso

Castropol
Address: Calle Malecón #107, between Genios and Crespo
Phone: (53) 7 861-4864
Cuisines: Cuban and International
Average price: $8.00 to $14.00 CUC
Hours of operation: Daily from noon to midnight
Payment options: Cuban Peso, Cuban Convertible Peso, U.S. Dollar, and Euro

La Flor de Loto
Address: Salud #313, between Gervasio and Escobar
Phone: (53) 7 860-8501
Cuisines: Chinese and Cuban
Average price: $7.00 CUC and under
Hours of operation: Daily from noon to midnight
Payment options: Cuban Peso and Cuban Convertible Peso

Castas & Tal
Address: Galiano #51, on the corner of San Lázaro
Phone: (53) 7 864-2177

Cuisine: Fusion
Average price: $8.00 to $14.00 CUC
Hours of operation: Daily from noon to midnight
Payment options: Cuban Peso, Cuban Convertible Peso, U.S. Dollar, and Euro

Come y Calla

Address: Neptuno #670, between Gervasio and Belascoaín
Cuisines: Chinese, Cuban, and International
Average price: $7.00 CUC and under
Hours of operation: Daily from 10:30 AM to 1 AM
Payment options: Cuban Peso, Cuban Convertible Peso, U.S. Dollar, and Euro

Mango Habana

Address: Calle Industria #352, between San Miguel and San Rafael
Phone: (53) 7 866-0396
Cuisines: Cuban, Italian, and International
Average price: $8.00 to $14.00 CUC
Hours of operation: Daily from noon to midnight
Payment options: Cuban Peso, Cuban Convertible Peso, U.S. Dollar, and Euro

Café Tilín

Address: Galiano #119, between Ánimas and Trocadero
Phone: (53) 7 864-4790
Cuisine: International
Average price: $7.00 CUC and under
Hours of operation: Daily from 10 AM until the last patron leaves
Payment options: Cuban Peso, Cuban Convertible Peso, U.S. Dollar, and Euro

El Levant

Address: Águila, between Reina and Dragones
Phone: (53) 5 805 0696
Cuisine: International
Average price: $7.00 CUC and under
Hours of operation: Monday through Friday from 11 AM to midnight; Saturday and Sunday from 11 AM to 2 AM
Payment options: Cuban Peso, Cuban Convertible Peso, U.S. Dollar, and Euro

Nazdarovie

Address: Malecón #25, between Prado and Cárcel (second floor)
Phone: (53) 7 860-2947
Cuisine: Slavic
Average price: $7.00 CUC and under
Hours of operation: Daily from noon to midnight

Payment options: Cuban Peso, Cuban Convertible Peso, U.S. Dollar, and Euro

Chang Wang Chung Tong

Address: San Nicolás #517, between Zanja and Dragones
Phone: (53) 7 862-1490
Cuisines: Chinese, Cuban, and International
Average price: $8.00 to $14.00 CUC
Hours of operation: Daily from noon to 11 PM
Payment options: Cuban Peso, Cuban Convertible Peso, U.S. Dollar, and Euro

Café Arcángel

Address: Concordia #57, between Galeano and Águila
Phone: (53) 7 867-7495
Serves light fare.
Average price: $7.00 CUC and under
Hours of operation: Sunday through Friday from 8:30 AM to 9 PM; and Saturday from 8:30 AM to midnight
Payment options: Cuban Peso, Cuban Convertible Peso, U.S. Dollar, and Euro

Wong Tong Ja Tong

Address: Dragones #414, on the corner of Campanario
Phone: (53) 7 863-2068
Cuisines: Chinese, Cuban, and International
Average price: $7.00 CUC and under
Hours of operation: Daily from noon to midnight
Payment options: Cuban Peso and Cuban Convertible Peso

El Cantonés

Address: Manrique #564, second floor, between Dragones and Salud
Phone: (53) 7 863-2981
Cuisine: International
Average price: $7.00 CUC and under
Hours of operation: Daily from noon to midnight
Payment options: Cuban Peso and Cuban Convertible Peso

Ming Chih Tang

Address: Manrique #513 (bajos), between Zanja and Dragones
Phone: (53) 7 863-2966
Cuisines: Chinese and International
Average price: $7.00 CUC and under
Hours of operation: Daily from noon to 11 PM
Payment options: Cuban Peso and Cuban Convertible Peso

El Zarzal
Address: Concordia #360, second floor, between Lealtad and Escobar
Phone: (53) 7 862-5952
Cuisines: Cuban and International
Average price: $7.00 CUC and under
Hours of operation: Daily from noon to 11:30 PM
Payment options: Cuban Peso and Cuban Convertible Peso

Notre Dame des Bijoux
Address: Gervasio #218, between Concordia and Virtudes
Phone: (53) 7 860-6764
Cuisine: Cuban
Average price: $7.00 CUC and under
Hours of operation: Daily from noon to midnight
Payment options: Cuban Peso, Cuban Convertible Peso, U.S. Dollar, and Euro

See Man
Address: Zanja #306, between Lealtad and Escobar
Phone: (53) 7 878-6484
Cuisines: Chinese and Cuban
Average price: $7.00 CUC and under
Hours of operation: Daily from noon to 11 PM
Payment options: Cuban Peso

Viejo Amigo
Address: Dragones #356, between San Nicolás and Manrique
Phone: (53) 7 861-8095
Cuisines: Chinese, Cuban, and International
Average price: $7.00 CUC and under
Hours of operation: Daily from noon to midnight
Payment options: Cuban Peso, Cuban Convertible Peso, U.S. Dollar, and Euro

La Gitana
Address: San Lázaro #208, between Águila and Blanco
Phone: (53) 7 866-6800
Cuisine: International
Average price: $8.00 to $14.00 CUC
Hours of operation: Daily from 11 AM to midnight
Payment options: Cuban Peso, Cuban Convertible Peso, U.S. Dollar, and Euro

Torresson

Address: Malecón #27, between Prado and Cárcel
Phone: (53) 7 861-7476
Cuisines: International and Vegetarian
Average price: $8.00 to $14.00 CUC
Hours of operation: Daily from noon to midnight
Payment options: Cuban Peso and Cuban Convertible Peso

Jared

Address: Zanja #165, between Manrique and San Nicolás
Phone: (53) 7 867-2063
Cuisine: International
Average price: $8.00 to $14.00 CUC
Hours of operation: Daily from noon to midnight
Payment options: Cuban Peso, Cuban Convertible Peso, U.S. Dollar, and Euro

Amistad de Lanzarote

Address: Amistad #211, between Neptuno and San Miguel
Phone: (53) 7 863-6172
Cuisines: Cuban and International
Average price: $8.00 to $14.00 CUC
Hours of operation: Daily from noon to midnight
Payment options: Cuban Peso, Cuban Convertible Peso, U.S. Dollar, and Euro

Bellomar

Address: Virtudes #169-A, between Industria and Amistad
Phone: (53) 7 861-0023
Cuisines: Cuban and International
Average price: $8.00 to $14.00 CUC
Hours of operation: Daily from noon to midnight
Payment options: Cuban Convertible Peso

El Maguey

Address: Amistad #111, between Ánimas and Virtudes
Phone: (53) 7 861-1701
Cuisines: Cuban and International
Average price: $7.00 CUC and under
Hours of operation: Daily from 11 AM to 1 AM
Payment options: Cuban Peso, Cuban Convertible Peso, U.S. Dollar, and Euro

Casa Miglis

Address: Lealtad #120, between Ánimas and Laguna
Phone: (53) 7 864-1486

Cuisines: International and Scandinavian
Average price: $15.00 to $21.00 CUC
Hours of operation: Daily from noon to 6 AM
Payment options: Cuban Peso, Cuban Convertible Peso, U.S. Dollar, and Euro

Las Delicias del Consulado

Address: Consulado #309, Suite B between Neptuno and Virtudes
Phone: (53) 7 863-7722
Cuisines: Cuban and International
Average price: $15.00 to $21.00 CUC
Hours of operation: Daily from 11 AM to midnight
Payment options: Cuban Peso, Cuban Convertible Peso, U.S. Dollar, and Euro

Casa Abel

Address: San Lázaro #319, on the corner of San Nicolás
Phone: (53) 7 860-6589
Cuisines: Cuban and International
Average price: $8.00 to $14.00 CUC
Hours of operation: Daily from noon to midnight
Payment options: Cuban Peso, Cuban Convertible Peso, U.S. Dollar, and Euro

La California

Address: Calle Crespo #5, between San Lázaro and Refugio
Phone: (53) 7 863-7510
Cuisines: Italian and International
Average price: $8.00 to $14.00 CUC
Hours of operation: Daily from noon to midnight
Payment options: Cuban Peso, Cuban Convertible Peso, U.S. Dollar, and Euro

A Mi Manera

Address: Calle Neptuno #919, between Aramburu and Soledad
Phone: (53) 7 870-9005
Cuisines: Cuban and Italian
Average price: $7.00 CUC and under
Hours of operation: Daily from noon to midnight
Payment options: Cuban Peso and Cuban Convertible Peso

La Bonita

Address: Galeano #209, between Concordia and Virtudes
Phone: (53) 5 290-0896
Cuisines: Cuban and International
Average price: $7.00 CUC and under
Hours of operation: Daily from noon to midnight
Payment options: Cuban Peso and Cuban Convertible Peso

Azúcar

Address: Mercaderes #315
Phone: (53) 5 293-1494
Cuisine: Cuban
Average price: $14.00 CUC and under
Hours of operation: Daily from 11 AM to midnight
Payment options: Cuban Peso and Cuban Convertible Peso

Cotorro District

El Resplandor

Address: Calle 95 #3808, between 38 and 40
Phone: (53) 5 276-8369
Cuisine: Cuban
Average price: $7.00 CUC and under
Hours of operation: Daily from noon to midnight
Currencies accepted: Cuban Peso

El Taller

Address: Calle 107 #2811, between 28 and 30
Phone: (53) 7 682-2778

Cuisine: International
Average price: $7.00 CUC and under
Hours of operation: Daily from noon to midnight
Currencies accepted: Cuban Peso

La Taberna

Address: Avenida 101 #3006, between 30 and 32
Phone: (53) 7 682-4608
Cuisines: Cuban, International
Average price: $7.00 CUC and under
Hours of operation: Daily from noon to midnight
Currencies accepted: Cuban Peso

Diez de Octubre

Cafetería 555

Address: Jorge #155, between Lagueruela and Gertrudis, El Sevillano
Phone: (53) 7 641-2742 and (53) 5 346-5426
Cuisine: Italian
Average price: $7.00 CUC and under
Hours of operation: Tuesday to Sunday, from 10 AM to 11 PM
Currencies accepted: Cuban Peso and Cuban Convertible Peso

El Chile Habanero

Address: Calle Durege #213, on the corner of Santa Emilia and Santos Suárez
Phone: (53) 7 642-2201
Cuisines: Cuban, Mexican, and Yucatecan
Average price: $8.00 to $14.00 CUC
Hours of operation: Daily from noon to midnight
Currencies accepted: Cuban Peso, Cuban Convertible Peso, U.S. Dollar, and Euro

El Mirador de Acosta

Address: Calle Acosta, corner ofVista Alegre, Víbora
Phone: (53) 7 698-4009
Cuisines: Cuban and International
Average price: $7.00 CUC and under
Hours of operation: Daily from 10 AM to midnight
Currencies accepted: Cuban Peso, Cuban Convertible Peso, U.S. Dollar, and Euro

La Orquídea

Address: Lagueruela #252, between Calle 5 and Calle 6, Lawton
Phone: (53) 7 698-8210

Cuisine: Cuban
Average price: $7.00 CUC and under
Hours of operation: Daily from noon to 11 PM
Currencies accepted: Cuban Peso

Los Curros

Address: Calle Santos Suárez #52, on the corner of Rabí, Santos Suárez
Phone: (53) 7 640-5822
Cuisines: Cuban and International
Average price: $7.00 CUC and under
Hours of operation: Daily from noon to midnight
Currencies accepted: Cuban Peso and Cuban Convertible Peso

Melesio Grill

Address: Calle Juan Delgado #676, between Freyre Andrade and Aranguren, Sevillano
Phone: (53) 7 642-4496
Cuisine: Cuban
Average price: $7.00 CUC and under
Hours of operation: Daily from noon to midnight
Currencies accepted: Cuban Peso and Cuban Convertible Peso

Rancho Coquito

Address: San Miguel #566, between Anita and Finlay, Víbora
Phone: (53) 7 641-4463
Cuisines: Cuban, Italian, and French
Average price: $7.00 CUC and under
Hours of operation: Daily from 11:30 AM to 11 PM
Currencies accepted: Cuban Peso, Cuban Convertible Peso, U.S. Dollar, and Euro

Villa Hernández

Address: Calle San Miguel #112, between Revolución and Gelabert, Sevillano
Phone: (53) 7 640-5250
Cuisines: Cuban
Average price: $8.00 to $14.00 CUC
Hours of operation: Wednesday to Sunday from noon to midnight
Currencies accepted: Cuban Peso, Cuban Convertible Peso, U.S. Dollar, and EuroArroyo Naranjo

Divino

Address: Calle Raquel, between Esperanza and Lindero
Phone: (53) 7 643-7734
Cuisine: Fusion
Average price: $8.00 to $14.00 CUC
Hours of operation: Tuesday to Sunday from noon to midnight
Currencies accepted: Cuban Peso, Cuban Convertible Peso, U.S. Dollar, and Euro

El Gallo de Oro

Address: #7 Callejón de Lucero, between Calzada de Managua and Santa Hortencia
Phone: (53) 7 644-4382
Cuisines: Cuban and International
Average price: $7.00 CUC and under
Hours of operation: Daily from 8 AM to midnight
Currencies accepted: Cuban Peso, Cuban Convertible Peso, U.S. Dollar, and Euro

Los Cascabeles

Address: San Juan #2541, between Calzada de Bejucal and Matanzas
Phone: (53) 7 643-7191
Cuisines: Italian
Average price: $7.00 CUC and under
Hours of operation: Daily from 9 AM to midnight
Currencies accepted: Cuban Peso and Cuban Convertible Peso

Rancho Manso

Address: Calzada de Managua #163, between Calle 1 and Miguel Viondi
Phone: (53) 5 232-9762
Cuisines: Cuban and International
Average price: $8.00 to $14.00 CUC
Hours of operation: Tuesday to Sunday from 10 AM to midnight
Currencies accepted: Cuban Peso, Cuban Convertible Peso, U.S. Dollar, and Euro

Guanabacoa

El Pavo

Address: Vía Blanca #11-A, between San Luis and D
Phone: (53) 7 797-6432
Cuisines: Cuban and International
Average price: $8.00 to $14.00 CUC
Hours of operation: Daily from noon to midnight
Currencies accepted: Cuban Peso and Cuban Convertible Peso

UFC

Address: Calle 3, between 10 and 11, Reparto Chivás
Phone: (53) 7 793-5919
Cuisine: International
Average price: $7.00 CUC and under
Hours of operation: Monday to Thursday from 10 AM to 11 PM; Friday to Sunday from 10 AM to midnight
Currencies accepted: Cuban Peso and Cuban Convertible Peso

Mangle Rojo

Address: Avenida 1 #2, between Calle 11 and Calle 12, Reparto Chivás
Phone: (53) 7 797-8613
Cuisine: International
Average price: $8.00 to $14.00 CUC
Hours of operation: Tuesday to Sunday from noon to 11 PM
Currencies accepted: Cuban Peso and Cuban Convertible Peso

Boyeros District

El Trébol

Address: Calzada de Bejucal, between Luz and Cuervo
Cuisine: Italian
Average price: $7.00 CUC and under
Hours of operation: Monday to Thursday from 11 AM to 10 PM; Friday from 11 AM to 11 PM
Payment options: Cuban Peso and Cuban Convertible Peso

Lacoste

Address: Avenida 225 #22506, between 210 and 211
Phone: (53) 5 293-7205
Cuisine: Cuban
Average price: $7.00 CUC and under
Hours of operation: Daily from 11 AM to 11 PM
Payment options: Cuban Peso and Cuban Convertible Peso

Doña Teresa

Address: Avenida 229 #21011, between 210 and 216
Phone: (53) 7 645-1861
Cuisines: Chinese, Cuban, Italian, and International
Average price: $7.00 CUC and under
Hours of operation: Daily from noon to 11 PM
Payment option: Cuban Peso

Tanokura

Address: Calle 403, between 180 and 184, Santiago de las Vegas
Phone: (53) 7 683 2173
Cuisines: Cuban and International
Average price: $7.00 CUC and under
Hours of operation: Daily from 9 AM to midnight
Payment options: Cuban Peso, Cuban Convertible Peso, U.S. Dollar, and Euro

Rancho Blanco

Address: Calle 190, between 17 and 19, Reparto Tessie
Phone: (53) 7 683-2992
Cuisine: International
Average price: $7.00 CUC and under
Hours of operation: Daily from noon to midnight
Payment options: Cuban Peso, Cuban Convertible Peso, U.S. Dollar, and Euro

Café Macondo

Address: Avenida Boyeros, between 100 and A
Phone: (53) 7 647-9544 and (53) 5 268-5797
Cuisine: Cuban
Average price: $7.00 CUC and under
Hours of operation: Daily from 11 AM to 11 PM
Payment options: Cuban Peso, Cuban Convertible Peso, U.S. Dollar, and Euro

Rancho Verde

Address: Santa Catalina #10633, between Avenida de los Ocujes and Palatino
Phone: (53) 7 641-6433
Cuisines: Cuban and International
Average price: $7.00 CUC and under
Hours of operation: Tuesday to Sunday from 12:30 PM to 11 PM
Payment options: Cuban Peso, Cuban Convertible Peso, U.S. Dollar, and Euro

Doña Ceci

Address: Calle 5 #1507, between Entrada and Calle 2
Cuisines: Cuban and International
Average price: $7.00 CUC and under
Hours of operation: Thursday to Tuesday from noon to 11 PM
Payment options: Cuban Peso, Cuban Convertible Peso, U.S. Dollar, and Euro

Doña Rosita

Address: Calle Blanquita #1932, between Calle 4 and Acosta
Phone: (53) 7 641-7156 and (53) 5 358-5328
Cuisines: Cuban and International
Average price: $8.00 to $14.00 CUC
Hours of operation: Daily from noon to 11 PM
Payment options: Cuban Peso, Cuban Convertible Peso, U.S. Dollar, and Euro

Leyendhabana

Address: Santa Rosa #217, between Infanta and Cruz del Padre
Phone: (53) 7 874-1421
Cuisines: Cuban and International
Average price: $7.00 CUC and under
Hours of operation: Daily from noon to midnight
Tuesday to Sunday from noon to 11 PM
Payment options: Cuban Peso, Cuban Convertible Peso, U.S. Dollar, and Euro

Cocktails, Coffee Shops, Music, and Tapas

There are times when you're in the mood for a drink, with music in the background, and perhaps some tapas to tide you over between meals. Here is a list of favorite places for drinks, music, and a little something.

Bodeguita del Medio

Calle Empedrado #207
Old Havana
Tel: (53) 7 867-1374

This remains one of the world's greatest bars. It's the place to have a mojito just to be able to say you had a mojito here while in Cuba. A band is almost always playing, and the ambiance evokes Ernest Hemingway, who made the place famous—and infamous.

Floridita

Obispo #557, on the corner ofMonserrate
Old Havana
Tel: (53) 7 867-1300

The Art Deco decor only makes enjoying a daiquiri that much more fun. Was it invented here? Does it matter? Enjoy the music—and the light fare is fantastic.

Café de Paris

Obispo and San Ignacio
Old Havana

This place is renowned for its music, not its food. Have a drink and enjoy fine Cuban music. Eat elsewhere.

Café Bohemio

San Ignacio
Old Havana
Tel: (53) 7 860-3722
Website: *http://www.havanabohemia.com/cafeacute-bohemia.html*

This is the best choice for a coffee shop in Old Havana, and it's right on San Ignacio Plaza. It has a full bar and the offerings are pleasant enough. A great place to people watch and enjoy the musicians who are almost always present in the plaza.

La Torre

Calle 17, on the corner of Calle M
Vedado
Tel: (53) 7 838-3088

Located on the 33rd floor of the FOCSA apartment building, this place has great cocktails and sweeping views of the ocean. The food is not great, but a drink with this view is an experience.

El Jerengue de Areito

Calle San Miguel #410, between Campanario and Lealtad

On Friday nights, people cram into this tiny venue for rumba and jazz. This place doesn't have a phone as this goes to press.

Privé Lounge

Call3 88-A #306, between Avenida 3 and Avenida 3-A
Miramar
Tel: (53) 7 209-2719

A laid-back lounge that evokes the style and feel of the 1940s.

Jardines del 1830

Malecón #1252, corner of Calle 20
Vedado
Tel: (53) 7 838-3091

Sunday night is salsa night at this spot, set in the ambient gardens of a grand colonial mansion. A great place to start the evening—or end it.

La Vitrola

San Ignacio, on the corner of Muralla
Old Havana
Tel: (53) 5 285-7111
Facebook: *https://www.facebook.com/pages/La-Vitrola/784372414944558#_=_*
Twitter: *https://twitter.com/BarLaVitrola*

This is one of the better tapas bar and restaurants in the area. A great place to sit out and enjoy the ambiance.

Basílica Menor de San Francisco de Asís

Plaza de San Francisco de Asis
Old Havana

Sunday performances of classical music at the basilica are an extraordinary experience. Sunday afternoons at 5 PM there are local ensembles playing as well.

Tipping at Restaurants

Cubans depend on earning hard currency (convertible pesos, U.S. dollars, and euros) to improve their lives.

As a general rule, tips are lower than in the U.S. Some restaurants will automatically add a 10% gratuity to the bill. If yours hasn't—most *paladares* don't add a tip to the bill—Cubans expect a tip between 10% and 12% at restaurants. A suggestion is to hand the waiter or waitress the tip yourself and thank them. It is also recommended that, given the scarcity in Cuba, you give them something they can use. This is the reason for packing bags of disposable razors, bottles of aspirin, travel-size toothpaste, and so forth.

RENTING CARS

Going for a drive?

Renting Cars in Cuba

If you are an American . . .

And you plan to rent a car in Cuba and you are a citizen or permanent resident of the United States, or you have a bank card issued by a U.S. bank, it's very likely that you won't be able to use a credit, debit, or other bank card to rent a car in Cuba. You will need to pay in cash and provide a security deposit in cash. Expect to need up to $500 USD for a security deposit. The only way around this is if you pay for your car rental prior to arriving in Cuba. This can be done through travel agencies or online.

If you are not an American . . .

Bank cards issued in most countries other than the United States can normally be used to rent cars in Cuba. It's recommended to make car rental reservations before arriving in Cuba. This can be done through travel agencies or online.

Rental Car Insurance

If you are an American . . .

Buy insurance! Your car insurance will not cover a rented vehicle in Cuba.

If you are not an American . . .

It's likely your bank card, charge card, or personal car insurance will cover your car rental in Cuba. It's always a good idea, however, to buy car insurance in Cuba.

Car Rental Agencies

Here is a comprehensive list of car rental agencies, their websites, addresses, and hours of operation throughout Cuba.

Cubacar
www.cuba-car.com

63

Havanautos

www.havanautos.com

Rex Car Rental

www.rexcarrental.com

Transtur Car Rental

www.transturcarrental.com

My Cuba Car

www.mycubacar.com

Vía Car Rental

http://carrentalcuba.net/via-cuba-official-website/

Rent a Car Cuba

www.rentacarcuba.com

Hiring Drivers and Special Car Rental Needs

Cubism offers comprehensive services for specific requests, such as getting a driver.

Cubism—Havana Car Hire

www.havanacarhire.com

Havana Offices:
Cubaism, Ltd.
Edificio Bacardi
Calle Monserrate #261
Suite 607
Old Havana
Tel: (53) 7 863-9555
Website: *www.havanacarhire.com*

Car Rental Locations Throughout Cuba

Cubacar Car Rental Locations

Following are Cubacar Car Rental locations by area.

Havana Airport

Cubacar: José Martí Airport Terminal 2
Address: Havana José Martí International Airport Terminal 2
Hours: 24 hours

Cubacar - José Martí Airport Terminal 3
Address: Havana José Martí International Airport Terminal 3
Hours: 24 hours

Vedado

Línea and Malecón (Tangana)
Address: Línea and Malecón, Vedado
Hours: 9 AM to 5 PM

Cubacar – Calle 3 and Paseo
Address: Calle 3 and Paseo
Hours: 24 hours

Cubacar - Hotel Nacional de Cuba
Address: Calle O, corner of Calle 21
Hours: 9 AM to 5 PM

Cubacar - Hotel Tryp Habana Libre
Address: Calle L, on the corner of Calle 23
Hours: 9 AM to 5 PM

Old Havana

Cubacar - Cruise Terminal, Havana Harbor
Address: Terminal de Cruceros, Avenida del Puerto
Hours: 9 AM to 5 PM

Cubacar - Hotel Parque Central
Address: Neptuno between Prado and Zulueta
Hours: 9 AM to 5 PM

Cubacar - Hotel Plaza
Address: Ignacio Agramonte #267
Hours: 9 AM to 5 PM

Cubacar - Hotel Sevilla
Address: Trocadero #55
Hours: 9 AM to 5 PM

Havana Centro

Cubacar - Galiano and Concordia
Address: Galiano and Concordia
Hours: 9 AM to 9 PM

Cubacar - Hotel Deauville
Address: Calle Galiano and Malecón
Hours: 9 AM to 5 PM

Miramar

Cubacar – Avenida 3 and 70
Address: Avenida 3 and Calle 70
Hours: 24 hours

Cubacar - Hotel Chateau Miramar
Address: Avenida 1 and Avenida 62
Hours: 9 AM to 9 PM

Cubacar - Hotel Copacabana
Address: Avenida 1, between 44 and 46
Hours: 9 AM to 5 PM

Cubacar - Hotel Neptuno
Address: Avenida 1 and 72, Playa
Hours: 24 hours

Cubacar - Kasalta
Address: Calle O, corner of Avenida 5
Hours: 9 AM to 5 PM

Cubacar - Miramar Avenida 1 and Calle O
Address: Avenida 1 and Calle O
Hours: 9 AM to 5 PM

Cubacar - Miramar 1 and 14
Address: Avenida 1 and 14
Hours: 9 AM to 5 PM

Cubacar - Miramar Pizza Nova
Address: Avenida 3 and 46
Hours: 9 AM to 5 PM

Cubacar - Playa 42 and 33
Address: 42 and 33, Playa
Hours: 9 AM to 8 PM

East Beaches and Varadero

Cubacar - Gran Vía
Address: Guanabo, Playas del Este
Hours: 9 AM to 5 PM

Cubacar - Hotel Tropicoco
Address: Hotel Tropicoco, Avenida Sur and Las Terrazas, Playa Santa María del Mar
Hours: 9 AM to 5 PM

Cubacar - Hotel Iberostar Varadero
Address: Carretera Las Molas Kilometro 16
Hours: 9 AM to 5 PM

Cubacar - Hotel Meliá Varadero
Address: Carretera de Las Morlas
Hours: 9 AM to 5 PM

Cubacar - Hotel Sol Palmeras
Address: Carretera de Las Morlas
Hours: 9 AM to 5 PM

Cubacar - Hotel Villa Cuba
Address: Hotel Villa Cuba
Hours: 9 AM to 5 PM

Cubacar - Varadero Airport
Address: Varadero Juan Gualberto Gómez International Airport
Hours: 24 hours

Cubacar - Varadero Calle 21
Address: Avenida 1 between 21 and 22

Hours: 9 AM to 5 PM

Jibacoa

Cubacar - Hotel Villa Trópico
Address: Hotel Villa Trópico
Hours: 9 AM to 5 PM

Jardines del Rey/Cayo Coco

Cubacar - Cayo Coco
Address: Rotonda Cayo Coco, Jardines del Rey
Hours: 24 hours

Cubacar - Hotel Meliá Cayo Coco
Address: Avenida de los Hoteles
Hours: 9 AM to 5 PM

Holguín

Cubacar - Guardalavaca
Address: Playa Guardalavaca
Hours: 9 AM to 5 PM

Cubacar - El Cocal
Address: Carretera Vía a Bayamo Kilometro 7.5
Hours: 9 AM to 5 PM

Cubacar - Holguín Airport
Address: Frank País International Airport
Hours: 24 hours

Cubacar - Hotel Pernik
Address: Avenida Jorge Dimitrov s/n (no number) Hotel Pernik
Hours: 9 AM to 5 PM

Cubacar - Pico Cristal
Address: Cafetería Pico Cristal Centro Ciudad
Hours: 9 AM to 5 PM

Villa Clara Province

Cubacar - La Catedral
Address: Calle Marta Abreu, between Alemán and Juan Bruno Zayas
Hours: 9 AM to 5 PM

Cubacar - Santa Clara Airport
Address: Airport Abel Santa Maria
Hours: 24 hours

Cubacar - Remedios
Address: Calle Solidaridad #3 between Ejido del Este and Marcelo Salado, Remedios
Hours: 9 AM to 5 PM

Sancti Spíritus/Trinidad

Cubacar - Cupet Trinidad
Address: Cupet Trinidad
Hours: 9 AM to 5 PM

Cubacar - Hotel Ancón
Address: Hotel Ancón, Peninsula Ancón, Trinidad, Sancti Spiritus
Hours: 9 AM to 5 PM

Cubacar - Hotel Brisas Trinidad del Mar
Address: Península Ancón, Sancti Spiritus
Hours: 9 AM to 5 PM

Cubacar - Infotur Trinidad
Address: Calle Maceo, corner of Simón Bolívar #163, Trinidad
Hours: 9 AM to 5 PM

Cubacar - Parque Sancti Spíritus
Address: Parque Serafín Sánchez, Sancti Spíritus
Hours: 9 AM to 5 PM

Camaguey Province

Cubacar - Florida
Address: Carretera Central Kilometro 532, Florida, Camaguey
Hours: 9 AM to 5 PM

Cubacar - Hotel Club Santa Lucía
Address: Avenida Tararaco s/n (no number) Playa Santa Lucia, Nuevitas, Camaguey
Hours: 9 AM to 5 PM

Cubacar - Camaguey Airport
Address: Avenida Finlay s/n (no number) Kilometro 7.6 Albaisa, Camaguey
Hours: 24 hours

Cubacar - Hotel Plaza
Address: Calle Van Horne No. 1, between Avenida and República, Camaguey
Hours: 9 AM to 5 PM

Cienfuegos

Cubacar - Cienfuegos Airport
Address: Cienfuegos Airport
Hours: 24 hours

Cubacar - Hotel Jagua
Address: Hotel Jagua
Hours: 9 AM to 5 PM

Las Tunas

Cubacar - Hotel Covarrubias
Address: Playa Covarrubias, Puerto Padre
Hours: 9 AM to 5 PM

Cubacar - Hotel Las Tunas
Address: Hotel Las Tunas, Las Tunas
Hours: 9 AM to 5 PM

Pinar del Río

Cubacar - Hotel Mirador de San Diego
Address: Calle 23 Final, San Diego de los Baños, Pinar del Río
Hours: 9 AM to 5 PM

Cubacar - Hotel Vueltabajo
Address: Calle Martí #103, corner of Rafael Morales, Pinar del Río
Hours: 9 AM to 5 PM

Cubacar - San Juan and Martínez
Address: Calle Francisco Rivera 134-A, between Ruiz Calderón and José María Padrón, San Juan and Martínez, Pinar del Río
Hours: 9 AM to 5 PM

Cubacar - Sandino
Address: Servicentro Oro Negro, Sandino, Pinar del Río
Hours: 9 AM to 5 PM

Cubacar - Hotel Pinar del Río
Address: Martí Final, Hotel Pinar del Río
Hours: 9 AM to 5 PM

Viñales

Cubacar - Hotel La Ermita
Address: Hotel La Ermita, Carretera de La Ermita Kilometro 1.5, Viñales
Hours: 9 AM to 5 PM

Granma Province

Cubacar - Hotel Marea del Portillo
Address: Hotel Marea del Portillo, Pilón, Granma
Hours: 9 AM to 5 PM

Cubacar - Hotel Sierra Maestra
Address: Carretera Central, Bayamo
Hours: 9 AM to 5 PM

Guantánamo

Cubacar - Baracoa
Address: Calle Martí, between Céspedes and Coronel Galano
Hours: 9 AM to 5 PM

Matanzas Province

Cubacar - Matanzas
Address: Avenida Playa Vista Alegre
Hours: 9 AM to 5 PM

Santiago de Cuba

Cubacar - Hotel Carisol los Corales
Address: Carretera Baconao, Santiago de Cuba
Hours: 9 AM to 5 PM

Cubacar - Hotel Casagranda
Address: Hotel Casagranda, Heredia No. 201, between San Pedro and San Félix
Hours: 9 AM to 5 PM

Cubacar - Hotel Las Américas
Address: Hotel Las Américas, Santiago de Cuba
Hours: 9 AM to 5 PM

Cubacar - Hotel Libertad
Address: Perez Carbo between Garzón and Enrramadas, Santiago de Cuba
Hours: 9 AM to 5 PM

Cubacar - Hotel Meliá Santiago
Address: Calle M, between Avenida de las Américas and Calle 4, RepartoSueño, Santiago de Cuba
Hours: 9 AM to 5 PM

Cubacar - Hotel San Juan
Address: Santiago de Cuba
Hours: 9 AM to 5 PM

Cubacar - Hotel Sierra Mar
Address: Carretera de Guamá, Santiago de Cuba
Hours: 9 AM to 5 PM

Cubacar - Santiago de Cuba Airport
Address: Antonio Maceo International Airport, Santiago de Cuba
Hours: 24 hours

Havanautos Car Rental Locations

Following are Havanautos Car Rental locations by area.

Havana Airport

Havanautos: José Martí Airport Terminal 3
Address: José Martí International Airport Terminal 3
Hours: 24 hours

Old Havana

Havanautos - Cruise Terminal, Havana Harbour
Address: Terminal de Cruceros, Avenida del Puerto
Hours: 9 AM to 5 PM

Havanautos - Hotel Parque Central
Address: Neptuno, between Prado and Zulueta
Hours: 9 AM to 5 PM

Havanautos - Hotel Plaza
Address: Hotel Plaza, Ignacio Agramonte #267
Hours: 9 AM to 5 PM

Havanautos - Hotel Sevilla
Address: Trocadero #55
Hours: 9 AM to 5 PM

Vedado

Havanautos – Calle 3 and Paseo
Address: Calle 3 and Paseo
Hours: 24 hours

Havanautos - Hotel Nacional de Cuba
Address: Hotel Nacional de Cuba, Calle O, corner of 21
Hours: 9 AM to 5 PM

Havanautos - Hotel Tryp Habana Libre
Address: Calle L corner of 23
Hours: 9 AM to 5 PM

Havana Centro

Havanautos - Galiano and Concordia
Address: Galiano and Concordia
Hours: 8 AM to 8 PM

Havanautos - Hotel Deauville
Address: Calle Galiano and Malecón
Hours: 9 AM to 5 PM

Miramar

Havanautos – Avenida 3 and 70
Address: Avenida 3 and 70, Playa
Hours: 24 hours

Havanautos - Hotel Chateau Miramar
Address: Hotel Chateau Miramar, Avenida 1 and 62, Playa
Hours: 9 AM to 9 PM

Havanautos - Hotel Copacabana
Address: Hotel Copacabana, 1 and 44, Playa
Hours: 9 AM to 5 PM

Havanautos - Hotel Neptuno
Address: 3 Avenida, between 72 and 74, Playa
Hours: 9 AM to 5 PM

Havanautos - Kasalta
Address: Kasalta, 5 and 2, Playa
Hours: 9 AM to 5 PM

Havanautos - Miramar 1 and 0
Address: Miramar 1 and 0
Hours: 9 AM to 5 PM

Havanautos - Miramar 1 and 14
Address: Miramar 1 and 14
Hours: 9 AM to 5 PM

Havanautos - Miramar Pizza Nova
Address: Restaurante Pizza Nova, 3 and 46, Playa
Hours: 9 AM to 5 P

Havanautos - Playa 42 and 33
Address: Playa 42 and 33
Hours: 9 AM to 5 PM

East Beaches and Varadero

Havanautos - Gran Vía
Address: Guanabo, Playas del Este
Hours: 9 AM to 5 PM

avanautos - Hotel Tropicoco
Address: Avenida Sur and Las Terrazas, Playa Santa María del Mar
Hours: 9 AM to 5 PM

Havanautos - Hotel Iberostar Varadero
Address: Carretera Las Morlas Kilometro 16
Hours: 9 AM to 5 PM

Havanautos - Hotel Sol Palmeras
Address: Hotel Sol Palmeras
Hours: 9 AM to 5 PM

Havanautos - Hotel Villa Cuba
Address: Hotel Villa Cuba
Hours: 9 AM to 5 PM

Havanautos - Varadero Airport
Address: Juan Gualberto Gómez International Airport
Hours: 24 hours

Havanautos - Varadero Calle 21
Address: Avenida 1 between 21 and 22
Hours: 9 AM to 5 PM

Jibacoa

Havanautos - Hotel Villa Tropico
Address: Hotel Villa Tropico
Hours: 9 AM to 5 PM

Jardines del Rey/Cayo Coco

Havanautos - Cayo Coco
Address: Rotonda Cayo Coco, Ciego de Ávila
Hours: 24 hours

Havanautos - Hotel Meliá Cayo Coco
Address: Avenida de los Hoteles
Hours: 9 AM to 5 PM

Holguín

Havanautos - Guardalavaca
Address: Playa Guardalavaca
Hours: 9 AM to 5 PM

Havanautos - El Cocal
Address: Carretera Vía a Bayamo Kilometro 7.5
Hours: 9 AM to 5 PM

Havanautos - Holguín Airport
Address: Frank País International Airport
Hours: 24 hours

Havanautos - Hotel Pernik
Address: Avenida Jorge Dimitrov s/n (no number) Hotel Pernik
Hours: 9 AM to 5 PM

Havanautos - Pico Cristal
Address: Cafetería Pico Cristal Centro Ciudad
Hours: 9 AM to 5 PM

Villa Clara Province

Havanautos - La Catedral
Address: Calle Marta Abreu between Alemán and Juan Bruno Zayas, Santa Clara
Hours: 9 AM to 5 PM

Havanautos - Santa Clara Airport
Address: Airport Abel Santa Maria, Santa Clara
Hours: 24 hours

Havanautos - Remedios
Address: Calle Solidaridad #3, between Ejido del Este and Marcelo Salado, Remedios
Hours: 9 AM to 5 PM

Sancti Spíritus/Trinidad

Havanautos - Cupet Trinidad
Address: Cupet Trinidad
Hours: 9 AM to 5 PM

Havanautos - Hotel Ancón
Address: Hotel Ancón, Peninsula Ancón
Hours: 9 AM to 5 PM

Havanautos - Hotel Brisas Trinidad del Mar
Address: Hotel Brisas Trinidad del Mar
Hours: 9 AM to 5 PM

Havanautos - Infotur Trinidad
Address: Calle Maceo, corner of Simón Bolívar #163, Trinidad
Hours: 9 AM to 5 PM

Havanautos - Parque Sancti Spíritus
Address: Parque Serafín Sanchez, Sancti Spíritus
Hours: 9 AM to 5 PM

Camaguey Province

Havanautos - Florida
Address: Carretera Central Kilometro 532, Florida
Hours: 9 AM to 5 PM

Havanautos - Hotel Club Santa Lucia
Address: Avenida Tararaco s/n (no number) Playa Santa Lucia, Nuevitas
Hours: 9 AM to 5 PM

Havanautos - Camaguey Airport
Address: Avenida Finlay s/n (no number) Kilometro 7.6 Albaisa
Hours: 24 hours

Havanautos - Hotel Plaza
Address: Calle Van Horne #1
Hours: 9 AM to 5 PM

Cienfuegos

Havanautos - Cienfuegos Airport
Address: Cienfuegos Airport
Hours: 9 AM to 5 PM

Havanautos - Hotel Jagua
Address: Hotel Jagua
Hours: 9 AM to 5 PM

Las Tunas

Havanautos - Hotel Covarrubias
Address: Hotel Covarrubias, Playa Covarrubias
Hours: 9 AM to 5 PM

Havanautos - Hotel Las Tunas
Address: Hotel Las Tunas, Las Tunas
Hours: 9 AM to 5 PM

Pinar del Río

Havanautos - Hotel Mirador de San Diego
Address: Calle 23 Final, San Diego de los Baños
Hours: 9 AM to 5 PM

Havanautos - Hotel Vueltabajo
Address: Calle Martí #103, corner of Rafael Morales
Hours: 9 AM to 5 PM

Havanautos - San Juan and Martínez
Address: Calle Francisco Rivera 134-A, between Ruiz Calderón and José María Padrón, San Juan and Martínez
Hours: 9 AM to 5 PM

Havanautos - Sandino
Address: Servicentro Oro Negro, Sandino

Hours: 9 AM to 5 PM

Havanautos - Hotel Pinar del Río
Address: Martí Final, Hotel Pinar del Río
Hours: 9 AM to 5 PM

Viñales

Havanautos - Hotel La Ermita
Address: Carretera de La Ermita Kilometro 1.5, Viñales
Hours: 9 AM to 5 PM

Granma Province

Havanautos - Hotel Marea del Portillo
Address: Hotel Marea del Portillo, Pilón, Granma
Hours: 9 AM to 5 PM

Havanautos - Hotel Sierra Maestra
Address: Carretera Central, Bayamo
Hours: 9 AM to 5 PM

Guantánamo

Havanautos - Baracoa
Address: Calle Martí between Céspedes and Coronel Galano
Hours: 9 AM to 5 PM

Matanzas Province

Havanautos - Hotel Meliá Varadero
Address: Hotel Meliá Varadero
Hours: 9 AM to 5 PM

Havanautos - Matanzas
Address: Avenida Playa Vista Alegre
Hours: 9 AM to 5 PM

Santiago de Cuba

Havanautos - Hotel Carisol los Corales
Address: Carretera Baconao
Hours: 9 AM to 5 PM

Havanautos - Hotel Casagranda
Address: Heredia No. 201, between San Pedro and San Félix
Hours: 9 AM to 5 PM

Havanautos - Hotel Las Américas
Address: Avenida Las Américas and General Cebreco
Hours: 9 AM to 5 PM

Havanautos - Hotel Libertad
Address: Perez Carbo between Garzón and Enrramadas
Hours: 9 AM to 5 PM

Havanautos - Hotel Meliá Santiago
Address: Calle M, between Avenida de las Américas and Calle 4, Reparto Sueño
Hours: 9 AM to 5 PM

Havanautos - Hotel San Juan
Address: Hotel San Juan
Hours: 9 AM to 5 PM

Havanautos - Hotel Sierra Mar
Address: Carretera de Guamá
Hours: 9 AM to 5 PM

Havanautos - Santiago de Cuba Airport
Address: Santiago de Cuba Airport
Hours: 24 hours

Rex Car Rental Locations

Following are Rex Car Rental locations by area.

Havana Airport

Rex: José Martí Airport Terminal 2
Address: José Martí International Airport Terminal 2
Hours: 8:30 AM to 8:00 PM

Rex - José Martí Airport Terminal 3
Address: José Martí International Airport Terminal 3
Hours: 24 hours

Old Havana

Address: Avenida Rancho Boyeros and Calzada Bejucal
Hours: 8:30 AM to 8:00 PM

Old Havana

Rex - Cruise Terminal, Havana Harbour
Address: Habana Cruise Terminal, Avenida del Puerto
Hours: 8:30 AM to 7.00 PM

Rex - Hotel Parque Central
Address: Neptuno, corner of Prado
Hours: 8:30 AM to 7:30 PM

Vedado

Rex - Línea and Malecón
Address: Línea and MalecónHours: 8:30 AM to 7:30 PM

Miramar

Rex – Avenida 5 and 92
Address: Avenida 5 and 92, Playa
Hours: 9:00AM to 8:00PM

Rex - Hotel Neptuno Tritón
Address: Calle 3, corner of Calle 74
Hours: 8:30 AM to 7:00 PM

East Beaches and Varadero

Rex - Hotel Iberostar Varadero
Address: Hotel Iberostar Varadero
Hours: 8:30 AM to 4:30 PM

Rex - Varadero Airport
Address: Varadero Juan Gualberto Gómez International Airport
Hours: 24 hours

Rex - Varadero Calle 36
Address: Calle 36 and Autopista
Hours: 8:30 AM to 7 PM

Jardines del Rey/Cayo Coco

Rex - Cayo Coco
Address: Hotel Sol Club Cayo Coco
Hours: 8 AM to 5 PM

Holguín

Rex - Brisas Guardalavaca
Address: Calle 2 #1 Playa Guardalavaca
Hours: 9:00AM to 4:30PM

Rex - Holguín
Address: Av. Jesús Menéndez, corner of Avenida Internacionalistas
Hours: 8:30AM to 5:30PM

Rex - Holguín Airport
Address: Frank País International Airport
Hours: 24 hours

Villa Clara Province

Rex - Santa Clara Airport
Address: Aeropuerto Internacional Abel Santamaría
Hours: 8:30 AM to 5:30 PM

Camaguey Province

Rex - Hotel Camaguey
Address: Carretera Central Este, Kilometro 4.5, Jayamá
Hours: 8:30 AM to 5:30 PM
Camaguey City

Rex - Camaguey Airport
Address: Ignacio Agramonte International Airport
Hours: 24 hours

Cienfuegos

Rex - Cienfuegos
Address: Calle 39 #1201, between 12 and 14, Punta Gorda
Hours: 8:30 AM to 5:30 PM

Pinar del Río

Rex - Hotel Pinar del Río
Address: Martí and Final Autopista
Hours: 9 AM to 5 PM

Ciego de Ávila Province

Rex - Ciego de Ávila
Address: Carretera de Ceballo, Kilometro 2.5
Hours: 8:30AM to 7:30PM

Santiago de Cuba

Rex - Santiago de Cuba
Address: Calle M, corner of Calle 5
Hours: 8:30 AM to 7:30 PM

Rex - Santiago de Cuba Airport
Address: Antonio Maceo International Airport
Hours: 24 hours

Vía Car Rental Locations

Vía Rental Car is the smallest rental car agency. It has locations in the following places.

Havana Airport

José Martí Airport Terminal 3
Address: José Martí International Airport Terminal 3
Hours: 9 AM to 9 PM

Vedado

Hotel El Bosque
Hotel Occidental Miramar
Hotel Tryp Habana Libre

Old Havana

AUSA
Hotel Mercure Sevilla
Hotel Parque Central
Hotel Saratoga
Museo de la Revolución

Miramar

Hotel H10 Panorama

Rent a Car Cuba Offices

Rent a Car Cuba has offices only in Havana. These are.

José Martí Airport - Terminal 2 and Terminal 3
Avenida Rancho Boyeros

Hotel Bellocaribe
Calle 158 and Avenida 32

Hotel Chateau Miramar
Avenida 1 and Playa

Hotel Meliá Cohiba
Calle 3, between Paseo and Calle 2

Hotel Comodoro
Avenida 3 and Calle 84

Terminal de Cruceros
San Ignacio #101, Old Havana

Hotel Las Praderas
Calle 230, between Calle 15 and Calle 17

Hotel Meliá Habana
Avenida 3, between 76 and 80, Miramar

Hotel Parque Central
Paseo del Prado and Neptuno

Hotel Vedado
Calle 25, corner of Calle O

Marina Hemingway
Avenida 5 and Calle 248, Santa Fé

Residencial Tarara
Calle 8, corner of Avenida 1, Playas del Este

Hotel Trip Habana Libre
Calle 23 and Calle M, Vedado

Am I Renting a Stolen Car?

Good question!

One out of three rental cars in Cuba are stolen by bored youth who want to go for a joyride. These cars are almost always abandoned in town and recovered by the rental agencies. But there are times when the police do not have the most complete information.

ALWAYS ASK IF THE CAR YOU ARE RENTING HAS BEEN REPORTED STOLEN TO THE POLICE. IF IT HAS, THEN ASK IF IT HAS BEEN REPORTED AS HAVING BEEN RECOVERED.

This Editor rented a car from an agency a block from the Hotel Nacional. He drove back to the hotel to pick up other visitors. After leaving the Hotel Nacional, he made a right turn and then another right when he reached the Malecón. Two blocks later he was pulled over for driving a stolen car. At the police station, a couple of blocks from the former U.S. Interests Section and current U.S. embassy, it was determined the car had, indeed, been stolen the previous week. It had also been recovered and returned to the rental agency. The police, however, had not been notified. The entire matter took about two hours to resolve.

Being pulled over in Havana for driving a stolen car should not be on your list of things to do in Cuba.

Nightlife & Sightseeing

NIGHTLIFE & CLUBS

When the sun goes down, the lights go on—most of the time. The variety of entertainment options in Havana continues to increase.

Fábrica de Arte Cubano
A former oil factory is one of Havana's most popular nightspots, the brainchild of X Alfonso.
Where?
Intersection of Calle 11 and Calle 26, Vedado
Tel: (53) 7 838-2260
Website: *www.fabricadeartecubano.com*

La Zorra y El Cuervo
This is one of Roberto Fonseca's regular haunts—and is the best place for jazz in Havana. The basement room—low ceilings, steps underground—adds to the ambiance of the place. Two drinks are included in the admission.
Where?
Calle 23, between Calle N and Calle O, Vedado
Tel: (53) 7 833-2402

Espacios
Is this a frat house? It feels that way, if a frat house had a contemporary bar and a grand garden filled with people lingering, enjoying live music.
Where?
Calle 10 #510, between Avenida 5 and Avenida 31, Miramar
Tel: (53) 7 202-2921

Gato Tuerto

This is a great spot for jazz, steps from the Hotel Nacional. It's a small venue, so keep that in mind.
Where?
Calle O, between Calle 17 and Calle 19
Tel: (53) 7 838-2629

Yellow Submarine

As the name suggests, it's a Beatles-themed spot, conveniently located in the Vedado. It doesn't open until 9 PM, but there's music until 2 AM.
Where?
Calle 17 and Calle 6, Vedado

Casa de la Música Miramar

This venue is great for big band shows—but it can get crowded, which is to be expected when the music is great.
Where?
Calle 20 #3308, on the corner of Calle 35, Miramar
Tel: (53) 7 202-3868

Cabaret Las Vegas

Believe it or not, many of the performers from the Tropicana Club also perform here. There's salsa music and nightly shows. It's a popular place with locals and tourists from Latin America. It's popular with the local LGBTQ community.
Where?
Calle Infanta #204, on the corner of Calle 25
Vedado
Tel: (53) 7 836-7939

Humboldt 52

A great place that is also favored by Havana's LGBTQ community, but everyone's welcome. Drag shows are, of course, to be expected—and dancing under a disco ball. It doesn't get going until after 1 AM. And who knows? You might run into Raúl Castro himself.
Where?
Calle Humboldt #52, between Infanta and Hospital, Centro
Tel: (53) 5 330-2989
Facebook: *www.facebook.com/humboldt52*

Diablo Tun Tun

This venue is the best for matinee performances. The stage is smaller and the crowd is a bit more into the music than into seeing and being seen, which is perfect if you love great music.
Where?
Calle 20 #3308, on the corner of Calle 35, Miramar
Tel: (53) 7 202-6147

El Gijones / Asociación Asturiana

The Havana Queens, a revue of Cuban dance forms performed by lovely dancing girls, is a splendid experience. It's a small venue, and the performance ends with the dancers heading out into the audience to dance with everyone.

Where?
Prado #309, on the corner of Virtudes, Old Havana
Tel: (53) 7 817-8778

El Tocororo

Foremost, this is a bar. A bar that has a stage. And a stage where terrific musicians perform nightly.

Where?
Calle 18, on the corner Avenida 3
Tel: (53) 7 202-4530

Tropicana Club

This is the closest thing to Las Vegas that Havana has—for now. It is pricey by Cuban standards—$100 USD—and popular. You will probably have to charm your concierge to snag tickets. (This is where those toiletries and sundries come in handy.) The Tropicana Club opened in 1939 at the Villa Mina and occupies a six-acre estate graced with lush tropical gardens.

Where?
Calle 72, between Calle 41 and Calle 42, Marianao
Tel: (53) 7 267-1717

Cabaret Parisién

A well-produced dance and music revue in the traditions of the Hotel Nacional, this is an enjoyable show that consistently draws people to the hotel.

Where?
On the grounds of the Hotel Nacional, Calle O on the corner of Calle 21, Vedado
Tel: (53) 7 836-3564

Maxim Rock

For the serious rockers in Havana, the place to go. Bands play every night, and a website provides current information.

Where?
Calle Bruzón #62, between Almendares and Ayestarán
Tel: (53) 7 877-5925
Website: *www.maximrock.com*

Café la Flauta Mágica

Located on the 10th floor penthouse with a rooftop pool, this jazz bar is the brainchild of Rembert Egues, who returned from Paris, where he was exiled, to launch this venture.

Where?

Calzada #101, between Calle L and Calle M, Vedado
Tel: (53) 7 832-3195

Don Cangrejo

Can you say Cuban circuit party? If you can, then this outdoor disco is reminiscent of late-night, noisy events in Key West or Miami Beach. Clearly for a younger crowd, the techno music and the bands keep the crowd dancing into the early hours.

Where?
Calle Avenida 1, between Calle 16 and Calle 18
Tel: (53) 7 207-4196

Bertolt Brecht Cultural Center

Also popular among the younger crowd, this is a good place to start or end the evening, especially if you're set to visit several clubs. The hippest Cuban musicians play here, and the crowd is cool.

Where?
Calle 13 #258, on the corner of Calle I
Tel: (53) 7 830-1354

Habana Café

Tickets are best secured through your concierge. The Buena Vista Social Club revue continues to pack them in night after night. Why not? It's a great show.

Where?
Avenida Paseo, between Calle 1 and Calle 3, interior of Meliá Cohiba Hotel, Vedado
Tel: (53) 7 833-3636, ext. 2710

Casa de la Música Centro Habana

The bands play with gusto, and the music flows freely and joyfully. This place will get your head in the right space for enjoying Havana at night.

Where?
Galiano, Centro
Tel: (53) 7 862-4165

Club Salsero Chévere

The best place to salsa in Havana? This is it. Where?
Avenida 3, between Calle 76 and Calle 80, Mirarmar
Tel: (53) 5 264-9692
Website: *www.salseandochevere.com*
E-mail: *pedro@saleseandochevere.com*

10 OLD HAVANA'S ETERNAL CHARM

Old Havana, La Habana Vieja, is the city's main attraction.

Old Havana is a World Heritage Site that attracts almost three million visitors a year.

Located in Havana's city center on the banks of the Bay of Havana, it has the second-highest population density in the city and comprises the original city of Havana during colonial rule. Not unlike other colonial cities built by the Spanish—San Juan, Santo Domingo, and Campeche—Old Havana is defined by fortifications that protected the city from attacks.

Founded in 1519 in the natural harbor of the Bay of Havana, it was the ideal shipment point for New Spain. Ships would arrive in Havana before continuing to Spain, and ships arriving from Europe would make call in Havana before continuing on to their final destinations.

Spanish galleons, laden with treasures, used Havana as their hub, linking the Old World and the New World. Wealth arrived in this port, and its economy reflected its importance. The city reflected Baroque and Neoclassical styles of architecture. Narrow streets conferred the sense of intimacy. The fortifications protected the Spanish settlers from pirate raids.

In 1555 Jacques de Sores, a French corsair, for example, invaded and burned Havana to the ground. Known as The Exterminating Angel, de Sores inflicted such devastation that the Spanish crown mandated massive fortifications as it rebuilt the city. In 1558 Bartolomé Sánchez was the engineer responsible for the construction of the Castillo de la Real Fuerza, which still stands today.

Under Sánchez's guidance, Old Havana was rebuilt to resemble Cádiz, a port in southwestern Spain that reflects a Moorish-Arab influence. This is apparent in the courtyards, narrow stone streets, alleys, arcades, convents, churches, and monumental structures.

Under the auspices of UNESCO, Old Havana is being restored.

Old Havana's Main Attractions

The Malecón is the broad seaside boulevard that runs along the seawall from the northern area of Old Havana all the way to the Almendares River.

Castillo del Morro, officially known as the Castillo de los Tres Reyes Magos del Morro, is the world-famous fortress standing watch over the entrance to the Bay of Havana. It is named after the biblical Magi and was designed by the Italian engineer Juan Bautista Antonelli. In 1762 the British captured the fort in the Battle of Havana, but control was returned to Spain under a treaty the following year.

La Cabaña, officially known as Fortaleza de San Carlos de la Cabaña, is located on the east side of the Bay of Havana. La Cabaña, boasting massive walls constructed in the eighteenth century, remains the most fearsome fortress the Spanish constructed in Cuba. Over the next two centuries following its construction, it served as a military base for Spain and then for the Cuban Republic. In 1959, after the Revolution, Che Guevara was placed in charge of La Cabaña. It served as a military prison where the revolutionary tribunals tried political prisoners, dissidents, and members of Batista's secret police, known as *Buró de Represión de Actividades Comunistas*. Since January 1959 Fidel Castro and Raúl Castro have had more than 1,000 men and women executed by firing squad at this location.

San Salvador de la Punta Fortress, located opposite the El Morro Castle, was constructed in 1590. It was united to El Morro in 1629 by a thick chain that prevented the entry of hostile ships from rival European powers.

Plaza de Armas is the main attraction in Old Havana and attracts all visitors. Since the late 16th century it has been the center of military events and political ceremonies.

94

Palacio de los Capitanes Generales, or the Palace of the Captains General (governors), is on the eastern side of the Plaza de Armas. Today it houses the Museum of the City.

Castillo de la Fuerza Real, or the Castle of the Royal Army, is one of the most important structures that flank the Plaza de Armas. The first large fortification in the city, reconstruction began in 1558 under the supervision of Bartolomé Sánchez; the original structure was razed by the French corsair Jacques de Sores.

Catedral de San Cristóbal, the most important structure in the Plaza de la Catedral, was built in 1748 on the orders of José Felipe de Trespalacios, the Bishop of Salamanca, Spain.

The Galician Center, located in the central park, was originally a social club for immigrants from Galicia; the Castro brothers are sons of such immigrants. Housed in the Theater Tacón, built in 1838, the Galician Center served as a social club between 1907 and 1914.

Gran Teatro de la Habana, originally the Theater Tacón, is the permanent theater company for the National Ballet of Cuba founded by the legendary Alicia Alonso. The theater also houses the García Lorca Concert Hall, the largest such venue in Cuba.

Museo de la Revolución, located in the former Presidential Palace, is famous for its display of *Granma*, the ship that brought Fidel Castro to Cuba from Mexico.

Basílica San Francisco de la Habana is the church and convent erected in 1608 in honor of San Francisco de Asis; the present structure was constructed in 1737.

Museo del Chocolate is not really a museum but the most elaborate chocolate shop in Cuba. When Fidel Castro was exiled in Mexico, he lived for a time in Mérida, Yucatán, as an expat, where he became a chocolate connoisseur. Chocolates from Mexico have been routinely shipped to him by diplomatic courier. The Museo del Chocolate is a charming conceit.

Lonja del Comcercio was Cuba's stock exchange until the Revolution. It now houses government offices.

Gaia Teatro, located on Calle Brazil #157, between Cuba and Aguiar, is an experimental performance arts theater offering workshops, community activities, and performance spaces.

Havana Central Railway Station, or La Habana Central, is the city's *Estación Central de Ferrocarriles*, or Central Railway Station. This is the main railway terminal in Havana and the largest train station in the country. The national railway company, the Ferrocarriles Nacionales de Cuba (FFCC), offers train service to the entire nation.

Here are the routes:

Train Route	Destination	Notes
#1	Santiago de Cuba	Offers First Class services with air-conditioning.
#3	Ciego de Ávila	
#11	Santiago de Cuba	
#11/30	Guantánamo	via Santiago de Cuba
#13	Bayamo	
#13/32	Manzanillo	via Bayamo
#15	Holguín	
#17	Sancti Spíritus	
#19	Cienfuegos	Evening departure
#21	Cienfuegos	Morning departure
#23	Pinar del Río	

11 HAVANA SIGHTSEEING

There are enough attractions apart from Old Havana to occupy visitors for a couple of weeks.

Old Havana has been restored. The rest of Havana has not. This makes for a dissonant experience, wandering through an unintended exhibition of urban decay and a city collapsing into ruins, most prominently along the Malecón. It's a fascinating glimpse into the limits of midtwentieth-century architecture left in disrepair for half a century. Take out your camera and document what will, without a doubt, not last much longer as the Castro regimes come to an end.

That doesn't mean that the Vedado, Habana Centro, and Miramar districts do not have astounding sights for visitors to enjoy.

97

Vedado

The Vedado is a neighborhood district that lies between Central Havana (*Habana Centro*) to the east and Miramar to the west. It is the most modern section of the city proper, constructed throughout the first half of the twentieth century. The northern area is bordered by the Malecón seawall, a popular place for pedestrian strolls. The main street is Calle 23, also known as La Rampa. The principal hotels in the Vedado are the Hotel Nacional de Cuba, Hotel Capri, La Habana Libre (the former Hilton Hotel), Hotel Riviera, and the Meliá Cohiba Hotel.

Following are key attractions in the Vedado:

United States Embassy is located on Calzado, between L and M Streets.

FOCSA Building, built in 1956, is the tallest building in Cuba. When it opened, it caused a national sensation, a harbinger of modern architecture and design.

Cine Yara is a classic cinema house.

José Martí Anti-Imperialist Plaza is located, conveniently, across from the U.S. embassy on the Malecón.

Helados Coppelia is located across from the Habana Libre Hotel. Before the Revolution it boasted 38 flavors of ice cream; today it is lucky to have two available.

Centro Hebreo Sefaradi and Synagogue is located across from the Víctor Hugo Park and is the most important Jewish synagogue and cultural center in Cuba.

Museum of Decorative Arts, located at Calle 17 #502, between Calle E and Calle D, is the former residence of María Luisa Gómez-Mena Vd. De Cagiga, Countess of Revilla de Camargo, sister of José Gómez-Mena, the proprietor of the Manzana de Gómez department store. The house was designed by French architects Virad and Destuque and constructed between 1924 and 1927. The Museum showcases most of her furnishings, which were abandoned when she fled. The most impressive pieces, however, are not on public view, but locked away in a cellar.

Monument to the Victims of the USS Maine stands on the Malecón, near the Hotel Nacional and the José Martí Anti-Imperialist Plaza.

Napoleonic Museum houses one of the most important collections from the 18th and 19th centuries of Napoleonic memorabilia outside Europe. The museum occupies the 1929 Florentine Renaissance-style mansion abandoned by Cuban politician Orestes Ferrara when he went into exile in Rome weeks afters the Revolution triumphed. The villa, named La Dolce Dimora, became a museum in 1961 simply because the Revolutionary government could not think of what to do with a residence

98

with such an astounding collection of treasures. The museum is on San Miguel, between Ronda and Mazón.

Universidad de la Habana is located across from the Napoleonic Museum. The University was founded on January 5, 1728, and is one of the first that Spain established in New Spain. This is where Fidel Castro studied law; Reinaldo Arenas was expelled from the University for expressing ideas other than those officially sanctioned by the government.

Cemeterio de Cristóbal Colón, or Colón Cemetery, rivals La Recoleta in Buenos Aires as one of the great historical cemeteries in Latin America. Designed and constructed by Spanish architect Calixto Arellano de Loira y Cardoso, he became the first person to be buried in the cemetery when he died before the project was completed. A visit to the cemetery, where there are legends and reported hauntings, is a great excursion.

National Theater of Cuba, or the Teatro Nacional de Cuba, is located on the Plaza de la Revolución.

Amadeo Roldán Theater, or the Teatro Amadeo Roldán, is the residence for the National Symphony Orchestra of Cuba, which has seasonal performances every Sunday.

John Lennon Park, formerly the Parque Menocal, is a public park with a bench, near the corner of 17th and 6th Streets, with a statue of former Beatle John Lennon. Sculpted by José Villa Soberón, it has an inscription reading, "You may say I'm a dreamer, but I'm not the only one," in Spanish (*"Dirás que soy un soñador pero no soy el único."*) The phrase, from the song "Imagine," remains a subtle affirmation of Cubans' aspirations for a future.

Hubert de Blanck Theater is a charming theater located on Calle Calzado, named in honor of Hubert de Blanck, the Dutch-born composer and musician who emigrated in Cuba.

José Martí Memorial, Monumento a José Martí, is a memorial to the Apostle of Cuban Independence. This star-shaped tower with its statue of Martí stands at the northern section of the Plaza de la Revolución. The monument, which stands 358 feet (109 meters), was designed by a team of architects under the direction of Enrique Luis Varela. The memorial is surrounded by six columns and gardens.

Havana Central (Habana Centro)

Lying between Old Havana and the Vedado, Havana Central is filled with attractions for tourists. Following are among the key attractions:

El Capitolio, or the National Capitol Building, was completed in 1929 and was Cuba's Congress until 1959. Today, it houses the Cuban Academy of Sciences. Modeled after the U.S. Capitol in Washington, D.C., it boasts the world's largest indoor statue. The Statue of the Republic *(La Estatua de la República)* is an idealized representation of Cuban nationalism modeled after Lily Valty, a Cuban model of great renown.

Edificio Bacardi was the largest office building in Cuba until the Revolution. It is located at Avenida Bélgica #261.

Plaza de Carlos III is a commercial, shopping, office, and hotel center.

Casa de la Música, on Galiano, is a popular destination for shopping.

Chinatown, or the Barrio Chino, much diminished since the Revolution, is close to the Capitolio.

Hospital Hermanos Ameijeiras is the leading medical facility in Cuba, apart from the ones that treat the political elite and foreign dignitaries.

Paseo del Prado is a grand concourse that divides Centro from Old Havana. The Paseo includes the entire length of Paseo José Martí, including the promenade's extension to the Malecón at the San Salvador de la Punta Fortress south to Neptuno; the street to the west of Parque Central; the street east of the Capitolio; and the area surrounding the Fuente de la India fountain.

Fuente de la India, a public fountain designed by Giuseppe Gaggini, is at the south of the Capitolio, between Monte and Dragones Streets and in front of the Hotel Saratoga. The figure representes Habana, the indigenous woman in whose honor Havana is named.

Manzana de Gómez was the first shopping mall in Cuba. Constructed by José Gómez-Mena Vila, the 1910 building occupied an entire city block. It was the first European-style shopping arcade in Cuba and one of the largest commercial centers in Latin America.

Miramar

Miramar is a sumptuous residential district. Before the Revolution, this was an upscale suburb boasting mansions and lavish homes. Today it houses many embassies, including the all-important Russian and Mexican embassies, as well as the Siboney Country Club, site of glamorous social events during the 1950s. Modern hotels, including the Meliá Oriente, Oasis Panorama, and Occidental Miramar, are located in this neighborhood. In recent years the Miramar Trade Center, or Centro de Negocios Miramar, opened, anticipating the opening up of Cuba.

Miramar's most prominent street is La Quinta Avenida, or Fifth Avenue, which runs through the district. Following are key attractions:

The Clock of Fifth Avenue is on Fifth Avenue and 10th Street. It was erected in 1924.

Casa de Alberto de Armas, a restored Beaux Arts mansion, was built in 1926 and designed by Jorge Luis Echarte. Located on 2nd Street.

Museum of the Ministry of the Interior, the Museo del Ministrerio del Interio, on 12th Street, is worth a visit.

Miramar Theater is on 18th Street.

Mexican Embassy is located on 12th Street. Mexican ambassador Gilberto Bosques played a pivotal role during the Cuban Missile Crisis and assisted John Donovan's efforts to win the release of prisoners from the failed Bay of Pigs invasion. (More than 1,100 people were detained and were traded for $53 million in food and medicine.

Russian Embassy lies between 62nd and 66th Streets. A monumental structure, it was designed by Basilio Piasecki and Alexander Rochegov.

Casa del Habano, between 14th and 16th Streets, is a great place for cigars. Smaller shops are found at the Meliá Habana and the Miramar Trade Center.

Karl Marx Theater is located in the Park of the Hanged. Prior to the Revolution it was the Teatro Blanquita. It is one of the city's most important venues, seating 5,500 people.

Park of the Hanged, or Parque de los Ahorcados, is between 24th and 26th Streets. The park boasts beautiful jagüey trees, or the *Ficus stahlii*, a species of *Ficus*, which create a beautiful space.

Iglesia San Antonio de Padua, located at 60th Street, was constructed in 1949 in the modernist style then popular.

Plaza Emiliano Zapata, Mexico's revolutionary hero, figures prominently in Cuban political thought.

Iglesia de Santa Rita de Casia, on 26th Street, was built in 1942 by renowned Cuban architect Víctor Morales.

Iglesia de Jesús de Miramar is located between 80th and 82nd Streets. Built in 1953, it has an organ with 5,000 pipes and massive paintings depicting the Stations of the Cross by Spanish artist César Hombrados Oñativa.

Prado Park features a Romanesque temple and a bust of Mahatma Gandhi.

Ecological Park Monte Barreto is located on 70th Street.

101

Iranian Embassy, at 30th Street and Fifth Avenue, boasts an exquisite collection of furniture seized from prominent Cubans who fled into exile.

Fifth Avenue Mansions are located all along the avenue; many are embassies of rogue nations, which in itself makes for a fun stroll.

El Ajibe Restaurant is noteworthy because it was featured in Anthony Bourdain's program *No Reservations*.

Hotel Barceló Habana is worth a stop for a drink in the lobby bar.

Meliá Occidental Hotel is a popular hotel in the district.

Miramar Trade Center is open for business.

Fusterlandia, located in Jaimitas, is an art installation now three decades in the making. The brainchild of José Fuster, this living monumental structure in inspired, according to the artist, by Pablo Picasso, but it evokes the aesthetics of Antoni Gaudí. It is certainly well worth a visit simply to enjoy its wonderful campiness.

Cine Miramar is located on Avenida 5 near Calle 90. The 600-seat movie house, built in the 1950s, was a cultural center in Miramar through the mid-1990s. During the Special Period, the end of Soviet subsidies made it impossible to repair and maintain it. The cinema is in disrepair today.

Oriental Park Racetrack was the site of the Havana-American Jockey Club of Cuba. It was founded in 1915 and was a thoroughbred horse-racing facility until the Revolution.

Baseball Estadio Latinoaméricano is located in the Cerro district, at Calle Pedro Pérez #302, between Patria and Sarabia.

The Malecón

The Malecón, whose official name is the Avenida de Maceo, is the broad seawall, or esplanade, that runs for five miles, from the Bay of Havana to the end of the Vedado district. It defines Havana, separating the city from the Straits of Florida.

Construction of this iconic feature began in 1901 during U.S. military occupation of the island. The Malecón was built to protect the city from the *nortes*, strong inclement weather during the fall and winter months.

Its broad and sweeping embrace of the city, however, has made it a pedestrian promenade at night for the city's residents. Teenagers hang out with their friends, lovers walk along holding hands, and fishermen spend hours seeing what they might catch. Note: Today, it is also the epicenter of prostitution and hustling, so be on the alert.

Despite its being a hotspot for prostitution and transgender people to socialize, the Malecón remains very popular among the city's residents, especially among the less privileged *Habaneros*, who have few alternatives for entertainment.

In 1923, the Malecón was extended to reach the Alemadares River, between K and L Streets. It is worth a stroll, especially the stretch between Havana Harbor and the U.S. Embassy. The buildings that line the Malecón are often in disrepair—some have collapsed into piles of rubble—but this, ironically, adds to the romantic appeal of this popular and spectacular destination.

Harbors and Rivers

Havana is defined by a harbor to the east and a river to the west.

Almendares River flows for about 30 miles. It originates east of Tapate and flows to the Straits of Florida. The Almendares provides Havana with its water supply. The river divides the Plaza de la Revolución, in the Vedado, from the Miramar district and the western neighborhoods.

Havana Harbor is the principal port for the nation, apart from the U.S.-occupied Guantánamo Bay Naval Base. During the Colonial period Spain struggled to prevent other European powers, particularly the British and the French, from raiding and attacking Havana. The Battle of Havana, a siege lasting two months, was launched by the British in 1762. This accounts for the fortifications that characterize the mouth of the harbor. Do note that Havana Bay comprises three distinct harbors: Marimelena, Guanabacoa, and Atarés. In the 18th-century the Fortaleza de San Carlos de la Cabaña, today known as La Cabaña or Fort of Saint Charles, was the site of mass executions after the 20th-century Revolution came to power. (Cubans are taught that claims mass executions following the 1959 Revolution are lies of American imperialism.)

Fortifications

La Cabaña, or the Fortaleza de San Carlos de la Cabaña (Fort of Saint Charles), is a fortress complex constructed in the eighteenth century. It is the third largest fortification in the Americas. The fort rises almost 200 feet from the harbor and is adjacent to the Morro Castle.

Castillo de la Real Fuerza, or the Castle of the Royal Force, is located on the western side of Havana Harbor, bordering the Plaza de Armas. The Castle was constructed to protect Havana from pirate attacks. It is the oldest stone fort in the Americans and was declared a World Heritage site by UNESCO.

Morro Castle, or the Castillo del os Tres Reyes Magos del Morro, guards the entrance to the Bay of Havana. Designed by Juan Bautista Antonelli, the castle was occupied by the British in 1762. It was returned to Spanish control the following year.

Castillo de San Salvador de la Punta is a fortress in the Bay of Havana. In 1559, to protect the city from pirate attacks and the landings of French corsairs, lookout posts were constructed. It served as an important defense for what is now Old Havana.

Castillo del Principe is located in the Loma de Aróstegui and served as an important military defense for Havana.

Torreón de la Chorrera, or the Fuerte de Santa Dorotea de la Luna de la Chorrera, is a tower that stands on a coral islet a short distance from the shore. The tower, completed in 1646, was an outlook to prevent enemy ships from entering into the mouth of the Almendares River.

Santa Clara Battery stands on the grounds of the Hotel Nacional. It has two remaining coastal guns. One is a Krupp, 280mm, and the other is an Ordóñez HSE Modelo 1892 rifle, 205mm. The Battery is part of the World Heritage Site designation that includes Old Havana.

Religious Sites

Havana Cathedral, or the Cathedral of the Virgin Mary of the Immaculate Conception (*La Catedral de la Virgen María de la Concepción Inmaculada de La Habana*), is located on the Plaza de la Catedral. It is one of eleven Roman Catholic cathedrals in Cuba. It serves as the seat of the Roman Catholic Archdiocese of San Cristóbal de la Habana.

Iglesia de Jesús de Miramar was constructed by Eugenio Cosculluela y Barreras in the Romanesque-Byzantine style. It is the second largest church in Cuba and boasts murals fourteen large murals by the Spanish painter Cesareo Marciano Hombrados y de Onativia. The church was consecrated on May 28, 1953.

Seminario de San Carlos y San Ambrosio was constructed for the Jesuits in the mid-eighteenth century; the order arrived in Cuba in 1689 and was expelled in 1767. In 1774 they were allowed to return and opened under the name of the Saint Carlos and Saint Ambrosio Royal School Seminary. In 1777 King Charles III of Spain declared it a Conciliate, making it equal in rank to Spanish seminaries.

Our Lady of Kazán Orthodox Catheral, or *La Catedral Ortodoxa Nuestra Señora de Kazán*, is under the jurisdiction of the Russian Orthodox Church.

Christ of Havana, or *El Cristo de La Habana,* is a sculpture of Jesus of Nazareth on a hilltop overlooking the Bay of Havana. It was designed by Cuban artist Jilma Madera in 1953.

The Basilica and Monastery of San Francisco de Asis, built between 1580 and 1591, is the seat of the Franciscan community in Cuba. The basilica was remoded, in the baroque style, in 1730.

Air and Flight Museum

Museo del Aire, once located in the southwestern suburbs, was relocated to the San Antonio de los Baños Airfield, approximately 30 miles (48 kilometers) southwest of Havana. It's difficult to visit because officials are ambivalent about how to manage requests for a tour.

School of Medicine

Escuela Latinoamericana de Medicina (ELAM), or the Latin American School of Medicine, is the leading international school of medicine in Cuba. It is an integral part of the Cuban health-care system. Established in 1999, as of 2013 it had 19,550 students from 110 countries, making it the largest medical school in the world.

Hailed as a leader in health care, Cuba trains thousands of doctors from the world over, and it has first-rate facilities for medical tourists (Americans traveling to Cuba for medical treatment were featured in Michael Moore's documentary *Sicko*) and for Cuba's ruling elite. Ordinary Cubans, however, unless they can offer gifts—bribes—to officials, routinely wait and wait to see doctors. It can take months to get an appointment and years to schedule surgery. (The same is true of socialized medicine in Canada or the U.K.) Often, pharmaceuticals are not available.

It is a paradox of the Revolution: spending lavishly to provide health care abroad while Cubans are forced to wait for health care.

The campus, however, is impressive.

105

12 OFF THE BEATEN PATH: U.S. FUGITIVES IN CUBA

There are scores of Americans living in Cuba who are fugitives from U.S. justice. After you have tired of sightseeing, seeking out a fugitive might be an intriguing pursuit . . .

One of the more surreal things to do in Havana is to look up some of the fugitives who have been granted asylum by Cuba. The U.S., especially now that diplomatic relations have been restored, is seeking the extradition of cop killers, hijackers, bomb makers, and other individuals it wants to prosecute.

In Havana, given that it is a fairly open city, it is possible to meet one of these fugitives; some would welcome being taken out for lunch, given their lives living in hiding.

Of course it helps to plan ahead and do research, but here are some of the more sought-after fugitives in Havana today:

1. Joanne Chesimard

Joanne Chesimard, who goes by the name of Assata Shakur, has been living in Cuba since 1984. A member of the Black Liberation Army, she shot Trooper Werner Foerster dead in 1973. Convicted of murder, she escaped in 1979.

She fled to Cuba where she was granted asylum and is now in her late 60s. The F.B.I. has a $2 million reward for her return to the U.S.

2. Guillermo Morales

Fighting for Puerto Rican independence led Mr. Morales to make and denotate bombs. He was sentenced to 99 years in prison for two bombings—in 1975 and 1977—that left five people dead and injured more than 60.

He escaped from Bellevue Hospital in New York in 1979, made his way to Mexico, and from there he fled to Cuba in 1988.

3. Víctor Manuel Gerena

In 1983 Víctor Manuel Gerena robbed a security company of $7 million. He then escaped from the U.S., making his way to Cuba. He was wanted by the F.B.I. Castro granted him asylum. Gerena currently lives in Havana.

4. William Potts

William Pott hijacked an airplane in 1984, diverting it to Havana. Jailed by Cuban authorities at first, he was subsequently granted asylum to spite Ronald Reagan. He now lives in Havana with his family. Pott has expressed the desire to return to the U.S. provided he is granted a pardon by current president Barack Obama.

5. Charlie Hill

Charlie Hill shot Robert Rosenbloom, a New Mexico State Trooper, dead in 1971. He then hijacked an airplane to Havana. He has been living in Havana since then.

6. Ishmael LaBeet

Ishmael LaBeet, accused of murdering eight people in St. Thomas in 1973, hijacked the airplane escorting him to the U.S. mainland, diverting it to Havana. He was granted asylum and lives in Havana.

Robert Vesco

Do note that the opportunity to meet other notorious fugitives has passed. Sadly, Robert Vesco, the legendary fugitive financier who is believed to have swindled more than $200 million, died years back. Mr. Vesco lived a life of leisure and luxury in Havana until 2007; he died of cancer.

This Editor was surprised by Mr. Vesco's great sense of humor, especially given his circumstances, over lunch in the summer of 2005.

Bounty Hunters

One final note: Although it might be possible to meet some of the scores of American fugitives living in Cuba, do not under any circumstances attempt to play bounty hunter. It may be tempting to kidnap a fugitive to collect a multimillion dollar reward in the U.S., but don't do it!

Cigars, Rum & Classic Cars

CIGARS

Think of Cuba and you think of cigars.

Think of cigars and you realize that a good cigar is like a good glass of wine: both reflect nature and nurture. That is to say, cigars depend on the quality of the leaf and craftsmanship of the cigar maker. And the quality of tobacco depends on many factors, natural and those informed by mankind.

Here, then, are the best cigars available in Cuba today. These Top Ten were determined by blind test No. 126 conducted by the editors of *Cigar Aficionado*.

These are the ones to enjoy during 2016.

Top Ten Cuban Cigars

1. Bolívar Corona Gigante
2. Bolívar Tubos No. 1
3. Montecristo Edmundo
4. Ramón Allones Perfecto Exclusivo Suiza
5. Montecristo No. 3
6. Romeo y Julieta Churchill
7. Vegueros Mañanita
8. Cohiba Robusto (Tubo)
9. Partagás de Luxe (Tubo)
10. Romeo y Julieta Romero No. 1 (Tubo)

Cigar Factories

Where are these wonderful cigars made?

Partagás

Calle San Carlos #816, between Sitio and Peñalver

Centro

The Partagás factory has been relocated to the site of the former El Rey del Mundo factory. They make Partagás, Bolívar, La Gloria Cubana, Ramón Allones, and Quai d'Orsay cigar brands.

H. Upmann

Belascoaín #852, between Peñalver and Desague Centro

This manufacturer has also changed location, now occupying the site of the old Romeo y Julieta location. The factory makes H. Upmanns and is subcontracted to make Montecristos, Romeos, and Cohibas.

La Corona
Avenida 20 de Mayo and Línea de Ferrocarril
Cerro

This location doesn't make La Corona cigars, which are no longer in production in Cuba. The plant, however, makes Hoyo de Monterrey, Cuaba, and Punch.

Franciso Donatién
Calle Antonio Maceo #157
Pinar del Río

This plant is a two-hour drive west of Havana, rather scenic since it meanders through the tobacco fields. It's known for making Trinidad Fundadores.

14 RUM

Cuba produces some of the world's best rums.

A royal decree, issued in 1539 by King Carlos V, placed Cuba on rum's map. During the colonial period, Cuba became an exporter of rum to Europe and throughout New Spain. In the 18th and 19th centuries Cuba gained worldwide renown for its rums.

The upheaval in Cuba's rum industry as a result of the Revolution—manufacturers were nationalized, and international patent disputes continue to this day—has not substantially affected the quality of the rum produced in Cuba.

Cuba today produces some of the more coveted brands, silky-smooth varieties ideal for classic drinks, including mojitos, Cuba libres, and daiquiris. Havana Club remains the most popular export rum. Here are the rum brands produced in Cuba:

Cubay
Havana Club
Ron Edmundo Dantes
Ron Legendario
Ron Mulata
Ron Santiago de Cuba
Ron Varadero

A rum tour begins at the Havana Club Museo del Ron in Old Havana. Although the museum is dedicated to Havana Club, there is considerable information on rum history and the rum industry in Cuba. The museum features authentic equipment, from a historic mule-drawn mill to oak casts. There is a very popular tasting room. The museum hours are 10 AM to 5 PM, Monday through Saturday. There are four tours a day (10 AM, noon, 2 PM, and 4 PM) in Spanish, English, and French. The cost is $5 CUC.

After the tour, head over to the Bodeguita del Medio and Floridita for a few rum drinks, in the spirit of Ernest Hemingway, famous for saying: "My mojito in La Bodeguita, my daiquiri in Floridita." Do note, however, that the Revolution has not been kind to either institution, though there is now a renewed effort to match the high standards of the Cuba of the 1940s and 1950s.

If Santiago de Cuba is on your itinerary, a visit to the (former) Barcardi Rum Factory is in order. Again, Revolution has intervened. The Bacardi family was exiled after their property was seized. Cuba cannot use Bacardi as a brand; Bacardi is now headquartered in the Bahamas and maintains lawsuits against the Cuban government, which are pending. (Because Cuba cannot use "Bacardi" as a brand; Havana Club is the brand used, which is also under legal dispute.) For the time being, Cuba produces domestic brands at the factory. There are no tours of the factory itself, but there is a small tasting room and gift shop that is pleasant after visitors admire the beautiful buildings.

These are the most popular brands available for sale to foreigners:

Havana Club Rum Brands

Añejo Blanco
Añejo 3 Years (Aged 3 years)
Añejo Especial
Añejo Reserva
Añejo 7 Years
Añejo 15 Years—Gran Reserva
Añejo Solera—San Cristóbal
Extra Añejo—Máximo
Cuban Barrel Proof
Company location:
Havana Club International, S.A.
Calle A #309, between Calle 13 and Calle 15, Vedado
Havana

Corporación Cuba Ron Brands

Ron CUBAY
Ron Santiago de Cuba
Aguardiente de Caña Sao Can
Company location:
Corporación Cuba Ron, S.A.
Calle 200 #1708, corner of Calle 17, Reparto Atabey
Havana

Museums

Havana Club Museo del Ron
Avenida del Puerto #262, between Sol and Muralla
Havana

Museo del Ron
Calle Bartolomé Masó #358, between Pío Rosado and Hartman
Santiago de Cuba

Master Rum-Makers

Havana Club is Cuba's premier rum. Cuba recognizes a few select artisans as master rum makers, *Maestros Roneros*. This designation requires a minimum of 15 years of dedicated rum-making experience. Master Rum Makers are responsible for every step in the production of making rum.

These are the four recognized *Maestros Roneros* working at Havana Club today.

115

José Navarro

First among equals, Don José was born in Palma Soriano in 1942. He has more than 40 years of experience in the rum industry. As he told a reporter, "The rum doesn't come from a magical combination. It is a cultural legacy, passed on from *Maestro Ronero* to *Maestro Ronero*, from heart to heart, from Cuban to Cuban."

Juan Carlos Gonzáles

Don Juan Carlos joined the quality control department of the Santa Cruz Distillery in 1976. A scientist, he has published more than 43 articles and research papers about rum making. In 2003 he was appointed as a *Maestro Ronero*.

Asbel Morales

The only *Maestro Ronero* actually born on the grounds of a distillery, Don Asbel studied chemical engineering and economics before joining Havana Club. He studied rum making at Manacas. When he was named a Master Rum Maker, he told a reporter: "You do not grow up thinking that you will become a *Maestro Ronero*. It's only when someone recognizes that skill within you and gives you the chance to express yourself that the possibility opens up."

CLASSIC CARS OF CUBA

When you think of Cuba, you think of classic American cars from a bygone era.

One of the unintended consequences of the U.S. trade embargo against Cuba has been to transform Cuba into a time capsule for American cars from the 1950s.

An estimated 60,000 American cars from the 1950s are in Cuba—and in running order. These "Yank tanks," or *máquinas,* refer to classic American cars, such as the 1958 Dodge or 1957 Chevrolet. Since the 1960 trade embargo it's been almost impossible for Cubans to purchase replacement parts for these vehicles. As a result, those on the road reflect Cuban ingenuity in how their owners have been able to adapt other parts, from simple lawn mowers to cannibalizing the engines of Soviet-era cars.

With diplomatic relations now reestablished, American car enthusiasts are newly interested in these cars. It's important to remember that private vehicles in Cuba can only be sold—*un traspaso*— provided that they were registered before the Revolution. If the current owner does not have this paperwork, then the car cannot be legally sold to you, or to anyone for that matter. In addition, there are restrictions on the export of these cars out of the country. These regulations are subject to change. At present, however, cars sold can be shipped to Mexico or the Cayman Islands.

Amigos de Fangio

Americans interested in classic American cars in Havana can start by visiting the Amigos de Fangio website. This is a nonprofit association that tries to join together all enthusiasts of the classic and vintage cars and motorcycles in Cuba.

Website: *www.amigosdefangio.org*

Museo del Automóvil

How can you not go? The Automobile Museum in Old Havana has 49 vehicles from 1905 to 1989, beautifully restored and ready to be admired.

Address:
Oficios #13, on the corner of Callejón de Jústiz
Old Havana
Hours: Tuesday through Sunday, 9 AM to 4:30 PM

Antique Automobile Club of America Museum

It is also a good idea to keep informed about cultural trips to Cuba for car enthusiasts arranged by the Antique Automobile Club of America Museum, which is based in Hershey, Pennsylvania. They sponsored one cultural trip to Cuba in 2015 that focused on rebuilding the bridges that have divided car lovers in Cuba and the U.S.

Website: *www.aacamuseum.org*

Renting a Classic Car

If you're interested in driving one of these beautiful classic cars—you can. Havana Vintage Car Tours is up and running. A family-run business, their fleet includes of a classic 1955 Oldsmobile convertible that took more than two years to restore.

For information on rates, drop by their offices or send them an e-mail.

Havana Vintage Car Tours
Ave 43 #8418, between Calle 84-A and Calle 86
Marianao
Havana
Tel: (53) 5 242-8987
E-mail: *fabiop85@nauta.cu*
Website: *http://www.havanavintagecartours.com/*

Havana Classic Car Tours

If you would rather not rent a car but want to hire one for a city tour or to drive you to Varadero Beach, here are companies that offer classic car tours.

Old Car Tours
Offers a wide range of classic car tours. Its stable includes vehicles by Chevrolet, Ford, Buick, Cadillac, Mercury, Dodge, Oldsmobile, and Pontiac.
Website: *http://www.oldcartours.com*

Havana Tour Company
Provides exceptional tours of Havana and Cuba. Their Havana tours aim to showcase the capital city's evocative history and its enchanting beauty along with its colonial core and enticing street theater.
Contact: Romey Chuit
Tel.: (53) 5 341-4873

Website: *www.Havanatourcompany.com*
E-mail: *support@havanatourcompany.com*
U.S. Toll Free: (877) 826-3633

Classic Car Tours

Offers a big-body 1951 Deluxe Mercury coupe with all the modern safety features and comforts, including air-conditioning and adult seat belts. This saloon car is available 24/7 with professionally trained chauffeurs, fully insured as required by law. The company is based in the United Kingdom.
Tel.: (44) 7826 356844
E-mail: *bookings@classiccartourscuba.com*
Website: *http://www.classiccartourscuba.com*

Cuba Accommodations

This company conducts city tours using classic cars.
Contact: Alain Tamayo
E-mail: *Alain@CubAccomodation.com*
Phone: (53) 5 827-3117
Website: *www.cubaccommodation.com/activity_details.asp?id_activity=14*

Rent or Tour

Havanacar allows you to rent a chauffeured classic car for short- or long-term rentals. It also offers tours in Havana and all around Cuba.

Havanacar

Calle 70 #2715
Playa
Havana
Facebook: *http://havanacar.net/car-rental--tours.html*
Website: *http://havanacar.net*

Havana Motor Club

The Havana Motor Club documentary is an excellent resource to better understand the joys and struggles of classic cars in Havana.

As their promo states: "*Havana Motor Club* tells a personal, character-driven story about Cuba's vibrant community of underground drag racers and their quest to hold Cuba's first official car race since shortly after the 1959 Revolution. It tackles how Cuba's recent reforms—the owning of property, allowance of small businesses, and greater exchange between Cubans, Cuban Americans, tourists, and other foreigners—have affected the lives of these racers and their families. One racer enlists the help of a Cuban American patron in Miami to bring in parts for his modern Porsche. His main competitor is a

119

renowned mechanic who uses ingenuity rather than resources to create a racing machine out of his 1955 Chevy Bel Air.

Another racer ponders whether he will participate in the race or sell his motor—one that he recovered on the ocean floor from a ship used to smuggle Cubans off the island—in order to flee Cuba on a raft headed to Florida. Meanwhile, the race itself is in jeopardy of coming to fruition due to factors ranging from its status as an elitist sport to the arrival of the Pope in Cuba. Through the experiences of these racers and their community, *Havana Motor Club* explores how Cuba is changing today but also what its future holds in light of Obama's recent move to normalize relations with the island nation."

More information at: *www.havanamotorclub.com*

Cuban Chrome

To get a better understanding of how Cubans live today, it is a good idea to see an episode or two of *Cuban Chrome* on the Discovery Channel.

The Discovery channel describes the show as a "groundbreaking new docu-series that explores the fascinating time warp that characterizes Cuban car culture. This is the first American television series to be produced entirely on location in Cuba."

The reality series follows Cuban car mechanics trying to keep vintage cars running. As the Discovery Channel describes the situation, after "the 1959 Cuban Revolution and the subsequent United States embargo, it has been illegal to import American cars to the island nation—as a result, Cuba's vintage American vehicles are frozen in time. For Cubans, these cars are not just a means of transportation, but a way of life. *Cuban Chrome* will give viewers an intimate look into this rarely seen country as they meet the men and women who put everything on the line to keep these classic cars running."

Cuban Chrome, however, is reminiscent of another reality show on the Discovery Channel: *Naked and Afraid*.

In *Naked and Afraid*, you can watch, with mock fascination, as "survivalists" try to make soup by boiling dirt in questionable water. All the while you know this is a game and that, 21 days later, the experiment is over. But it's entertaining to watch survivalists fight the elements in a controlled setting—cameramen, producers, and medics are on hand.

Compare that to *Cuban Chrome*, where the people have been stuck in this absurd situation for more than a half a century. Yes, it's amusing to see a Cuban mechanic try to fix a car by, say, taking this from a blender and that from a lawn-mower motor, but you know this show wouldn't exist if there were a Napa Auto Parts, Pep Boys, or even a Walmart across town.

Yes, they are clever in solving their problems, but the problems are stupid because they have no reason for existing in the first place.

The producers would do well by the men in the show—Ricardo Medel, Roberto Ordaz, Demetrio Montalvo, Fernando Barral, and Alberto Gutiérrez—by letting them spend a day shopping for auto parts in stores and ordering spare parts from the automobile manufacturers in Miami. If they did that, however, there wouldn't be a show.

In the meantime, American audiences are treated to watching "Clothed and Deprived"—men making soup by boiling dirt in questionable water with the hope that this will get the engine started so they can putz down the dusty road in nowhere Havana.

Cruising Down the Malecón

It's tremendous fun to cruise down the Malecón under the hot, hot sun.

Art & Shopping

16 ART SCENE & CONTEMPORARY ART COLLECTING

If you don't have contemporary Cuban art in your collection, you should.

Cubans living on the island have been so marginalized from the rest of the world that their art reflects an insular perspective, often not influenced by global trends. "I think there is a mystique and the association with the 'time-capsule island and all that's inaccessible," Rachel Weingeist, an adviser to Shelley and Donald Rubin on their Cuban art collection, told Beth Harpaz of the Associated Press in May 2015 during the Havana Biennial, which was established ni 1984.

The 2015 Biennial, in fact, created a sensation among American visitors who are now looking to Cuba as a source of exceptional art—long missing from the world scene.

Private Art Tours in Havana

It's possible to arrange for private art tours to get a more intimate knowledge of the contemporary Cuban art scene. Here are two resources:

Sachie Hernández is an art historian who offers tours for visitors and collectors alike. You can contact her at her Facebook profile: *https://www.facebook.com/profile.php?id=100001016827401*.

Susette Martínez conducts personalized tours to various galleries and artists' studios throughout Havana. To schedule an appointment call her at (53) 5 258-5678.

Museo de Bellas Artes

This art museum, officially named the National Museum of Fine Arts of Havana (*Museo Nacional de Bellas Artes de La Habana*), became a national treasure when it opened on February 23, 1913, under the leadership of Emilio Heredia. Today, the galleries showcase artworks from the colonial period to contemporary works of art. The exhibitions are well organized, and the galleries flow from one period to another. A fine introduction to Cuban aesthetics and sensibilities.

The museum is located at Calle Trocadero between Calle Zulueta and Calle Monserrate in Old Havana.

Tel: (53) 7 861-0241

Hous: Tuesday–Saturday, 9 AM to 5 PM; Sunday, 10 AM to 2 PM

Wilfredo Lam Center for Contemporary Art

This is a great place to visit to become familiar with contemporary Cuban art. Wilfredo Lam, often called the Cuban Picasso, is renowned throughout Cuba. The Center has a permanent exhibition of Lam's etchings and lithographs. There are also temporary exhibitions that feature Cuban and Latin American contemporary artists. Lam, a Cuban of mixed ancestry, hence his Chinese surname, studied art in Spain. He fought against Francisco Franco and fled to France during the Spanish Civil War. It was in France where he met Pablo Picasso, the poet André Breton, and French painters influential in the modernist movement. Although this is the Wilfredo Lam Center, be advised that his most impressive works are on view at the Museo de Bellas Artes.

Lam, ever a patriot, returned to Cuba in support the Revolution of 1959. Then, ever a patriot, he left for Paris, where he lived in exile until his death in 1982.

The Center is located in the elegant Casa del Obispo Peñalver, behind Havana's Cathedral. Hours are Monday–Saturday, 10 AM to 5 PM.

Address: Calle San Ignacio 22, Old Havana
Tel: (53) 7 861-3419

Cuban Artists (Living)

A general observation: Cuban artists working in Cuba tend to create apolitical art, while Cuban artists in exile are more adventurous in exploring artistic themes without any sense of self-censorship.

Here is a list of artists whose works are generating interest the world over:

Alejandro Arrechea, Abel Barros, José Bedia, Tania Bruguera, Alejandro Campins, Yoan Capote, Lizardo Chijona, Roberto Diago, Nelson Domínguez, Roberto Fabelo, Adrián Fernández, Carlos Garaicoa, Arién Guerra Porto, Alex Hernández, Eduardo Hernández Santos, Kcho, Glenda León, Kadir López, Norberto Marrero, Manuel Mendive, Enrique Giovanni Miralles Tartabull, Alejandro Montesino, Frank Mujica, Jorge Otero, René Peña, Michel "El Pollo" Pérez, Mabel Poblet Pujol, Poder, Carlos Quintana, René Francisco Rodríguez, Rubén Rodríguez, Santiago Rodríguez, Sandra Ramos, Tomás Sánchez, Carlos del Toro, Lino Vizcaíno

Cuban Artists (Deceased)

These artists are highly coveted and respected—and setting record prices at auctions throughout the world. They are also the source of inspiration for the current generation of Cuban artists, whether they are living on the island or in exile.

Belkis Ayón Manso (January 23, 1967—September 11, 1999). A painter and lithographer, Ayón is the greatest female artist Cuba has given the world. Her work, which explores Santería and the Afro-Cuban myth of Sikan and the men's secret society of Abakuá, has been declared national patrimony by

126

the Cuban government. The pieces outside Cuba are highly coveted. She committed suicide at the age of 32, the only way she could escape.

Carlos Enríquez (August 3, 1900—May 2, 1957). A painter and illustrator, Enríquez was inspired by both surrealism and modernsm to depict Cuba's culture, society, and landscapes. A bohemian at heart, his female nudes scandalized Cuban society, but his provocations catapulted him as a leader of the Cuban avant-garde. He is considered the best and most influential Cuban painter of the twentieth century, on a par with Wilfredo Lam.

Cundo Bermúdez (September 3, 1914—October 30, 2008). Bermúdez founded the Asociación de Pintores y Escultores de Cuba (APEC) in 1949 after having lived in Mexico. He studied at the Academy of San Carlos. His work influenced Cuban artists throughout the second half of the twentieth century.

Wilfredo Lam (December 8, 1902—September 11, 1982). Lam is credited with reviving Afro-Cuban art as a bold affirmation of Cuban identity. He lived and painted in Europe and is often called the Cuban Picasso. Today, he is considered the Cuban painter with the strongest cultural perspective of the Cuban identity as depicted in his paintings.

Mario Carreño y Morales (May 23, 1913—December 20, 1999). Carreño studied at the Real Academia de Bellas Artes de San Fernando in Madrid, Spain, in 1934. From there he went to Paris where he studied at the Académie Julian and the Ecole des Arts Appliqués before returning to Cuba. His work remains emblematic of Cuban art in the twentieth century, although he fled the Revolution and lived in exile in Chile.

Havana Galleries for Contemporary Art

Here is a list of galleries in Havana worth a visit.

3/31 Art Space
Calle 31, corner of Calle 34
Playa
Tel.: (53) 7 202-3749

7 y 60
Avenida 7, corner of Calle 60
Miramar
Tel.: (53) 5 239-5584

Alan Manuel
Calle San Carlos #34, between Morell and Alfredo Zayas
Loma de Chaple, Santos Suárez
Tel.: (53) 7 640-2104

Capote Studio (El Bunker)
Calle 23 #1355, between Calle 18 and 20
Vedado
Tel.: (53) 7 833-0018

Esterio Segura Studio
Calzada del Cerro #1313, on the corner of Calle Carvajal
Cerro
Tel.: (53) 7 870-5431

Factoría Habana
Calle O'Reilly #308, between Habana and Aguiar
Old Havana
Tel: (53) 7 864-9518

Galería Habana
Calle Línea #460, between Calle E and Calle F
Vedado.
Tel.: (53) 7 832-7101

Galería Villa Manuela
Calle H #406, between Calle 17 and Calle 19
Vedado
Tel.: (53) 7 832-2391

Kcho Estudio Romerillo
Avenida 7, on the corner of Calle 120
Playa
Tel.: (53) 7 208-0966

William Pérez and Marlys Fuego
Estudio Alcázar
Calle Reina #210, Lower Level, on the corner of Calle Manrique
Centro Habana
Tel.: (53) 5 325-5524

How to Purchase Art in Cuba

The U.S. Office of Foreign Assets Control is as confused about what is going on as everyone else. In theory, cultural material is exempt from import restrictions imposed by the trade embargo. In practice, determination of what can and cannot be imported is arbitrary and capricious. Sounds like what one would expect from a bureaucracy. With this caveat, you may want to consult with an American Customs Broker about importing artworks into the U.S.

Now, before you can take art *into* the U.S., it has to get *out* of Cuba.

Two steps are involved. First, pay the artist for the work of art. The artist is required to provide a receipt. The second step is to take the piece of art and that receipt to the National Patrimony Office, where you pay an export fee. The National Patrimony Office will provide you with an export document that confirms that the piece of art is not part of Cuba's patrimony.

If you are interested in purchasing a piece of art by an artist whose work is considered to be part of Cuba's patrimony, such as Wilfredo Lam or Belkis Ayón, it will be necessary to prove provenance. As a general rule the work of famous artists cannot leave Cuba.

The way to avoid these steps, of course, is to purchase art from galleries in Mexico and the U.S. that specialize in contemporary Cuban art.

Galleries in the U.S. and Mexico

Galleries in the U.S. and Mexico now represent many Cuban artists. This is a list of galleries to consider if you are interested in adding the work of Cuban artists to your collection. F. R. Gillette in Hudson, New York, for example, has the largest collection of Belkis Ayón's work available today outside Cuba. François Valcke in Mérida, Mexico, has one of the most impressive collections of work by mid-career Cuban artists available at present.

California

Couturier Gallery
Attn: Darrell Couturier

166 N. La Brea Avenue
Los Angeles, CA 90036
Tel.: (323) 933-5557
Website: *www.couturiergallery.com*
E-mail: *cg@couturiergallery.com*

Florida

Gallery on Greene

Attention: Nance Frank
606 Greene Street
Key West, Florida 33040
Tel.: (305) 294-1669
Website: *www.galleryongreene.com*
E-mail: *galleryongreene@bellsouth.net*

Cernuda Arte

Attention: Ramón Cernuda
3155 Ponce de Leon Boulevard
Coral Gables, FL 33134
Tel.: (305) 461-1050
Website: *www.cernudaarte.com*
E-mail: *cernudaarte@msn.net*

Nuance Galleries Tampa

Attn: Robert Nuance
804 South Dale Mabry
Tampa, FL 33609
Tel.: (813) 875-0511
Website: *www.nuancegalleries.com*
E-mail: *nuancegalleries@earthlink.net*

New York

Magnan Metz Gallery

Attn: Alberto Magnan
521 West 26 Street
New York, NY 10001
Tel.: (212) 244-2344
Website: *www.magnanmetz.com*
E-mail: *info@magnanmetz.com*

F. R. Gillette

Attn: Rick Gillette
217 Warren Street, 2nd Floor
Hudson, NY 12534
Tel.: (646) 483-9109
Website: *www.frgdesignart.com*
E-mail: *frg@frgdesignart.com*

Mexico

Galería Tataya

Attn: François Valcke
Calle 72 #468, between Calle 53 and Calle 55
Barrio Santiago
Mérida, Yucatán, Mexico
Tel.: (011) 52 999-928-2962
Website: *www.tataya.com.mx*
E-mail: *francois@tataya.com.mx*

Creating a Portfolio of Contemporary Cuban Art

As a result of the 2015 Biennial in Havana, many U.S. and Latin American collectors have begun to augment their representation of Cuban artists in their holdings. Some of the more promising Cuban artists are already represented.

Here are three galleries that represent artists every serious collect should consider including in their collection. Galería Tataya, additionally, has been granted an official export license by the Cuban government; this opens doors to foreign collectors in unexpected ways.

Couturier Gallery

Artists represented: Belkis Ayón, Abel Barroso, Raúl Corrales, Carlos Estevez, José Figueroa, Aimee Garcia, Alberto Korda, Alexis Lago, Ibrahim Miranda, Carlos Montés de Oca, Elsa Mora, Cirenaica Moreira, and René Peña.

F. R. Gillette

Artists represented: This gallery specializes in works by Belkis Ayón currently located outside Cuba.

Galería Tataya

Artists represented: Lizardo Chijona, Arien Guerra Porto, Eduardo Hernández Santos, Norberto Marrero, Enrique Giovanni Miralles Tartabull, Alejandro Montesino, Poder, Rubén Rodríguez, Carlos del Toro, and Lino Vizcaíno.

131

Poster Art

In addition to fine art, poster and graphic design in Cuba is spectacular. If you are interested at all in graphics and poster, check out this source:

Poster Art/Graphic Design: *http://cuba.slanted.de*

Foreign Gallery Officially Authorized for Export by Cuba

Galería Tataya is the only gallery officially authorized by the Cuban government for the export of art. If you are interested in buying art and having all tax and export requirements seamlessly fulfilled, contact Francois Valcke to have his gallery act as an intermediary.

Since July 2015, he has been offering guidance to Cuban artists traveling to Mexico to purchase materials and furnishings to open their own galleries throughout Havana.

Francois Valcke of the Galería Tataya is the best bet for anyone interested in adding contemporary Cuban art to his or her collection. Mr. Valcke is the most authoritative connoisseur and dealer of the current art culture in Havana.

Galería Tataya
Attn: François Valcke
Calle 72 #468, between Calle 53 and Calle 55
Barrio Santiago
Mérida, Yucatán, Mexico
Tel.: (011) 52 999-928-2962
Website: *www.tataya.com.mx*
E-mail: francois@tataya.com.mx

Art and Freedom of Expression

When thinking about contemporary Cuban art, it's important to keep one general observation in mind: Cuban artists working in Cuba tend to self-censor.

In consequence, Cuban art produced in Cuba has almost no political overtones or themes. This is in sharp contrast to the more powerful and provocative art Cubans produce when they are outside Cuba, both in terms of content and the ideas explored.

American Friends of the Ludwig Foundation of Cuba

The Ludwig Foundation of Cuba has, since 1990, been at the vanguard of promoting and helping Cuban art, theater, and dance.

Anyone interested in participating in a leading forum for helping build better relations with Cuba through the arts should contact this organization for more information.

132

American Friends of the Ludwig Foundation of Cuba

Attn: Carole Rosenberg, President
3 East 69 Street, Suite SR2
New York, NY 10021
Tel.: (2120 628-3494
Website: *www.aflfc.org*
E-mail: *CRosenberg@aflfc.org*

SHOPPING: SOUVENIRS & STOLEN TREASURES

The best shopping in Cuba

No one goes to Cuba to shop. Other than cigars, rum, and contemporary Cuban art, there is very little to buy in Cuba. The Cuban economy is that exhausted. Yes, there are all manner of knickknacks and tchotchkes available—Cuban flags, postcards with Che's picture, and so forth—but most of it is the kind of stuff suitable for a rummage sale in Chula Vista, California, or a flea market in Opa-Locka, Florida.

With that caveat, consider the following observation: The best shopping in Cuba is not at a store. It is at a bank.

Since the Revolution, millions of Cubans have been forced into exile. Depending on the policies at the time of their departure, it may or may not have been possible to take their personal valuables with them. I refer to jewelry, family heirlooms, watches, and so forth. Often times, these were confiscated by Revolutionary authorities when Cubans were about to leave.

So what happened to the gold, silver, jewelry, diamonds, emeralds, sapphires, rubies, watches, and other family heirlooms confiscated?

Funny you should ask.

Jewels, Diamonds, Watches & Plundered Treasures

Confiscated jewelry and valuables were sent to the Central Bank. At the Central Bank they were inventoried, appraised, and placed in vaults. Over the years, Communist Party officials have helped themselves to these items for their wives, mistresses, daughters, or themselves.

Many pieces have also been given to visiting dignitaries as gifts over the decades.

During the economic hardship of the Special Period after the collapse of the Soviet Union, the Cuban government allowed the jewelry to be sold to visitors to raise cash. This Editor learned of this from a Mexican diplomat who was returning to Mexico and wanted to take something back for his daughter, whose birthday was the following week.

"Come on," he said. "Let me show you something."

In the mid-1980s when the Banco Financiero Internacional, S.A., was founded, the bulk of the jewelry confiscated by Cuban authorities over the decades was transferred to its Vedado branch. (The bank's headquarters are in the Miramar neighborhood.)

Upon arriving at the bank, the Mexican diplomat was well received by officials. He explained what he wanted—as if we were in a jewelry store. The bank official/salesperson made recommendations for a gift for his daughter. The bank official/salesperson disappeared for about 20 minutes and then returned with two trays holding dozens of pieces of jewelry. The Mexican diplomat settled on an emerald-encrusted brooch. He paid in U.S. dollars. Government officials set prices arbitrarily and far below current market value.

I was asked if I wanted to purchase anything. "A watch, perhaps?" I declined. After we left, the Mexican diplomat said he had shopped there many times, as had colleagues from the diplomatic corps. "The Iranians and Chinese are crazy for Art Deco stuff," he said. Then he commented that the vintage jewelry was incredible—like something from *Connoisseur* magazine, the defunct publication Thomas Hoving edited.

Now you know: the best shopping in Havana has been, for decades, at the Banco Financiero Internacional where the plundered jewels taken from Cubans fleeing their country are available for sale at discounted prices.

The ethics of these purchases aside, the reality is Cuban exiles who believe they may recover jewels and family heirlooms seized by the Revolution are not going to be happy to learn that these items may have been sold off to diplomats and foreign businessmen.

Are plundered treasures still for sale? It's unclear if officials will sell to ordinary tourists or if the clientele remains limited to diplomats and foreign dignitaries. Try your luck:

Banco Financiero Internacional, S.A.

Línea #1

Vedado

Havana

Banco Financiero Internacional, S.A.

A note about this bank and its jewelry vault: The bank was inscribed as a joint-stock company under Decree-Law No. 84 issued on October 13, 1984. Banco Financiero Internacional, S.A., was founded on November 3, 1984, and went into operation two days later.

Among its authorized operations, the following are included:

- To put cash in and pay it out from demand and/or term deposit accounts.
- To receive and grant loans or other forms of financial credits.
- To handle transfers of funds to or from other countries.
- To buy and sell precious metals, freely convertible currency and securities.
- To buy and sell national currency which is legal tender.
- To receive deposits of securities denominated in foreign currency, in custody or in trust; provide services of administration of property, financial studies and others; and carry out brokering activities.
- To issue Letters of Guarantee.
- To establish correspondent agreements with other banking entities.

The omission that the bank will sell plundered jewelry is clearly an oversight in the bank's Mission Statement.

T-shirts & Knickknacks

No luck getting a diamond tiara at the bank? Then settle for a T-shirt from Old Havana. Here are two fun gift shops:

Clandestina
Villegas #403, between Brasil and Muralla

This store is a testament to the entrepreneurial spirit emerging in Cuba. Owned by Cuban Idania del Río and Spaniard Lere Fernández, it sells clever T-shirts, posters, and other souvenirs. A bestselling item is the 99% DISEÑO CUBANO T-shirt.

Piscolabis Bazar-Café
San Ignacio #75, between Empedrado and O'Reilly

A fun selection of gifts and books, along with coffees and coffee cakes.

Tattoos

If it's 2015 and you're in Williamsburg, Brooklyn, and the guy next to you, drinking weak cacao tea at the dreadful Mast Brothers Brew Bar, tells you that he wants to get inked in Havana, then perhaps you might also consider acquiring a Cuban tattoo.

136

La Marca

This is the first tattoo parlor allowed to open in Cuban since the Revolution closed them all as bourgeois decadence. Officials continue to express some concern that this one exists at all. Communist officials believe tattoos are not in keeping with Marxist-Leninist principles. If *The Communist Manifesto* has a discussion on tattoos, I must have missed it.

In any case, La Marca's proprietor, Leo Canosa, is a talented artist and skilled in his craft.

Obrapía #108-C, between Oficios and Mercaderes
Old Havana
Tel: (53) 7 863-8026
Website: *http://www.lamarcabodyart.com*
Facebook: *https://www.facebook.com/LaMarcaBodyArtGallery*

Havana Hair Salon: Arte Corte Papito's

If a tattoo is too permanent a souvenir for you, perhaps a post-Revolution coif? Gilberto Valladeres, known as Papito, returned from years in Mexico, where he worked on his free-market skills. Now, he is taking advantage of the new opportunities in the emerging Cuba. His hair salon, for men, women, and bald hipsters who need their beards trimmed, is a virtual community and cultural center.

Is he good?

This is from a review titled, "Papito's: The Most Beautiful Hair Salon in Cuba," by Victoria Alacalá: "Loquacious like all good barbers, Gilberto Valladares (Papito) speaks at the same speed and enthusiasm as his hands handle the scissors. However, his conversations don't involve home runs made by his favorite baseball team or inappropriate comments about the beautiful woman who lives across the street. Neither does he attempt to captivate his clientele by talking of the merits of a new hair dye that will soon hit the market or how many liters of silicone a certain movie star has in her body. Instead, Papito talks of his projects, his most recent find for a future hairdressing museum, or a new addition to his art collection: To the Last Hair. It's therefore hardly surprising that we should find, seated in Papito's salon, a popular TV announcer determined to change her look or a renowned Cuban art curator waiting for a traditional haircut."

Arte Corte Papito's

Calle Aguiar #10, between Pena Pobre and Monserrate
Old Havana
Hours: Noon to 6 PM, Monday through Saturday

Centro Cultural Antiguos Almacenes de Depósito San José

If the exuberance of a marketplace where buyers and sellers set prices for merchandise is what you want, then this is it. This open-air flea market, located in an old shipping warehouse, remains the most popular place for Cubans and visitors to mingle as they see what's available. Of course everything that can have Che's face on it is for sale, but there are guayabera shirts, leather goods, jewelry, wood carvings, and a good number of other items that may be considered souvenirs.

This is where the Editor found a Spanish-language copy of *The Communist Manifesto* in Braille for blind Marxists. As if there were any other kind.

Centro Cultural Antiguos Almacenes de Depósito San José
Avenida Desamparados and Avenida San Ignacio
Old Havana
Hours: 10 AM to 6 PM, Monday through Saturday

Memorias Librería

This is a remarkably charming antiquarian bookstore. It's clear that the last few hidden collections of books—in the possession of the government or private individuals—are being liquidated, book by book. In addition to a sweeping collection of books, there are lots of memorabilia dating back decades before the Revolution.

Is it good?

If you're into postcards, posters, old coins, vintage magazines, and items from the 1930s, it's a great place to spend a few hours. If this were a normal country, everything here would be listed on eBay.

Memorias Librería
Ánimas #57, between Paseo de Martí and Agramonte
Old Havana
Hours: 9 AM to 5 PM, Tuesday through Sunday
Tel: (53) 7 862-3153

Casa de Carmen Montilla

Carmen Montilla was a Venezuelan artist who lived in Havana until her death in 2004. That alone tells you she was an eccentric and incorrigible character. The shop, which could be considered a gallery to the artist, showcases Montilla's work and—increasingly—also the work of up-and-coming contemporary Cuban artists.

Go and see if any of the works speak to you.

Casa de Carmen Montilla
Oficios #164
Old Havana
Hours: 10:30 AM to 5:30 PM, Tuesday through Saturday; and 9 AM to 1 PM on Sundays

Galería Víctor Manuel

If Casa Carmen Montilla has emerging Cuban artists, then this shop, which functions as a gallery, located in a privileged spot in the Plaza de la Catedral, shows where the new Cuba is headed: First World prices for works of art.

This is the most high-end gallery in Havana, set in a stunning baroque building, filled with an impressive collection of luxurious collectibles set against the backdrop of this proletarian paradise. Take a look at the fine silver jewelry and the extraordinary wooden figurines.

Galería Víctor Manuel

Plaza de la Catedral
Old Havana
Hours: 9 AM to 9 PM, Monday through Saturday

Palacio de la Artesanía

Housed in a former eighteenth-century palace, this is a shopping mall filled with souvenirs and other knickknacks that only busloads of tourists would love.

And guess what?

The busloads of tourists who come here love it all. Handicrafts, Cuban flags, Che memorabilia, cigars, musical instruments, and CDs are entertaining to rummage through—and this is an ideal location for those mandatory gifts for people back home.

Palacio de la Artesanía

Cuba #64
Old Havana
Hours: 9 AM to 7 PM, Daily

Promociones de ICAIC

This shop offers a terrific selection of original Cuban movie posters. Did you ever year of Luminito Fernández, who's now living in Mérida, Mexico? He's one of the principal Cubans responsible for protecting Cuban films after the economic collapse during the Special Period, a remarkable feat especially after the deprivations the arts endured in the late 1990s. Anyone who loves cinema owes a debt to Luminito Fernández.

Snap up these posters and souvenirs because the supplies are limited—and as Cuba opens up, they will soon be gone.

Promociones de ICAIC

Calle 23 and Calle L
Hours: Noon to 6 PM, Monday to Saturday

139

Promociones de ICAIC
At Café Fresa y Chocolate
Calle 23 and Calle 12
Hours: Noon to 6 PM, Monday to Saturday

Galerías de Paseo

Located across from the Hotel Meliá Cohiba, this is virtually the only place in Havana to find designer clothing and upscale merchandise. Its prices exclude everyone other than wealthy Cuban entrepreneurs and Cuba's Communist elite. And, of course, foreign tourists.

Galerías de Paseo
Paseo and Calle 1
Old Havana
Hours: 9 AM to 6 PM, Monday to Saturday; 9 AM to 1 PM on Sundays

Longina Música

If you're into music, this is a fine spot. Located in a pedestrian mall, there are guitars, maracas, bongos, and all kinds of other musical instruments and sheet music at reasonable prices.

Longina Música
Obispo #360, between Habana and Compostela
Old Havana
Hours: 10 AM to 7 PM, Monday to Saturday; 10 AM to 1 PM on Sundays

Antiques

Antiques?

Remember when the Revolution abolished private property? That included everything in everyone's home, including families' furnishings. When Cubans were forced into exile, they first had to apply for an exit visa. Shortly thereafter, Revolutionary authorities showed up at their homes and took an inventory of everything.

One blender? Check. One Tiffany lamp? Check. One Andy Warhol? Check.

Prior to departure, another inventory was taken to make sure that everything that belonged to the Revolution was being left behind for the Revolution. (This precluded people leaving from giving things to friends or family left behind.) As the number of Cubans fleeing reached hundreds of thousands, the Revolution was confronted with taking an inventory of everything—and of appraising its value.

There were some very, very wealthy Cubans who left mansions filled with furnishings behind. Consider María Luisa Gómez-Mena Viuda de Caigaga, Countess of Revilla de Camargo. Not only was she a noblewoman, but her brother, José Gómez-Mena Vila, was the owner of Manzana de Gómez, the largest department store in Latin America at the time. This family had a superb collection of furnishings. When the Revolution seized the Countess of Revilla de Carmargo's home, officials were so impressed by the quality of the furnishings in her home that her house became a museum: Museo de Artes Decorativas.

Once when this Editor went to visit, he had an appointment with the director; he was accompanied by an authority who had worked for decades at Sotheby's in the U.S. The director gave us a tour of the house. Each step of the way the gentleman from Sotheby's offered new insights about the pieces. When we finally reached the master bedroom, it was clear that the furniture in that room was not original to the house when the Countess lived there.

"Who's sleeping in her bed?" the director was asked.

"It isn't Goldilocks," she said, smiling.

Revolutionary officials, of course, had, throughout the decades, helped themselves to specific pieces of furniture left behind by their owners. In consequence, Havana is shabby, but not chic.

This largess was extended to friends of the Cuban government. When in Havana, if you have an opportunity to have dinner at the private residence of Iran's ambassador, for example, don't fail to show up. The furnishings are exquisite, more Shah than Ayatollah. This Editor was certainly impressed.

Care to buy a few antiques?

There are three "authorized" depositories for selling off these plundered furnishings. They are located in various places in the Mirarmar area of Havana; their addresses change because at this point many of the items for sale are consolidated now that raising cash for new enterprises has made liquidating furnishings more urgent. The best bet is to ask someone at your hotel or your host at an AirBNB; they can point you in the right direction.

There are, however, other, more stable "shops" selling furnishings. Cubans are now selling whatever of value remains in their possession either to launch a business or to begin a new life in exile.

Here are some places that sell antiques and vintage furniture:

Belkis

Calle 2 #697, between Calle 25 and Calle 27
Tel.: (53) 7 830-4124

At this point, almost all the furniture is gone, but there is a wide selection of crystal, porcelain, and glassware.

Milagro

Calle A #610, between Calle 25 and Calle 27, Vedado
Tel: (53) 7 833-6140
By appointment only, in late afternoon and evening.

Mirtha

Calle 6 #601, between Calle 25 and Calle 27, Vedado
Tel.: (53) 7 836-0695

A modest selection of furniture, but there are a good number of chandeliers and ceramic vases.

Ibrahim

Calle 35 #251, corner of Calle 4, Vedado
Tel.: (53) 7 883-3272

This shop has furniture and specializes in clocks.

Elia Rodríguez

Calle 4 #305, between Calle 13 and Calle 15, Vedado
Tel.: (53) 7 830-1725

This shop has a reasonable selection of furniture.

In addition, you may want to visit a few online listings to see the kinds of items still available. These three sites have prices quoted in CUCs, although U.S. dollars are welcome.

Porlalivre.com

Site: *http://habana.portalivre.com*

Cuba Clasificados

Site: *http://cu.clasificados.st/antiguedades*

La Habana Compra y Venta

Site: *http://la-habana.comprayventa.org/arte-y-antiguedades*

If the selections, after almost six decades of plundering, are slim, do note that the process of "liquidating" these warehouses intensified during the Special Period. Latin American visitors were encouraged to buy decorative objects while in Havana. Latin American antiques dealers were invited to buy furnishings by the container to ship back to their home countries. The result is that the most desirable antiques, sadly, were exported long ago.

All is not lost, however. It turns out that many Cubans privileged enough to travel back and forth between Cuba and Mexico have made it a business to sell these items. In Mérida, there are two companies that sell furniture acquired in Cuba. One is Barrio Santiago, and the other is in Colonia García Ginerés. The former is owned by a Cuban and the latter by a Mexican. The Cuban has five warehouses in Havana filled with antiques and decorative objects he has bought from the government over the years.

Cuban exiles have little hope of ever finding the family possessions they left behind when they were forced to flee. And if Pope Francis is curious to know where some of the treasures plundered from Catholic churches in Havana under Communist rule are, a good number made their way into the hands of collectors through shops in Mérida, Mexico.

The Cuban citizen who sells Havana furnishings in Mérida requested that his name and number not be included in this guide. Messages to him, however, will be forwarded by contacting the Editor. A Mexican dealer who has, over the decades, handled an untold number of items from Havana on consignment in his store is Roberto Guzmán. His contact information is below:

El Bazar

Roberto Guzmán
Calle 19 #201-D, between Calle 22 and 24 Street, Colonia García Ginerés
Mérida, Yucatán
Tel: 52 (999) 157-6636

The Cultures of Cuba & Santería

CULTURES OF HAVANA

Exploring Havana's cultures

The African Diaspora in Cuba

"The Casa de África was founded in 1986 in a colonial palace in Old Havana to showcase the history and culture of Africa. There are valuable collections from 27 African countries, based on the collection of researcher Fernando Ortiz, who first used the term Afro-Cuban, and also on the African collection of Fidel Castro, which consists principally of pieces sent by grateful recipients of Cuban aid. The institution does research on the countries represented in its collections, especially those that had a direct influence on Cuba's culture. It preserves many ethnographic pieces because they are valuable practical laboratories for theoretical ethnographic conceptions. It has an advisory council made up of specialists in the different social sciences who provide valuable professional support for the institution's work," the Casa de Africa states on its website.

The Africa House Museum is considered the most important study center and a place where researchers, ethnologists, linguists, and students of African and Afro-Cuban history can present their findings in Cuba.

Casa de África
Alberto Granados
Obrapía #157, between San Ignacio and Mercaderes
Old Havana
E-mail: *africa@cultural.ohch.cu*
Tel: (53) 7 61-5798

Jews of Cuba

There are two synagogues in Havana and there is a Jewish cultural center.

To quote the website *www.jewishcuba.org*:

"Religious persecution in the fifteenth century brought Jewish life to an end in Spain. The Spanish Inquisition gave Jews the choice to either convert to Catholicism or be expelled. Most Jews left for points east in the Mediterranean or north to France or the Netherlands. Those who stayed converted, but many continued to practice Judaism secretly. These 'pretenders' of Catholicism were called *los Marranos*, which referred to the pork they would eat in public for show their support of Catholicism. Many Marranos headed for the 'New World' where they established their communities, complete with synagogues. In Spanish-controlled territories, however, while less threatened by the local government, the practice remained secret. In Cuba where the Inquisition was strong it was very difficult to continue

147

Jewish practices even in secret. These 'New Christians' left for other locations in the New World or were absorbed into the general Spanish population of Cuba.

"Cuba saw many waves of Jewish immigration after the Spanish-American War. During the 1920s, with the tightening of immigration quotas into the United States, Jews, mainly from Turkey and Eastern Europe, settled all over the island. Young men from Eastern Europe, both single and married, came to make a better life or to wait until they could get permission to immigrate to the U.S. Many quickly became successful peddlers and small businessmen. The married ones sent to Europe for their families and bought homes. Single men either sent to the 'old world' for wives or intermarried with the Cuban Catholic population. Those from Turkey and other Sephardic Jews tended to arrive as family units. Since life in Havana was more expensive than in the countryside and more opportunities for economic success existed in other cities, the Sephardic influence became widespread across the island."

Centro Sefaradi
Calle 17, on the corner of Calle E
Tel: (53) 7 832-6623
E-mail: *judiosefarad@yahoo.com*

Beth Shalom Temple
Calle I, on the corner of Calle 13
Vedado
Tel: (53) 7 832-8953
E-mail: *beth_shalom@enet.cu*

Casa de la Comunidad Hebrea de Cuba
Calle I #259, on the cornr of Calle 13
Vedado
Tel: (53) 7 832-8953
E-mail: *patronato-ort@enet.cu*

A visit to Finca Vigía is highly recommended.
The Finca Vigía Foundation
Website: *www.fincafoundation.org*

Ernest Hemingway

Ernest Hemingway is more than a person. He is, in Cuba, a state of mind. His life in Cuba and his love for Cuba represent the best of what is American in the Cuban imagination. If Fidel Castro told the Cubans "Be like Che," then Cubans tell Americans, "Be like Papa."

His home in Cuba, Finca Vigía, is located about 10 miles east of Havana and is open to the public. The nonprofit in charge of taking care of Hemingway's home declares: "The Finca Vigía Foundation, a small American non-profit working in Havana, has navigated the shoals of US/Cuban relations to create a bi-national project that has saved one of the most significant monuments of American literature. In doing so, the Foundation has built bridges between Cuban and American professionals, won the support of both governments, and provided training for Cuban preservationists. Hemingway loved Cuba and Cubans still love Hemingway. *Finca Vigía*—consisting of a large main house, numerous outbuildings, and extensive gardens—was Hemingway's primary home from 1939 to 1960. This is where he wrote standing at his typewriter, where he entertained, where he pitched endless innings of baseball with the neighborhood children. Most important for contemporary purposes, Finca Vigía was where Hemingway gathered the things he prized: animal trophies, fishing rods, paintings, thousands of photographs, the original manuscripts and galleys of his stories and novels, his correspondence and his journals, and a personal library of almost nine thousand volumes. No other Hemingway place—in Paris, Key West, or Idaho—comes close to the significance of *Finca Vigía* in Havana."

Are they doing a good job? Here is what Valerie Hemingway wrote in *Smithsonian Magazine* in an article titled "Hemingway's Cuba, Cuba's Hemingway," published in August 2007: "The Finca Vigía had been my home too. I lived there for six months in 1960 as Hemingway's secretary, having met him on a sojourn to Spain the previous year, and I returned to the finca for five weeks in 1961 as a companion to his widow, Mary. (Later, I married Ernest's youngest son, Gregory; we had three children before we divorced in 1987; he died in 2001.) I well remember the night in 1960 when Philip Bonsall, the U.S. ambassador to Cuba and a frequent visitor, dropped by to say that Washington was planning to cut off relations with Fidel Castro's fledgling government, and that American officials thought it would be best if Hemingway demonstrated his patriotism by giving up his beloved tropical home. He resisted the suggestion, fiercely. As things turned out, the Hemingways left Cuba that summer so Ernest could tend to some writerly business in Spain and the United States; his suicide, in Idaho on July 2, 1961, made the question of his residency moot. Shortly thereafter, Mary and I returned to Cuba to pack up a mass of letters, manuscripts, books and paintings and ship them to the United States, and she donated the finca to the Cuban people. I visited Cuba briefly in 1999 to celebrate the centennial of Ernest's birth and found his home, by then a museum, essentially as Mary and I had left it almost 40 years before."

Hamel Callejón / Hamel Alley

Each Sunday there is exuberance of music, visual art, and dance in Havana, focused on the island's proud Afro-Cuban traditions. The rest of the week there are splendid murals, theater, and crafts. The Callejón de Hamel, or Hamel Alley, is a small backstreet in Cayo Hueso, adjacent to the Vedado district in Centro. It is a high temple to Afro-Cuban culture focusing on West African peoples and traditions.

Here is now the *Havana Times* described it:

> "The project emerged in 1990, on April 21, 1990, to be exact, when Salvador decided to paint his first mural in a public space in front of his house. In 1989, he had already painted a mural in Old Havana's *Casa de Africa*," Elias Asef, assistant to visual artist Salvador Gonzalez and the project's manager and leader, tells us. He adds that the precursors of the alley take us back the mid-19th century, when a German-American immigrant surnamed Hamel settled in the place and established a construction materials plant there.
>
> " 'I define the project as a series of murals and sculptures in a public space devoted to the environment. There is no religious proselytism here, we only try to divulge some of the symbols of cultures and religions of African origin, such as Santería, *Palo de Monte* and the *Abakua* society, through theatrical stagings.'
>
> "This cultural project has allowed young people from the neighborhood to socialize, fraternize and have a space where they can contribute to the spiritual and personal development of residents and visitors constructively. No few of them began as musicians (today professionals), playing rumba rhythms in the alley, and several have participated in the regular performances staged Sunday mornings (such as Yoruba Andabo, Calve y Guaguanco, Los Muñequitos de Matanzas and Frank Fernandez, among other illustrious representatives of Cuban music). The alley has also been the venue of the Wemilere Festival and, recently, it was awarded the Cubadisco Festival Award for its cultural promotion activities."
> —*Ernesto Gonzalez Diaz and Milot Septiem*

Callejón de Hamel
Calle Espada and Calle Araburu

The Surfers of Havana

Believe it or not, after the anti-Semitism of the Revolution, there are now more surfers than Jews in Cuba. Be mindful that authorities still look with suspicion at anyone surfing, lest that individual aspire to surf to Key West. You are advised to obey the police patrolling the beaches.

With that caveat, surfers hang near the Russian Embassy in Miramar, down Calle 70. There's also good surfing along the eastern beaches at Las Playas del Este, also known as Guanabo. The Havana Surf Club has a free e-book on surfing in Cuba. The book is filled with interesting facts: "In the 15th century Spanish explorers noted Peruvian fishermen would surf the waves back to shore on craft made of reeds after fishing the offshore reef."

If you are interested in this primer, you can download the e-book here:

150

http://www.havanasurf-cuba.com/assets/cubansurfingmanuel.pdf.

Finally, if you want to earn surf karma, you might consider taking a gently used board with you to Cuba; enjoy it while you're there, and then donate it to the club. Boards are difficult to find in Cuba.

Havana Surf

Website: *www.havanasurf-cuba.com*

The Arabs of Cuba

"In Havana, Arabs settled mainly in Barrio Monte, where many established textile, clothing, and watch and jewelry businesses along Monte Street. But the abolition of private enterprise after the 1959 revolution fragmented the trade-oriented Arab community. Many left for the United States, others departed for Mexico and South America, and little was left behind to distinguish the Arab barrio. . . . The UAC's library, salon, restaurant, and meeting hall create a focus for cultural activities and provide something like a home and family life for Arab students from overseas studying in Cuba. The UAC hosts receptions for visiting Arab dignitaries, offers a Saturday-morning lecture series on Middle Eastern culture or politics, and publishes a magazine, *El Arabe,* which covers events in the Middle East as well as local activities.

Although most Arab immigrants to Cuba in the last century have been Christians, a significant minority have been Muslim. Both church and mosque watched their congregations dwindle as the 1959 revolution brought dialectical materialism to Cuba, but in recent years there has been a gradual but widespread return to spiritual roots. As a result, an increasing number of Cuban converts to Islam now attend Friday prayers at the mosque, alongside Arab diplomats and students from abroad."—*Bill Strubbe and Karen Wald, writing in* Aramco World.

Unión Arabe de Cuba

Prado #256 between Ánimas and Trocadero

Havana

Website: *www.unionarabecuba.org*

THE PEOPLE YOU WON'T MEET

Alas, you're too late.

Here are some of the colorful personalities whose charismas and memories still inform Havana. As you meander through this grand city, their stories will enrich your visit. These are some of the people who gave Havana its grand ambiance and haunting sense of history.

Natalia Revuelta Clews

Known as one of the most beautiful and glamorous women in the world three-quarters of a century ago, Natalia, known as Naty, was a socialite who fell in love with Fidel Castro. She introduced him to high society, gave him her fortune, and aided his revolution. She became his lover and she became pregnant by him, giving birth to a daughter in 1956.

This being a Cuban Revolution story, you know it ends miserably. Fidel accompanied her to parties, took her money, and enjoyed her carnal company. Although he did not deny his daughter with her, he nonetheless left her. Upon his triumphant return from exile in Mexico in 1959, Fidel Castro asked for her support once again. In love with him, she gave him everything he asked of her. But when the Revolution's triumph ended, he ended their relationship forever.

Naty never went into exile, hopeful he would come back to her. Without any means left, she was shuffled from one government position to another in the Revolutionary government, never wanting, but not quite thriving.

Stories about Naty's mad affair with Fidel are legendary. Her well-to-do friends, including María Luisa Gómez-Mena Vd. de Cagiga, let her and Fidel carry on in her grand mansion. (María Luisa Gómez-Mena Vd. de Cagiga's home is today the Museum of Decorative Arts.) Other locations where whirlwind trysts took place were the Hotel Nacional and the Hotel Capri. Fidel doesn't dance, so she never took him to the Tropicana. But others did; Naty was very active on Havana's social scene.

This is how she described her social life at Havana's tennis club to Vanity Fair before Fidel knocked her up: "The loudspeaker would announce, 'Naty Revuelta, teléfono,' and it would be 'Hello. This is Errol Flynn' or 'This is Edward G. Robinson.' One day, a friend called me over to the bar where he and Ernest Hemingway were having a drink and playing dice. My friend said, 'Naty, Mr. Hemingway wants to meet you.' I said, 'How do you do?' Hemingway said, 'I wanted to meet you because you remind me of my cats.' And I said, 'Well, why?' He said, 'Your eyes, your eyes.' A compliment."

Alina, the daughter she had with Fidel, eventually fled Cuba; Naty was thus left alone, abandoned by the man she loved and left behind by the daughter who could not bear to live a life of nothingness, officially relegated to oblivion by her father.

As you meander about Vedado, retrace Naty Revuelta's scandalous adventures.

Asunción Durán Moré and Florentina Durán Moré

These women are sisters who survived the sinking of the RMS Titanic. Five of the passengers aboard that doomed oceanliner were bound for Cuba. Servand Ovies Rodríguez, a first-class passenger, drowned in the waters of the North Atlantic. The other Cubans, all in second-class accommodations, survived: Julian Padrón Manet, Emilio Pallas Castello, and the sisters Asunción Durán Moré and Florentina Durán Moré.

When the survivors managed to arrive in Havana weeks after the sinking, the sisters, who were aboard Lifeboat #12, claimed that they had prayed to the Virgin of Charity, Cuba's patron saint, who intervened and saved them. The story was sensational, especially when other Latin Americans aboard the Titanic had perished. (The two passengers bound for Mexico, both traveling in first class, drowned.) The sisters also said that they had made a promise to the Virgin of Charity: they would toss a rose in the waters off the Malecón once a week in memory of those who died. The lore remains that, at night along the Malecón, the two Cuban women, sisters born in Barcelona, Spain, who lived their lives in Cuba, were faithful mourners, remembering those lost in the greatest maritime disaster in human history.

The sisters kept their promise, walking to the Malecón each Sunday evening after dusk, making the sign of the cross, offering a prayer, and tossing a single rose into the waters.

The sisters died in the late 1950s and are buried in the Colón Cemetery.

William Morgan

William Morgan, known as *el comandante Yankee*, fought alongside Fidel Castro and was part of the rebels who strode victoriously into Havana. He was, of course, to meet a horrific end.

He married a Cuban, Olga María Rodríguez, had a child, and wanted to be a farmer. A simple man from Ohio, when he was in Havana, as a *comandante* of the Revolution, he stayed at the Capri Hotel and loved to walk down to Centro to eat at Sloppy Joe's.

His ghost haunts the Cuban imagination to this day, and his memory is legendary. Why? He was an American idealist who fought the good fight against a dictator, only to be executed by another dictator.

That's not how he saw things at the time, however. At a time when Americans were enthralled by the charismatic and enigmatic Fidel Castro, William Morgan, in 1958, sent a statement to the *New York Times* to explain his participation in the Cuban Revolution.

The statement, published under the headline "Why I Am Here," read, in part:

> I am here because I believe that the most important thing for free men to do is to protect the freedom of others. I am here so that my son, when he is grown, will not have to fight or die in a land not his own, because one man or group of men try to take his liberty from him. I am here because I believe that free men should take up arms and stand together and fight and destroy the groups and forces that want to take the rights of people away.

Morgan would be stripped of his American citizenship by the State Department. Two years later Castro arrested him, and, after a trial, he was executed on March 11, 1961.

153

Gilberto Bosques

Gilberto Bosques served as Mexico's ambassador to Cuba during the Revolution. A career diplomat who had befriended Castro in Mexico, Bosques had also served as Mexico's top diplomat to France during World War II. After the Nazis invaded Paris, Mexico relocated its embassy to Marseilles. It was there that Bosques launched one of the most comprehensive humanitarian efforts by issuing exit visas to almost 45,000 men, women, and children fleeing dictatorships in Germany, Italy, and Spain.

"We did what we had to do to save people," Bosques later said.

He only stopped when the Gestapo stormed the Mexican diplomatic compound, housed at the Castile Reynarde, and arrested everyone, holding them as prisoners of war for almost a year.

What does this have to do with Cuba? The Nazis taught Bosques to recognize evil when he saw it.

As Mexico's ambassador to Cuba, although he was a personal friend of Fidel Castro's and had helped Castro secure Mexican support, Bosques realized that the Revolution had taken a sinister turn. "When they began to declare people to be enemies of the State and when Che, at the United Nations, boasted that the executions would continue, I knew I had to do something," he said.

Bosques then embarked on a clandestine program to give false Mexican passports to Cubans desperate to escape. At that time, Mexico's Secretariat of Foreign Relations allowed provinces to issue their own passports, and Bosques was able to issue Mexican travel documents that would allow Cubans to escape to Mérida, which was served with flights on Mexicana Airlines. Hundreds of Cuban Jews and others targeted by the Revolution are believed to have escaped Cuba as Mexicans thanks to Bosques.

It is believed Fidel Castro learned of what was going on, but Soviet leader Nikita Khrushchev insisted that Bosques remain at his post because Bosques was working to relay messages between Moscow and Washington, D.C., during the Cuban Missile Crisis; Bosques had helped John Donovan negotiate the release of prisoners captured during the failed Bay of Pigs invasion. Bosques was also instrumental in defusing tensions between the United States and the Soviet Union. Indeed, Richard Grabman credits Bosques with being instrumental in averting World War III.

His presence is still felt throughout Havana, and many history buffs pay their respects by placing flowers at the gates of the Mexican Embassy in Havana, located at Calle 12 #518, corner of 7th Avenue, Miramar, Havana.

Leopoldo Fernández Salgado

Leopoldo Fernández Salgado was a Cuban comedian whose wit entertained people throughout Cuba and Latin America for decades. His character, José Candelario Tres Patines, or Pototo, was the star of the radio show *La Tremenda Corte*.

With the advent of television, his comedy *Filomeno Pototo* became a staple of Cuban TV viewing. Along with Aníbal de Mar, who played the judge, the comic program offered levity about life in the tradition of comedy pursued in the United States by their compatriot Desi Arnaz.

Throughout the 1940s and 1950s Tres Patines was a fixture along the Paseo del Prado in Centro, charming fans and being a gracious host to friends—fellow actors and comedians—from other Latin American countries. As a pioneer in broadcast comedy on television in the Spanish-speaking world, the humor presented, while naïve by today's standards, had an edge; it challenged and mocked authority, often with a critical political edge.

The Revolution brought an abrupt end to his career in Cuba. His familiar presence along the Paseo del Prado became an aching absence once he left for exile. (He would entertain friends and guests in the bar at the Hotel Saratoga.) Aníbal de Mar, his comedic partner, was also exiled, but the chemistry they had created proved elusive to duplicate.

Leopoldo moved to Mexico in the mid-1960s. The Monterrey radio station XEFB-AM produced the radio show, and in 1966 it was adapted for television by XET-TV 6. The show was a success; it became one of the first TV programs Mexico exported to other Latin American countries. Leopoldo then traveled throughout Latin America. In Mexico, he lived in Monterrey and Veracruz, visiting Mexico City and Mérida, before he moved permanently to Miami. It was there that he died on November 11, 1985.

Cubans old enough to remember Leopoldo Fernández point out that when Tres Patinas was forced into exile, Cuba lost its sense of humor.

Félix Varela

If there's a spiritual presence that's palpably felt throughout Old Havana it is that of Félix Varela, a Roman Catholic priest and independence leader who was born in Havana in 1788. This was when Cuba and Florida were part of New Spain. Born in Havana, Félix Varela grew up in St. Augustine, Florida. He returned to Havana to study to become a priest at the San Carlos and San Ambrosio Seminary. Ordained at the age of 23 at the Catedral de La Habana, he served in the Diocese of San Cristóbal de La Habana.

Varela studied philosophy, and he argued that the nations of the New World should not be subject to European powers. In 1821 he represented Cuba at the *Cortés Generales* in Madrid, where he petitioned the crown for independence. He also published an essay calling for the abolition of slavery. These notions did not sit well with European powers. When France invaded Spain in 1823 to restore King Ferdinand VII, Félix Varela was charged with treason and sentenced to death.

Before he could be arrested, he fled to Gibraltar. From there, he arrived in New York, where he founded *El Habanero*, the first Spanish-language newspaper in the United States. In 1837, he was named Vicar General of the Diocese of New York, which included the entire state of New York and northern New Jersey.

Always the voice of reason and a champion of freedoms—for the nations of Latin America to be independent republics, for all men and women to be free from the bondage of slavery, for everyone to be free to express his or her opinions—he is considered the philosopher who emboldened Cubans to yearn for emancipation and self-determination.

"As long as there is thought in Cuba, we will have to remember him, the one who taught us how to think," José de la Luz y Caballero, a leading Cuban intellectual, has said of him.

In 1998 Oswaldo Payá and the Christian Liberation Movement formed the Proyecto Varela, a pacifist movement calling for democratic political reform in Cuba. (In March 2003 Cuba arrested 75 dissidents, including 25 Proyecto Varela members, in a move that garnered worldwide condemnation.)

155

The Cuban government for its part created the Orden Félix Varela, without irony, an honor bestowed to those who have contributed to spreading Cuban culture worldwide. There is a movement for his canonization after having been declared a Servant of God. On Easter Sunday 2012 the Archdiocese of New York and the Archdiocese of Miami announced that the Vatican had declared Father Varela "Venerable," meaning his life is worthy of veneration.

His importance is such that he is now considered to be a common inspiration for the reconciliation of the Cuban people.

It is said that his presence can be felt from the Plaza de Armas to the University of Havana, where he is buried in the Aula Magna.

Reinaldo Arenas

An acclaimed writer of his generation, Reinaldo Arenas was a teenager when the Revolution came to power. The enthusiasm he felt for the promise of change quickly disappeared; he was gay and the Revolution considered divergent sexuality to be bourgeois decadence that had to be eradicated. There was no place for gays and lesbians in a Marxist-Leninist state.

He studied philosophy at the University of Havana. There, as a student, he would sit on the steps reading and daydream about being free one day. He secretly wrote his stories while working at the Biblioteca Nacional José Martí, located at the Plaza de la Revolución. He became an editor at the Cuban Book Institute. When his writings for *La Gaceta de Cuba*, a literary magazine, angered officials, he was arrested and charged for "ideological deviation," a phrase for being queer. He was imprisoned at El Morro Castle. He continued to write clandestinely and, when discovered, he was beaten.

Defiant, Reinaldo's writings openly discussed his homosexuality, and he openly declared he was gay.

In 1980, as part of the Mariel Boat Lift, he was deported to the U.S. Gone were the days when he could spend time on the steps of the University of Havana and dream of a future. Seven years later, he was diagnosed with AIDS. Three years later, he committed suicide, leaving several finished manuscripts. In his suicide note, he left a message to the Cuban people:

> Due to my delicate state of health and to the terrible depression that causes me not to be able to continue writing and struggling for the freedom of Cuba, I am ending my life. . . . I want to encourage the Cuban people abroad as well as on the Island to continue fighting for freedom. . . Cuba will be free. I already am.

His autobiography, *Before Night Falls*, became a *New York Times* bestseller in 1993. It was made into a critically acclaimed film, staring Javier Bardem and directed by Julian Schnabel.

María Teresa Mestre y Batista

María Teresa is probably the only person in the world, apart from Fidel and Raúl Castro, who is better off because of the Cuban Revolution. The daughter of José Antonio Mestre y Álvarez and María Teresa Batista y Falla, her family fled Cuba after the Revolution. In New York, María Teresa attended the Lycée Français.

A privileged exile, she studied ballet, took singing classes, mastered Alpine skiing, and studied in Santander, Spain, and Geneva, Switzerland. In 1980 she completed her studies at the Graduate Institute of International Development Studies in Geneva, where she met a fellow student who would become her future husband: Prince Henri.

María Teresa, through her father, is a descendant of the Espinosa de los Monteros, a noble Spanish family, which made the romance between her and Prince Henri acceptable to the prince's family.

And that is how María Teresa, a Cuban refugee, became the Grand Duchess of Luxembourg when she married her prince charming in February 1981. She and the Grand Duke Henri have five children: Guillaume, Hereditary Grand Duke of Luxembourg, Prince Félix, Prince Louis, Princess Alexandra, and Prince Sébastien.

Her parents, while in exile in New York, reminisced about their former lives in the Vedado district of Havana, but it can be said that their daughter is better off today than she would have ever been had the family not been forced to flee the Revolution.

20 SANTERÍA

What is Santería?

As you walk around Havana you will notice women dressed in white dresses. They are followers of Santería, an Afro-Cuban religion.

Santería, which is also known as Regla de Ochá or La Regla de Lucumí, is a syncretic religion that combines beliefs of the West African mythology of the Yoruba people and Roman Catholicism. It evolved throughout the Caribbean among black slaves who combined the teachings of Christianity and some elements of the beliefs of the indigenous peoples of the Americas.

Key components include drumming, dance, animal sacrifice, and the belief in communicating with ancestors and deities through divination.

This is how Ernesto Pichardo explains it in *Santería in Contemporary Cuba*:

> The colonial period from the standpoint of African slaves may be defined as a time of perseverance. Their world quickly changed. Tribal kings and their families, politicians, business and community leaders all were enslaved and taken to a foreign region of the world. Religious leaders, their relatives and their followers were now slaves. Colonial laws criminalized their religion.
>
> They were forced to become baptized and worship a god their ancestors had not known who was surrounded by a pantheon of saints. The early concerns during this period seem to have necessitated a need for individual survival under harsh plantation conditions. A sense of hope was sustaining the internal essence of what today is called Santería, a misnomer (and former pejorative) for the indigenous religion of the Lukumi people of Nigeria. In the heart of their homeland, they had a complex political and social order. They were a sedentary hoe farming cultural group with specialized labor.
>
> Their religion, based on the worship of nature, was renamed and documented by their masters. Santería, a pejorative term that characterizes deviant Catholic forms of worshiping saints, has become a common name for the religion. The term santero(a) is used to describe a priest or priestess replacing the traditional term Olorisha as an extension of the deities. The orishas became known as the saints in image of the Catholic pantheon.

The black women dressed in white are wonderful. They are friendly and charming. Whenever I'm in Havana, I strike up a conversation with several of them.

At first they may appear to be like the fake "psychics" doing readings in New York and many European cities. In Havana, however, while these ladies would welcome the chance to make some money from you, the interaction has a different quality.

Be willing to engage in conversation with them. If you do, have a few presents—toiletries, over-the-counter medicines, candy, rum, cigars—in your backpack. Also consider making a contribution, $5 to $10 CUCs is appropriate. Don't be afraid to accept an invitation into their homes. They have their altars and paraphenalia in their residences. These altars are adorned with shells, saints, carved masks, colored beads, bottles of rum, coins, candles, incense, and so forth. (NOTE: Use common sense when entering a stranger's home anywhere in the world.)

The "readings" they give are conversations about life, faith, how to be at peace with the world. They may or may not offer to "anticipate" your destiny, or answer any questions. In one of the more memorable visits I made to the home of one of these women, she asked, after we had been drinking rum for a while, what I wanted to know about Cuba.

What did I want to know? I thought about it. Then I told her I had one question: *Why has this Revolution been so severe?*

She laughed, clapped her hands, and said it was a secret. But it was a secret she would disclose. I asked if I could reveal the secret to others once I knew it. She paused, thought about it, stood up, and replied that *one full year* would have to pass before I could disclose the reason why the Cuban Revolution was so severe.

We made a deal. She stood up, took a sip of rum, lit a cigar, and began to dance. A man, her aide, played the drum, and she danced furiously. After a 15-minute performance, she was ready. She told me the answer.

This occurred in 2009. Thus, keeping my end of the bargain, I will now disclose why the Cuban Revolution has been so severe—*from the perspective of Santería.*

This is what she said:

> *Los gallegos son un pueblo ibérico sin ritmo. Por lo tanto, no saben bailar. Los gallegos no saben bailar y por ello no saben la alegría de la vida. Fidel es hijo de gallegos y Fidel no sabe bailar. Fidel no sabe bailar y por esta razón su revolución es un fracaso como él es un fracasado.*

In English, this means: "The Galicians are an Iberian people without rhythm. As such, they do not know how to dance. The Galicians do not know how to dance, and that is why they do not know the joy of life. Fidel is the son of Galicians, and Fidel does not know how to dance. Fidel does not know how to dance and it is for this reason his revolution is as much of a failure as he is a failure."

It was a great revelation; I invited her and her assistant to dinner.

What will Santería reveal to you?

The Revolution & a Cuban Primer

CHRONOLOGY OF THE CUBAN REVOLUTION

The Cuban Revolution has certainly been momentous.

Following is a chronology of key events since Fidel Castro seized power in January 1959.

1958 December: Castro and his men seize control of several towns in eastern and central Cuba.

1959 January: President Fulgencio Batista flees Cuba the same day that Fidel Castro's men enter Santiago de Cuba. Manuel Urrutia is named president of Cuba four days later.

1959 January: Taking control, Fidel orders summary trials and execution by firing squads of officials associated with the ousted Batista government. Over the next 11 months 954 Cubans are executed, most under the direction of Che Guevara.

1959 February: Fidel Castro is named premier of Cuba.

1959 March: Castro makes a national speech in which he addresses the problem of racism in Cuba. Today, Cuba remains governed by descendants of white European males.

1959 May: The Cuban government enacts the Agrarian Reform Law limiting land ownership to 1,000 acres; all larger proprieties are nationalized. The first property seized is Las Manacas, his family's farm. His mother is enraged.

1959 July: Osvaldo Dorticós Torrado becomes president of Cuba, replacing Manuel Urrutia. Dorticós remains in office until December 2, 1976.

1959 October: Revolutionary leaders, including Huber Matos, are imprisoned or, as happened to Camilo Cienfuegos, disappear without a trace as the Revolution devours its own.

1960 February: Soviet Deputy Prime Minister Anastas Mikoyan visits Havana to establish a trade and political agreement between Cuba and the USSR.

1960 March: The French freighter *La Coubre*, carrying 76 tons of munitions from Belgium, explodes in Havana harbor. Castro blames the U.S., fueling anti-American sentiment.

1960 March: The Revolutionary government takes control of Cuba's radio stations.

1960 March: U.S. President Dwight Eisenhower signs an executive order authorizing C.I.A. director Allen Dulles to train Cuban exiles for a covert operation.

1960 May: The Revolutionary government nationalizes all of Cuba's newspapers; freedom of the press and free speech are abolished.

1960 June: Anti-Castro guerrillas in eastern and central Cuba take up arms against Castro. The Revolutionary government fights back against the Escambray Revolt, or the War Against the Bandits.

1960 June: Professional and middle-class Cubans begin leaving Cuba, most settling in Miami as the Cuban Diaspora becomes a phenomenon.

1960 July: The Revolutionary government, accusing the U.S. of interventions, nationalizes all U.S. businesses and commercial properties.

1960 September: Fidel Castro visits New York to address the United Nations, where Soviet Premier Nikita Khrushchev embraces him.

1960 September: The Revolutionary government establishes Committees for the Defense of the Revolution (CDRs) on every block. The CDRs report to government officials on the activities of residents of each neighborhood.

1960 October: The Revolutionary government nationalizes all Cuban-owned private enterprises and rental apartment buildings and seizes commercial bank accounts. The abolition of all private property and the shutting down of all free enterprise business begins; the Cuban Revolution is declared Communist.

1960 October: The U.S. imposes an embargo prohibiting all exports to Cuba, except foodstuffs and medical supplies.

1960 December: Operation Peter Pan (*Operación Pedro Pan*) begins. The airlift of more than 14,000 Cuban children, whose parents are not allowed to leave Cuba but who want to get their children out, begins. The airlift ends in October 1962 when the U.S. closes all airports to Cuban flights during the Cuban Missile Crisis.

1961 January: Castro proclaims 1961 as the Year of Education *(Año de la Educación)* and the Year of Literacy *(Año de la Alfabetización)*. Havana professionals are sent to rural communities throughout Cuba in a mass literary campaign.

1961 January: The U.S. and Cuba sever diplomatic relations. Embassies in both Washington, D.C., and Havana are closed.

1961 April: The Revolutionary government establishes the Pioneers, a Communist youth organization. The indoctrination of Cuban youth begins.

1961 April: The U.S. uses Cuban exiles and other proxies for an invasion of Cuba. Known as the Bay of Pigs, without adequate air support the invasion fails. More than 1,100 Cubans are arrested. John Donovan will be sent to Cuba to negotiate for the release of captured American citizens, and Cuban exiles are captured.

1961 May: The Revolutionary government nationalizes private and religious schools. Education is nationalized.

1961 August: The Revolutionary government changes the currency, and all personal bank accounts are seized.

1961 September: The Revolutionary government suspends all outdoor religious processions; religious authorities, primarily priests and rabbis, are expelled from the country.

1961 December: Castro declares himself a Marxist-Leninist and pledges allegiance with the Soviet Union.

1962 January: Cuba is suspended from the Organization of American States (OAS); many member states begin to break off diplomatic relations with Havana. Mexico alone maintains a full diplomatic presence in Havana without interruption.

1962 April: Mexico's ambassador to Cuba, Gilberto Bosques, begins to issue Mexican passports to Cubans persecuted by Castro. Hundreds of Cuban Jews flee Havana with false Mexican papers.

1962 August–October: U.S. President John F. Kennedy is briefed of the presence of surface-to-air missile batteries in Cuba. The Cuban Missile Crisis begins when the U.S. establishes an air and sea blockade. Kennedy threatens to invade Cuba if the missile bases are not dismantled. Kennedy warns that a nuclear attack launched from Cuba would be considered a Soviet attack on the U.S. and vows full retaliation. Mexican ambassador Gilberto Bosques begins back-channel communications between the U.S., the Soviet Union, and the Cubans after Nikita Khrushchev locks out Fidel Castro from negotiations with Kennedy.

1962 October: Khrushchev agrees to remove Soviet nuclear missiles from Cuba. The U.S. agrees to remove missiles from Turkey. The U.S. agrees not to invade Cuba.

1962 November: The U.S. ends its Cuban air and sea blockade, satisfied that the missile bases have been dismantled and Soviet jets will leave Cuba before the end of the year.

1962 November: The Revolutionary government suspends the exodus of Cubans. Thousands of Cuban families are divided.

1965 November: The Revolutionary government resumes allowing Cubans to flee for exile in Mexico and the U.S. Many Cuban parents now begin to be reunited with their "Pedro Pan" children.

1967 October: Che Guevara is captured and executed in La Higuera, Bolivia.

1975 November: The Revolutionary government sends troops to Angola and occupies that nation immediately after its independence from Portugal. General Raúl Díaz Argüelles is in charge of Cuban military forces in Angola. General Arnaldo Ochoa leads Cuban military engagements during a decade of revolutionary involvement in African wars, primarily in Mozambique and Ethiopia.

1976 September: The Revolutionary government enshrines universal free health care in the Cuban Constitution. The World Health Organization praises Cuba as a model for other countries.

1976 December: Fidel Castro assumes the title of President of the State Council. He is named Head of State, Head of Government, and Commander in Chief of the Armed Forces.

1979 January: The Revolutionary government permits exiles to visit their families in Cuba, provided they use Cuban passports and are subject to all Cuban laws while in Cuba. More than 100,000 exiles return to visit their homeland and families.

1980 April: The Revolutionary government announces that anyone who wants to leave Cuba may depart by sea. The result, the Mariel Boat Lift, results in an exodus of more than 150,000 people to the U.S. The Revolutionary government uses this as an opportunity to empty jails and mental hospitals, sending criminals and the insane to the U.S.

1980 May: The Mariel exodus provides a cover for Cuba to lash out at the LGBTQ community. Fidel Castro arrests and deports an estimated 40,000 gays, lesbians, and transgender Cubans who are sent to Florida from the port of Mariel. The most famous members of the LGBTQ community expelled from Cuba are Pedro Zamora, who went on to appear on MTV's *Real World: San Francisco*, and Reinaldo Arenas, whose book *Before Night Falls* became a major motion picture.

1985 May: Cuba diagnoses its first case of HIV/AIDS in a soldier returning from Mozambique. Draconian measures are taken against individuals with HIV/AIDS, who are rounded up and sent to internment camps.

1989 July: General Arnaldo Ochoa, a Hero of the Revolution and commander of Cuban military forces in Africa, and the third most powerful man in Cuba after Fidel and Raúl, is executed by firing squad. Ochoa's popularity threatened Castro's hold on power.

1991 December: The Soviet Union is dissolved. This ends more than $6 billion in annual subsidies to Havana. Soviet military personnel and advisers leave Cuba. The subsequent economic hardship is called the Special Period, or *Período Especial*.

1996 February: The Revolutionary government arrests or detains more than 150 dissidents. This crackdown, the largest since the 1970s, garners worldwide condemnation.

1998 January: Pope John Paul II visits the island, declaring that Cuba must open up to the world and that the world must reach out to Cuba.

1999 November: Christian activist Óscar Elías Biscet is arrested for organizing religious gatherings in the cities of Havana and Matanzas. He is released in 2002, only to be rearrested in 2003 along with scores of other dissidents.

1999 November: Elián González is rescued off the Florida Keys, setting off an international custody battle.

2002 September: U.S. President George W. Bush establishes the Guantánamo Bay detention camp at Guantánamo Bay Naval Base. The detention camp, over Cuban objections, holds unlawful combatants captured in Afghanistan, Iraq, and other countries as part of America's War on Terror.

2003 April: The Revolutionary government arrests 78 writers, poets, dissidents, and librarians. All are found guilty of treason. They are sentenced to jail; books and publications from several independent libraries are confiscated or destroyed.

2003 April: Cuba taxes transactions in U.S. dollars; the euro becomes the hard currency of choice.

2006 July: Raúl Castro assumes presidential duties while Fidel Castro recovers from an illness the nature of which is not disclosed. The Revolutionary government, fearing a U.S. invasion during this transition from one Castro to the other, places the Cuban military on highest alert, and all reservists are called into active duty.

2008 February: Fidel Castro leaves office. Raúl Castro is elected president by the National Assembly, becoming Cuba's leader.

2009 January: President Barack Obama issues an executive order to close the Guantánamo Bay detention camp; the U.S. Senate votes to keep it open. As of 2015, more than a hundred prisoners remain in custody.

2014 December: U.S. President Barack Obama announce the reestablishment of diplomatic relations between the U.S. and Cuba.

2015 July: The United States and Cuba reestablish diplomatic relations. Embassies are reopened in Havana and Washington, D.C.

2015 October: Cuban authorities, fearing the repercussions of greater economic expectations, crack down on dissidents, focusing on the Ladies in White (*Damas de Blanco*).

CUBAN POLITICAL POWER & DISSIDENTS

Cuba adopted a communist political system two years after the 1959 Revolution.

Its constitution defines it as a Marxist-Leninist state "guided by the principles of José Martí, and the political ideas of Marx, the father of communist states, Engels, and Lenin."

Political Structure

The **Executive** power is exercised through the Council of State and the Council of Ministers. Legislative power is exercised through the unicameral National Assembly of People's Power.

Fidel Castro held the offices of president of the Council of State, president of the Council of Ministers (at times referred to as prime minister), first secretary of the Communist Party, and commander in chief of the Revolutionary Armed Forces. Today, Raúl Castro holds these positions.

Judiciary authority is exercised through the People's Supreme Court. The constitution states that all civil liberties, including the right to disagree with the state, can be denied to anyone; opposition to the government is defined as opposition to the Cuban people's right to build socialism. Dissidents are routinely imprisoned as a danger to the state.

Political Parties

The only political party is the Communist Party of Cuba.

Cuban Leaders

Communist Party of Cuba

- First Secretary: Raúl Castro Ruz
- Second Secretary: José Ramón Machado
- Members of the Politburo: Raúl Castro Ruz, José Ramón Machado, Ramiro Valdés Menéndez, Abelardo Colomé Ibarra, Esteban Lazo Hernández, Ricardo Alarcón de Quesada, Miguel Díaz-Canel Bermúdez Mario, Leopoldo Cintra Frías, Ramón Espinosa Martín, Álvaro Lopez Miera, Salvador Valdés Mesa, Mercedes López Acea, Marino Murillo Jorge, and Adel Yzquierdo Rodríguez
- Members of the Secretariat: José Ramón Machado Ventura, Esteban Lazo Hernández, Abelardo Álvarez Gil, José Ramón Balaguer Cabrera, Víctor Gaute López, and Olga Lidia Tapia Iglesias

167

Officers of the Council of State

- President: Raúl Castro Ruz
- First Vice President: Miguel Díaz-Canel Bermúdez
- Vice Presidents: Abelardo Colomé Ibarra, Ramiro Valdés Menéndez, Juan Esteban Lazo Hernández, Gladys María Bejerano Portela, and José Ramón Machado
- Secretary: Homero Acosta Álvarez

Council of Ministers

- President: Raúl Castro Ruz
- First Vice President: Miguel Díaz-Canel Bermúdez
- Vice Presidents: José Ramón Fernández Álvarez, Marino Alberto Murillo, Ulises Rosales del Toro, Ramiro Valdés Menéndez, Ricardo Cabrisas Ruíz, and Antonio Enrique Lussón Batlle
- Minister of the Interior: Abelardo Colomé Ibarra
- Minister of the Armed Forces: position vacant

National Assembly of People's Power

- President: Esteban Lazo Hernández
- Vice President: Jaime Alberto Crombet Hernández-Baquero
- Secretary: Miriam Brito Sarroca

Committees for the Defense of the Revolution

To maintain power and control dissent, Cuba established the Committees for the Defense of the Revolution (CDR) in September 1960. These are networks of neighborhood surveillance posts. The CDRs are designed to monitor the population, report on "counterrevolutionary" activity, distribute government information, report on neighbors' associations, and authorize residents' gatherings in their own homes (dinner parties, birthday parties, social gatherings, etc.). It is the responsibility CDR officers to monitor the activities of each person in their respective blocks.

As the stamina for revolution wanes, the CDR offices on each block, often designated by faded tin plaques on the wall by the front door of a house, are today often manned an elderly woman, the neighborhood busybody sitting on her front step keeping an eye on the people on the block.

Press Censorship

Cuba is the only authoritarian regime in the Americas, according to the 2010 Democracy Index. The Press Freedom Index ranks Cuba's press censorship to be comparable to that in North Korea.

168

All media in Cuba operates under the jurisdiction of the Communist Party's Department of Revolutionary Orientation. Its mission is to develop and coordinate all "propaganda strategies" throughout the island nation.

This guidebook is not authorized to be sold in Cuba.

Opposition Groups

Ladies in White

The *Damas de Blanco*, Ladies in White, is an opposition movement founded in 2003 by the wives and female relatives of imprisoned political dissidents. The women attend Mass each Sunday dressed in white clothing. They pin a photograph of their imprisoned relatives and the number of years to which they have been sentenced on their clothing. After Mass, they walk through the streets in silence. The color white symbolizes peace, and the group's purpose is to shame the government.

The group is modeled after the Mothers of the Plaza de Mayo, or *Asociación Madres de la Plaza de Mayo*, in Argentina. This was an association of mothers whose children "disappeared" during the military dictatorship's "Dirty War" between 1976 and 1983. The Mothers of the Plaza de Mayo are credited with having accelerated the downfall of Argentina's dictatorship.

In Cuba, the Ladies in White was formed in 2003 after 75 human rights advocates, independent journalists, and librarians were arrested, tried, and sentenced to terms of up to 28 years in prison. This mass roundup of dissidents is known as the Black Spring of 2003.

Cuban authorities accused the dissidents of "acts against the independence or the territorial integrity of the state." This included "illegal organizations," "hijacking" the Cuban constitution, and "terroristic" collaboration with foreign media.

Laura Pollán formed, and led, the organization two weeks after the dissidents were arrested. The Cuban government labeled the women as a "subversive association of Yankee-backed terrorists."

The women are routinely attacked by angry mobs, which often hurl insults, eggs, and trash at them. They are beaten; some have been stripped naked and shoved in the gutter. The police routinely follow them and arrest them, throwing them into police buses. They are often kept incommunicado for days.

The Ladies received the Sakharov Prize for Freedom of Thought conferred on them by the European Parliament in 2005. Cuba did not allow the any member to travel to France to receive the award.

In 2010, Cardinal Jaime Lucas Ortega y Alamino appealed to government officials on behalf of the group. Since then, the ladies have been allowed to protest outside his church.

Laura Pollán died in 2011 at a state-run hospital; Berto Soler is the group's current leader.

Since the reestablishment of diplomatic relations with the U.S., there has been an intensification of state violence against the women.

Travel Advisory

Cuba, Cuban leaders are nervous about the changes now unfolding.

With the reestablishment of diplomatic relations between the U.S. and ng in Cuba. While they want to move to a more open, market-driven economy, they also want to keep complete political control.

In consequence, violence against all dissidents has increased. Visitors to Cuba are advised to be vigilant and stay away from any gathering—mob—that assembles around the Ladies in White or other protestors. Violence against protestors continues to escalate in the Miramar, Vedado, Havana Centro, and Cotorro areas.

Dissident Organizations

In addition to the Ladies in White, there are other organizations—all considered subversive by authorities—that do not believe Cuba should be a one-party system.

These include:

The Varela Project.
The organization, named after Father Félix Varela, an eighteenth-century Roman Catholic priest, calls for a referendum, by secret ballot, to reestablish a free press, the right to form political parties, establishment of press enterprise, and for the right of Cubans to travel. The government responded by calling for its own referendum that made socialism "untouchable," adding that the "revolutionary process of socialism cannot be reversed" in Cuba.

Yo No Coopero Con La Dictadura, or "I Do Not Cooperate with the Dictatorship."
This is an organization of peaceful civil resistance. Its acts of civil disobedience are peaceful. Members, for instance, wear shirts with the slogan *Yo sí quiero el cambio*," meaning "I do want change." Its six principles are: "I do not repudiate, I do not assist, I do not snitch, I do not follow, I do not cooperate, and I do not repress." At mandatory public gatherings, when workers are ordered to attend public gathering in a show of solidarity with the government, they signal their repudiation of the regime by crossing their arms over their chests.

Christian Liberation Movement.
Founded by political activist and dissident Oswaldo Payá, this is a Roman Catholic movement calling for the reestablishment of democracy in Cuba. The European Parliament awarded him the Sakharov Prize for Freedom of Thought in 2002. Payá died in a car accident under mysterious circumstances in 2012. He was 60.

The Lawton Foundation.
Established by Óscar Elías Biscet, the group strives to promote the "defense of human rights inside Cuba" and to "denounce" the violations of these rights. Biscet was arrested, tried, and sentenced to 25 years in prison for crimes "against the sovereignty and integrity of Cuban national territory." In 2007 U.S. President George W. Bush presented Biscet with the Presidential Medal of Freedom. After

170

years of appeals by the United Nations, the European Union, and Mexico, he was released on March 11, 2011.

Cuban Democratic Directorate.

This nongovernmental organization, based in the U.S., was formed at the International Congress of Cuban Youth for a Free Cuba held in Miami Beach, Florida. The CDD began primarily as an advocacy group comprised of students and professionals, under the age of 40, who wanted to contribute to the restoration of democracy in Cuba. The organization is a member of the Centrist Democrat International and International Democratic Union.

The Assembly to Promote Civil Society.

An initiative of Marta Beatriz Roque, this organization works to coordinate activities of dissidents and opposition organizations in Cuba. An economist by training, she, along with Vladimiro Roca, Félix Bonne, and Rene Gómez Manzano, were arrested in 1997 for publishing an academic paper titled "The Homeland Belongs to All," which called for political and economic reform. The "Gang of Four" were tried for "sedition" and imprisoned. She was released in 2002 after staging a hunger strike. That year she was awarded the Heinz R. Pagels Human Rights of Scientists Award of the New York Academy of Sciences. She is considered Cuba's leading female dissident.

Dissident Blogger

Yoani Sánchez is the leading dissident Cuban voice in cyberspace. Her blog has won awards from nations around the world, and she is a champion for defending human rights.

Anyone interested in the state of Cuban thinking about current events should visit her blog:

Yoani Sánchez: *http://www.14ymedio.com/blogs/generacion_y*

Tourists' Rights

Under Cuban law, as a tourist, you do not have the right to engage in any political activity or event whatsoever. Furthermore, you do not have the right to express any political opinion that runs counter to the policies of the Cuban Communist Party. You risk deportation—or imprisonment—for saying anything, writing anything, or attending any political event that is not supportive of the Cuban government.

Best advice: Always say *"Soy amigo de Cuba,"* meaning "I'm a friend of Cuba," and keep all other opinions to yourself.

171

A CUBAN PRIMER: QUESTIONS ANSWERED

Visitors to Cuba are often struck by things they find odd—and don't know who to ask.

Following are questions that foreign tourists and visitors in Cuba have asked time and again as the Editor developed this guide.

When Did Fidel Castro Become Communist?

Fidel Castro can best answer that question for himself. Here is what he told a student at the University of the Concepción, Chile, on November 18, 1971:

> "I was the son of a landowner—that was one reason for me to be a reactionary. I was educated in religious schools that were attended by the sons of the rich—another reason for being a reactionary. I lived in Cuba, where all the films, publications, and mass media were 'Made in USA'—a third reason for being a reactionary. I studied in a university where out of fifteen thousand students, only thirty were anti-imperialists, and I was one of those thirty at the end. When I entered the university, it was as the son of a landowner—and to make matters worse, as a political illiterate!
>
> "... And mind you, no party member, no Communist, no socialist or extremist got hold of me and indoctrinated me. No. I was given a big, heavy, infernal, unreadable, unbearable textbook that tried to explain political economy from a bourgeois viewpoint—they called that political economy!
>
> "And that unbearable book presented the crises of overproduction and other such problems as the most natural things in the world. It explained how in Britain, when there was an abundance of coal, there were workers who didn't have any, because by the inexorable natural and unchangeable laws of history, of society and nature, crises of overproduction inevitably occur, and when they do, they bring unemployment and starvation. When there's too much coal, workers will freeze and starve!
>
> "So that landowner's son, who had been educated by bourgeois schools and Yankee propaganda, began to think that something was wrong with that system, that it didn't make sense ...
>
> "As the son of a poor man who later became a big landowner, I had the advantage of at least living in the countryside, with the peasants, with the poor, who were all my friends. Had I been the grandson of a landowner, it's quite possible that my father would have taken me to live in the capital, in a super aristocratic neighborhood and those positive factors at work on me wouldn't have been able to survive the influence of the milieu. Egoism and other negative traits we human beings have would have prevailed.
>
> "Luckily, the schools I studied in developed some of the positive factors. A certain idealistic rationality; a certain concept of good and evil, just and unjust; and a certain spirit of

172

rebelliousness against impositions and oppression led me to an analysis of human society, and turned me into what I later realized was a utopian Communist. At the time, I still hadn't been fortunate enough to meet a Communist or read a Communist document.

"Then one day a copy of the Communist Manifesto—the famous Communist Manifesto!—fell into my hands and I read some things I'll never forget. . . . What phrases, what truths! And we saw those truths every day!

"I felt like some little animal that had been born in a forest which he didn't understand. Then, all of a sudden, he finds a map of that forest—a description, a geography of that forest and everything in it. It was then that I got my bearings. Take a look now and see if Marx's ideas weren't just, correct, and inspiring. If we hadn't based our struggle on them, we wouldn't be here now! We wouldn't be here!

"Now then, was I a Communist? No. I was a man who was lucky enough to have discovered a political theory, a man who was caught up in the whirlpool of Cuba's political crisis long before becoming a full-fledged Communist. . . .

"I went on developing. Afterwards, I had the opportunity to know imperialism more concretely than I had through Lenin's book. I got to know imperialism—the worst and most aggressive of all. . . . And I believe life has given me a better understanding of reality. It has made me more revolutionary, more socialist, more Communist."

How Did Cuba Celebrate the First Year of Revolution?

When Fidel Castro entered Havana in January 1959, he set up offices in the presidential suite at the Havana Hilton, which is now known as the Habana-Libre Hotel.

He returned there to celebrate the first year of the Revolution. He threw a grand gala to say goodbye to the 1950s and to welcome both a new year and new decade: the 1960s. Who was Fidel Castro's personal guest of honor? American boxer Joe Louis.

Here is an excerpt from Carlos Franqui's book, *Family Portrait with Fidel,* describing the scene:

To bid farewell to 1959 and to greet the new and, as we would soon see, decisive 1960, we had an official dinner in the Habana-Libre. The mix at our table was a bit odd: Fidel, Celia, my wife, Margot, and I. Then two guests of "Revolución," Giselle Halimi and Claude Faux, French writers and lawyers, friends of Sartre and Simone de Beauvoir, who would themselves soon visit the island. And Joe Louis, the American mulatto who had knocked out the Aryan great white hope, Max Schmeling, was Fidel Castro's personal guest.

Louis wasn't scarred or physically smashed up; he was mentally beaten, punchy. I was a fan of his and remembered the party we had in my hometown with the blacks when he beat Schmeling. But what Louis meant as a symbol wasn't lost on me: Fidel was warning me again. For him, sports were more important than culture. Back in the Sierra, Fidel had wanted us to broadcast scenes from the war on Radio Rebelde while Che and I insisted on reading poetry.

I remembered that on our trips to New York and Washington Fidel had refused to go to art museums, preferring to have his picture taken in the zoo. I remembered when he refused to support our petition to have the Cintas painting collection sent to Cuba. But, for all that, we still had room to maneuver, and "Revolución" still retained some autonomy. "Lunes," the Monday literary supplement edited by Guillermo Cabrera Infante, annoyed some but impressed everyone.

When Did Castro Declare the Cuban Revolution to Be Socialist?

The Revolution triumphed on January 1, 1959. Less than a year and a half later, Fidel Castro declared the Cuban Revolution to be socialist. Here is an excerpt from Fidel Castro's long and rambling speech, delivered on May 2, 1961, less than two weeks after the failed Bay of Pigs invasion, in connection with May Day celebrations:

"Distinguished visitors from Latin America and the entire world, combatants of the armed forces of the people, workers: We have had fourteen and a half hours of parading. (Public chanting adoration) I think that only a people imbued with infinite enthusiasm is capable of enduring such tests. Nevertheless, I will try to be as brief as possible. . . .

We are very happy over this attitude by the people. . . .

We have been witnesses, all of us Cubans, of every step taken by the Revolution, so maybe we cannot realize how much we have advanced as fully as can be understood by visitors, particularly those visitors from Latin America, where today they are still living in a world very similar to the one we lived in yesterday. It is as if they were suddenly transported from the past to the present of our Revolution, with all its extraordinary progress as compared to the past. We do not intend tonight to stress the merit of what we have done. We merely want to locate ourselves at the point where we are at the present.

We had a chance today to see genuine results of the Revolution on this May Day, so different from the May Days of the past. Formerly that date was the occasion for each sector of labor to set forth its demands, its aspirations for improvement, to men who were deaf to the working-class interests, men who could not even accede to those basic demands because they did not govern for the people, for the workers, for the peasants, or for the humble; they governed solely for the privileged, the dominant economic interests. Doing anything for the people would have meant harming the interests that they represented, and so they could not accede to any just demand from the people. The May Day parades of those days marked the complaints and protest of the workers.

How different today's parade has been! How different even from the first parades after the Revolution triumphed. Today's parade shows us how much we have advanced. The workers (light applause) now do not have to submit themselves to those trials; the workers now do not have to implore deaf executives; the workers now are not subject to the domination of any exploiting class; the workers no longer live in a country run by men serving exploiting interests. The workers know now that everything the revolution does, everything the government does or can do, has one goal: helping the workers, helping the people. (Applause)

Otherwise, there would be no explanation for the spontaneous sentiment of support for the Revolutionary Government, that overflowing good will that every man and woman has expressed today. (Applause)

Fruits of the Revolution are seen everywhere. . . . We saw the pupils of the schools for young peasants of the Zapata swamps parade by, the swamps that the mercenaries chose for their attack. We saw thousands and thousands of peasants who are studying in the capital and who come from distant mountain areas or from cane cooperatives or from people's farms parade. We saw the young girls studying for children's club work. And we saw also what is going into the rural areas. The volunteer teachers paraded and also representatives of the 100,00 young people on their way to the interior to wipe out illiteracy. Where does this strength come from? It comes from the people, and it is devoted to the people in return. . . .

Art, culture, university professions, opportunities, honors, elegant clothes were only the privilege of a small minority, a minority represented today with that grace and humor shown by some worker federations in their imitations of the rich. . . .

And so one can see today the unity of the humble people who are fighting for the poor. Workers of every profession; manual laborers and intellectual workers; all were marching together, the writer, artist, actor, announcer, doctor, nurse, clinical employer. Marching together in great numbers under the flag of the national education workers union were the teachers, employees of the Education Ministry. (Applause)

Today we have had a chance to see everything worthwhile in our country, everything produced in our country. We have understood better than ever that there are two classes of citizens, or rather there were two classes of citizens; the citizens who worked, produced, and created and the citizens who lived without working or producing. These latter were parasites. . . .

Those who paraded today were the working people who will never resign themselves to work for the parasites. . . . (Applause)

The motherland of today where we have won the right to direct our destiny, where we have learned to decide our destiny, a motherland which will be now and forever—as Martí wanted it—for the well-being of everyone and not a motherland for few!

What kind of morality and what reason and what right do they have to make a Negro die to defend the monopolies, the factories, and the mines of the dominating classes? What right have they to send the Puerto Rican of Latin blood, of Latin tradition, to the battlefields to defend the policy of large capitalists and monopolies? This concept of motherland and this danger to their security to which they refer is the danger of the monopolies. You can understand what concept they have of morality, law, and rights, to send the Negroes of the South and the Puerto Ricans to the battlefields to fight for them. This is their concept of motherland only when the interests of the privileged classes are liquidated, and when a nation with its wealth becomes a nation for everyone, the wealth for everyone, and opportunity and happiness for everybody.

This happiness now belongs to those youths who paraded, and the families who know that their children can have a school, receive scholarships, and go to the best universities abroad, a privilege enjoyed only by the richest families. . . .

These enthusiastic people are the discouraged people of yesterday. The difference is that yesterday they worked for others and today they work for themselves. (Applause)

Think of the men who died in recent battles and decide whether a single drop of blood was worth being lost to defend the past. Consider that these workers and youths, the children of workers, fell ten to twelve days ago to defend what we have seen today. They fell to defend this enthusiasm, this hope, and this joy of today. That is why when today we saw a happy face or a smile full of hope, we thought that each smile of today was flower over the grave of the fallen hero. . . .

What would have happened to our workers, wives, sisters, and factories? What would have happened if imperialism had established even a single beachhead on our territory? What would have happened if the imperialists succeeded in taking one part of our territory, and from there, with Yankee bombs, machine guns, and planes, would have launched an armed attack against us?

175

Let us not talk about what would have happened if the imperialist had won. There is no sadder picture than a defeated revolution. . . . That is why we were thinking that every smile today was like a tribute to those who made possible this hopeful day. The blood that was shed was the blood of workers and peasants, the blood of humble sons of the people, not blood of landowners, millionaires, thieves, criminals, or exploiters. The bloodshed was the blood of the exploited of yesterday, the free men of today. The bloodshed was humble, honest, working, creative blood—the blood of patriots not the blood of mercenaries. It was the blood of militiamen who voluntarily came to defend the Revolution. It was spontaneously offered blood to defend an ideal. . . . It was not an ideal of those who came to recover their lost wealth. It was not the ideal of those who always lived at the expense of others. It was not the ideal of those who sell their soul for the gold of a powerful empire.

Humble, honest blood was shed by the fatherland in the struggle against the mercenaries of imperialism. But what blood, what men did imperialism send here to establish that beachhead, to bleed our revolution dry, to destroy our achievements, to burn our cane? It was to be a war of destruction.

We can tell the people right here that at the same instant that three of our airports were being bombed, the Yankee agencies were telling the world that our airports had been attacked by planes from our own air force. They cold-bloodedly bombed our nation and told the world that the bombing was done by Cuban pilots with Cuban planes. This was done with planes on which they painted our insignia.

If nothing else, this deed should be enough to demonstrate how miserable are the actions of imperialism. It should be enough for us to realize what Yankee imperialism really is and what its press and its government is. . . . This should serve to keep us alert and to understand that the imperialists are capable of the most monstrous lies to cover the most monstrous deeds.

U.S. leaders publicly confessed their participation—without any explanation which they owe the world for the statements made by Kennedy that they would never participate in aggression—and save us the effort of finding proof.

The invaders came to fight for free enterprise! Imagine, at this time, for an idiot to come here to say that he fought for free enterprise! As if this people did not know what free enterprise is! It was slums, unemployment, begging. One hundred thousand families working the land to turn over 25 percent of their production to shareholders who never saw that land. How can they come to speak about free enterprise to a country where there was unemployment, illiteracy, and where one had to beg to get into a hospital? The people knew that free enterprise was social clubs, and bathing in mud for the children. . . .

How can one of those who never knew labor say that he came to shed the people's blood to defend free enterprise?

The death of thousands of children for lack of medicine and doctors did not bother the free enterprise men. There was never an agrarian reform law because congress was in the hands of the rich. Even though the constitution said the land must be returned to the Cubans, and even though in 1959 the 1940 constitution had been in effect nineteen years, no law took land away from the Yankee monopolies, which had huge expanses.

The Batista group took over through a coup sponsored by imperialism and the exploiting class; they needed such a man as Batista, so that the rural guard would serve the landowners against the peasants. (Applause) It did not matter to them that the nation was being plundered. The landowners did not give anybody modern weapons to fight that regime; they gave arms to that bloody regime itself, not caring about how it violated the constitution. Now that their privileges have ended, they found a Yankee government willing to give them arms to come here and shed the blood of workers and peasants. (Applause)

A revolution expressing the will of the people is an election every day, not every four years; it is a constant meeting with the people, like this meeting. The old politicians could never have gathered as many votes as there are people here tonight to support the Revolution.

What do they want? Elections with pictures on the posts. The Revolution has changed the conception of pseudo-democracy for direct government by the people.

What were the political parties? Just an expression of class interests. Here there is just one class, the humble; that class is in power, and so it is not interested in the ambition of an exploiting minority to get back in power.

It would be absurd for us to try to tell the people of the United States what system of government they must have, for in that case we would be considering that the United States is not a sovereign nation and that we have rights over the domestic life of the United States.

Rights do not come from size. Right does not come from one country being bigger than another. That does not matter. We have only limited territory, a small nation, but our right is as respectable as that of any country, regardless of its size. It does not occur to us to tell the people of the United States what system of government they must have. Therefore it is absurd for Mr. Kennedy to take it into his head to tell us what kind of government he wants us to have here. That is absurd. It occurs to Mr. Kennedy to do that only because he does not have a clear concept of international law or sovereignty. Who had those notions before Kennedy? Hitler and Mussolini!

They spoke the same language of force; it is the fascist language. We heard it in the years before Germany's attack on Czechoslovakia. Hitler split it up because it was governed by a reactionary government. The bourgeoisie, reactionary and pro-fascist, afraid of the advance of a socialist system, preferred even domination by Hitler. We heard that language on the eve of the invasion of Denmark, Belgium, Poland, and so forth. It is the right of might. This is the only right Kennedy advances in claiming the right to interfere in our country.

The U.S. government says that a socialist regime here threatens U.S. security. But what threatens the security of the North American people is the aggressive policy of the warmongers of the United States. What threatens the security of the North American family and people is the violence, that aggressive policy, that policy that ignores the sovereignty and the rights of other peoples. The one who is threatening the security of the United States is Kennedy, with that aggressive policy. That aggressive policy can give rise to a world war; and that world war can cost the lives of tens of millions of North Americans. Therefore, the one who threatens the security of the United States is not the Cuban Revolutionary Government but the aggressor and aggressive government of the United States.

We do not endanger the security of a single North American. We do not endanger the life or security of a single North American family. We, making cooperatives, agrarian reform, people's ranches, houses, schools, literacy campaigns, and sending thousands and thousands of teachers to the interior, building hospitals, sending doctors, giving scholarships, building factories, increasing the productive capacity of our country, creating public beaches, converting fortresses into schools, and give the people the right to a better future—we do not endanger a single U.S. family or a single U.S. citizen."

When Did the Executions Begin?

Again, the Revolution triumphed on January 1, 1959. By the time New Year's Eve rolled around, 954 executions had been carried out throughout the country.

The executions began almost immediately. On January 1, Fidel Castro was in the city of Santiago de Cuba. He made a speech in which he stated:

> "This time the Revolution will not be frustrated! This time, fortunately for Cuba, the Revolution will achieve its true objective. It will not be like 1898, when the Americans came and made themselves masters of the country."

Everyone associated with the deposed dictator was declared an enemy of the Revolution. On January 12, 75 men were shot by firing squad in Santiago de Cuba. The men were members of Senator Rolando Masferrer's private army.

The following day, Fidel Castro, in Havana, announced that revolutionary tribunals would continue "until all criminals of the Batista regime are tried."

On January 23, Havana's sports stadium became a venue for public military tribunals. Major Jesús Sosa, an officer in Batista's army, was the first sentenced to death by firing squad. There were more than 18,000 spectators in the stadium and almost 300 reporters from throughout Cuba and the foreign press.

The three judges presiding were Dr. Humberto Sori Marín, Major Raúl Chibas, and Major Universo Sánchez.

By the end of January, revolutionary tribunals were established throughout Cuba. Public executions were broadcast on the evening news and over the radio. Newsreels of some of the executions are posted on YouTube. Search "Cuba," "1959," and "execution" for videos.

Who Were the Foreigners Who Fought with Fidel?

Three foreigners fought alongside Fidel Castro: Ernesto "Che" Guevara, from Argentina; Eloy Gutiérrez-Menoyo, from Spain; and William A. Morgan, from the United States.

Che Guevara's first post was to head the *Comisión Depuradora*, or revolutionary tribunal, which was responsible for executing those found guilty. It outraged many Cubans that Che, a foreigner in Cuba, was deciding which Cubans would live or die. Che's presence in Cuba proved so disruptive to the Cuban political scene, especially after he advocated for a nuclear attack on the U.S. during the Cuban Missile Crisis, that Fidel Castro sent him on foreign assignments to get him out of Cuba. His final mission was to foment revolution in Bolivia where he was captured and executed. He was 39.

Eloy Gutiérrez-Menoyo grew disenchanted with Fidel Castro's socialist policies and fled to Miami in January 1961. He formed Alpha 66, a group comprised of Cuban exiles, in order to overthrow the Castro government. In October 1964, he led a group of men back into Cuba to fight in the mountains. What he and Fidel Castro had done when trying to overthrow Batista, Gutiérrez-Menoyo was now doing to Castro. He and his men were captured. "Eloy, I knew you would come, but I also knew I would catch you. And you realize, of course, that we are going to shoot you," he quoted Fidel Castro as telling him when he was interviewed by George Volsky for the *New York Times Magazine* in 1987.

He was not executed, however, but was sentenced to 30 years in prison. He was released in 1986 after repeated requests by Prime Minister Felipe González of Spain. He returned to Miami and, in 1993, established *Cambio Cubano* (Cuban Change) to work as a loyal opposition in Cuba. In 1995, Fidel Castro agreed to meet with him. He was then allowed to travel back and forth between the U.S. and Cuba. In 2003 he was allowed to settle in Havana. "Cuba cannot continue to corner itself, trying to convince the world that there is democracy, when a one-party system will never be a democracy," he said. He never was allowed to establish an opposition party in Cuba, however. He died of a heart attack on October 26, 2012. He was 77.

William Morgan fought alongside Fidel Castro. He was known as *el Comandante Yankee*, the Yankee Commandant. When the Revolution turned Communist, he distanced himself from Fidel Castro. He was arrested in October 1960 and was accused with plotting to lead counterrevolutionaries against the Revolution. He was tried and convicted of treason. Morgan was executed before a firing squad at La Cabaña on March 11, 1961. He was 32.

Why Is There an Embargo?

Imagine waking up in the morning and finding out that the president had issued a decree abolishing private property. Your home, your car, your business—even your furnishings, including the pajamas you were wearing—now belonged to the state. That's precisely what happened in Cuba when Fidel Castro declared the Revolution to be Marxist-Leninist. And it was the seizure of American properties—from ITT's telephone system to Citibank's banking operations—that resulted in a confrontation between Washington, D.C., and Havana.

The position of the U.S. was that, if Cuba wanted to nationalize American businesses and properties, it could do so as part of its sovereign right, but that it had to compensate the owners and shareholders of the assets being expropriated. Havana balked. An embargo was imposed.

For Cuban citizens facing the seizure of their businesses, homes, furnishings, and everything else, there was little recourse. They could either go along, becoming good comrades of the Revolution—or they could choose exile. Hundreds of thousands—now numbering millions—chose exile.

When will the embargo end?

It will take an act of Congress to lift the embargo. One of the major obstacles is that Havana has to begin the process for compensating the companies and American citizens whose properties were expropriated. It is estimated that American companies and private citizens have claims against Cuba that, in 2015 dollars, approximate $9 billion.

This figure does not include claims by American citizens who were born in Cuba or individuals who have not filed claims for properties seized.

In the summer of 2015 the *New York Times* Editorial Board called for ending the embargo. "Over the decades, American presidents and lawmakers have stiffened and at times loosened the embargo. Yet, the web of laws and regulations enacted in a failed attempt to change the regime in Havana through coercive means remains largely frozen in time," the editorial, published August 3, 2015, read. "With the United States and Cuba restoring diplomatic relations, a significant majority of Americans and an overwhelming majority of Cubans want the embargo repealed. It is time for Congress to help make engagement the cornerstone of American policy toward Cuba."

Cuba, however, has not acknowledged any obligation to compensate the owners of properties and assets seized.

There is, however, a precedent that may end the stalemate. In 1986, Cuba and Spain agreed to a process for adjudicating claims against Cuba by Spanish citizens whose properties and assets were seized by the Revolution. This agreement has been applied to settle, claim by claim, each dispute. A similar process can be negotiated with Cuba, which would allow for the lifting of the embargo.

If Havana and Washington, D.C., approach the matter with magnanimity, the broad framework for settling American claims against Cuba could be reached in the course of the next few years.

Why Are Black People in Cuba So Disenfranchised?

In March 1959, Fidel Castro gave a landmark speech attacking racism in all its forms and vowing to work for the full integration of people of color in his new Cuba. The lack of progress strikes many visitors as very peculiar. To see such stark racial disparities among Cubans is a major failure of the Revolution: the darker one's skin, the greater the chances that he or she is less privileged.

The Castro brothers, Fidel and Raúl, are the sons of a white European male immigrant to Cuba. Like many white Cubans, the Castros are from the impoverished province of Galicia in northwestern Spain who left for the New World searching for a better life. Known as *gallegos*, the ruling government of Cuba is comprised primarily of white men who are descendants of white European immigrants.

As a visitor you will not be able to miss the harsh reality of Cuban life: the darker one's skin, the lower one's position in society. Cubans who look like Desi Arnaz are at the top, and Cubans who look like Celia Cruz are at the bottom.

To learn about racism in Cuba today, here are two books. The descriptions are provided by the publishers.

Pichón: Race and Revolution in Castro's Cuba: A Memoir

Revolutionary black nationalist Carlos Moore breaks three decades of silence to challenge Castro's legacy in this controversial, behind-the-scenes memoir that explores the Revolution from a perspective of a *pichón*, the racist Cuban term for a black of Haitian or West Indian descent. After more than thirty years in exile, continually under the threat of retribution from the Cuban regime, Moore steps forward to reveal the truth: Fidel's Revolution was a success for white Marxists. But for Cuban blacks, the Revolution was basically business as usual, a cover-up of their ongoing struggle for racial, political, and social enfranchisement. Fidel Castro and his men rose from the ranks of the patriarchal, white Spanish-Cuban elite, and the Revolution did not weaken those ties.

Race in Cuba: Essays on the Revolution and Racial Inequality

As a young militant in the 26th of July Movement, Esteban Morales Domínguez participated in the overthrow of the Batista regime and the triumph of the Cuban Revolution. The revolutionaries, he understood, sought to establish a more just and egalitarian society. But Morales Domínguez, an Afro-Cuban, knew that the complicated question of race could not be ignored, or simply willed away in a post-revolutionary context. Today, he is one of Cuba's most prominent Afro-Cuban intellectuals and its leading authority on the race question.

Available for the first time in English, the essays collected here describe the problem of racial inequality in Cuba, provide evidence of its existence, constructively criticize efforts by the Cuban political leadership to end discrimination, and point to a possible way forward. Morales Domínguez surveys the major advancements in race relations that occurred as a result of the revolution, but does not ignore continuing signs of inequality and discrimination. Instead, he argues that the revolution must be an ongoing process and that to truly transform society it must continue to confront the question of race in Cuba.

Where Did Che Get His Rolex?

Unlike most of the proletariat, Ernesto "Che" Guevara sported a fashionable Rolex GMT Master 1675, not a Timex.

He never bought his Rolex, however. He appropriated it, part of the plunder of the Revolution. He showed it off during his time in Cuba and while fomenting revolution around the world. Félix Rodríguez, a Cuban exile drafted by the Central Intelligence Agency, assembled a team to track down and bring Che to justice in Bolivia; Rodríguez, in turn, appropriated Che's Rolex.

As A. Morgan writes in "Timeless Manhunt" in *www.thewatch.watchfinder.co.uk,* this is how Che met his end—and how his Rolex came into the possession of a Cuban exile.

> On October the 8th, 1967, Rodríguez assembled one thousand, eight hundred U.S. trained Bolivian troops around Guevara's encampment, and it wasn't long before Guevara was captured. As Rodríguez was under cover as a Bolivian Army Major, when the orders came in from the Bolivian President, René Barrientos, that Guevara was to be executed on the spot, there was little he could do to stop it. He appealed to Barrientos to let him take Guevara to Panama for questioning, but his mind was made up; Guevara had to die.
>
> Under Barrientos' instructions, Guevara was shot nine times all over his body to give the appearance that he had died in a gunfight. He writhed on the floor as each subsequent round was pumped into him, into his legs, his arms, his throat and fatally, into his chest. He died at 1:10pm on October the 9th, seven years after Rodríguez had first begun his manhunt. The last thing Rodríguez did before leaving Guevara's corpse was to take the watch off his wrist; a Rolex GMT Master 1675 that he had been wearing since the Cuban revolution. Rodríguez still has it to this day.

That Rolex watch, before Che took possession of it, is believed to have been the property of José Felipe Romero, a Mexican national living in Cuba who was declared an enemy of the Revolution and deported to Mexico—without his watch.

181

Does the Cuban Government Recognize Any Responsibility for Expropriations?

No and yes.

The Cuban Government's official position is that everyone who left did so voluntarily and abandoned their property.

In reality, the Cuban government formally accepted the obligation to reimburse individuals and companies whose properties and assets were seized under certain circumstances. Cuba, for instance, entered into an agreement with Spain in 1986 in which it established a fund to reimburse Cubans exiled in Spain for their assets seized in Cuba by the Revolution. The 1986 agreement stipulated that Cuba would pay, over a period of 15 years, almost $40 million in compensation for seized assets to Cubans who are also Spanish citizens. It is an imperfect agreement—and some Cuban families were excluded by name from this agreement—but it marked the first time Cuba accepted an obligation to Cuban exiles.

As for claims against Cuba by U.S. citizens and corporations, the Foreign Claims Settlement Commission, an independent agency at the Department of Justice, has almost 9,000 applications against Cuba on file. While most of these are by American corporations, including Coca-Cola, Citibank, and Colgate-Palmolive, there are thousands of individuals who lost businesses, homes, and other properties after the Revolution. Almost 6,000 of these claims had been certified as valid by 1971. The value, at the time, was $1.9 billion, which, with interest, is estimated to be $8 billion today.

If you believe you have a claim against the Cuban government, you can contact the Foreign Claims Settlement Commission at the Department of Justice or the 1898 Company, a firm that specializes in representing claims against the Cuban Government.

Foreign Claims Settlement Commission
U.S. Department of Justice
950 Pennsylvania Avenue, N.W.
Washington, DC 20530-0001
E-mail: *info.fcsc@usdoj.gov*
Telephone: (202) 616-6975

Jordi Cabarrocas
1898 Company
Santander International Tower
1401 Brickell Avenue, Suite 420
Miami, FL 33131
Website: *www.1898.es*

Be advised that the FCSC is not presently authorized to accept claims by U.S. nationals for property seized by Cuba. On July 6, 1972, the Commission completed a program involving claims against Cuba under Title V of the International Claims Settlement Act of 1949, as amended. In addition, the

Commission conducted a second Cuba claims program in 2006; the completion date for that program, however, was August 11, 2006. This is consistent with 70 Fed. Reg. 46,890 (August 11, 2005).

If, however, you have a claim against the government of Cuba that has not been adjudicated in the Commission's claim program, you might want to contact your representative and senator to ask that the International Claims Settlement Act of 1949 be amended to reflect the need to adjudicate claims by U.S. nationals now that diplomatic relations have been restored.

Another option is to contact the Department of State's Office of International Claims and Investment Dipsutes to request the assistance of the U.S. government in pursuing a claim. The website for more information is
www.state.gov/s/l/c7344.htm.

Why Are There No Pets in Havana?

Did you notice that as well?

As a general rule, dogs are expensive pets to have. They have to be fed. They need toys. They need leashes. Visits to veterinarians cost money. As a result, only a few Cubans can afford to have mankind's best friend as pets. That's why there are almost no dogs in Havana.

Cats are different; they require much less care because they are both resourceful and independent. So why are there so few cats in Havana?

The answer is not pleasant, so skip this section if you don't want to know. Having continued to read past the warning in the previous sentence, here's the answer: *they were eaten in the 1990s.*

It's not an urban myth. During the Special Period in the 1990s after Soviet subsidies ended, Cuba was facing malnutrition and the threat of starvation in certain areas. People trapped cats and ate them.

Don't believe me? Consider this report prepared on behalf of the Canadian Medical Journal Association (CMJA):

> Manuel Franco and colleagues have analyzed some of the health consequences of Cuba's socioeconomic collapse in 1990–1995, when the country lost the funding from the Soviet Union on which it had relied for the previous 30 years. During this period, Cubans essentially experienced a famine: adults had an average daily protein intake of 15–20 g and lost an average of 5%–25% of their body weight. Franco and colleagues neglected to mention many of the negative physical, mental and social consequences of this so-called Special Period.
>
> The famine in Cuba during the Special Period was caused by political and economic factors similar to the ones that caused a famine in North Korea in the mid-1990s. Both countries were run by authoritarian regimes that denied ordinary people the food to which they were entitled when the public food distribution collapsed; priority was given to the elite classes and the military. In North Korea, 3%–5% of the population died; in Cuba the death rate among the elderly increased by 20% from 1982 to 1993. Thirty thousand Cubans fled the country, and thousands of these emigrants drowned or were killed by sharks in the Gulf of Mexico.
>
> Cuba finally accepted US donations of food, medicines and cash in 1993, and a system of private farmers' markets was set up in 1994 to provide easy access to locally grown food.

The title of the report is "Health Consequences of Cuba's Special Period"; it was published July 29, 2008 and is available at *www.cmaj.ca*.

On one trip, when I was discussing the deprivations during the Special Period, I met a woman who admitted that her family resorted to eating cats at the end of the 1990s. I asked what it tasted like—with the caveat that I didn't want to hear that it tasted like chicken. Iguanas taste like chicken, but cats? She laughed. Cats, she told me, taste like rabbit. "If we eat Bugs Bunny, why not Sylvester the Cat?" she said.

Now you know: Cuban cats were eaten in stews. If you're in Havana, you're in a city where people ate their pets.

Why Is Senator Marco Rubio So Hostile to Cuba?

It's odd, isn't it? Marco Rubio really is hostile to anything that would ease conflict with Cuba.

Marco Rubio, you may recall, got into trouble when he misrepresented his own family's history. In October 2011, the news media reported that his characterization that his parents, Mario Rubio and Oriales García de Rubio, had been forced to flee Castro's Revolution, was a fabrication. Senator Rubio backtracked, offering the following explanation: "The real essence of my family's story is not about the date my parents first entered the United States. Or whether they traveled back and forth between the two nations. Or even the date they left Fidel Castro's Cuba forever and permanently settled here. The essence of my family story is why they came to America in the first place, and why they had to stay."

Well, details do matter. The fact is that the Rubios immigrated to the U.S. in 1956, three years before Fulgencio Batista was overthrown. The Rubios opposed Batista and supported Fidel Castro. When the Revolution triumphed, the Rubios returned to Cuba, as did many other Castro supporters, known as Fidelistas. The Rubios supported Castro and returned to Cuba thinking they could participate in making the Revolution a success.

Not unlike many other Fidelistas, however, the Rubios realized they had bet on the wrong horse, that Castro was a Marxist-Leninist, and that there was no place for them in Castro's Cuba. Humilated by Castro, they subsequently returned to the U.S. in 1961, this time as political *refugees*, and not ordinary *immigrants*. The Rubios did not immigrate to the U.S.; they were Cuban refugees granted political asylum in the U.S. There is a difference between being a *willing* immigrant and an *unwilling* political refugee seeking asylum.

Senator Rubio's hostility to improving relations with Cuba while the Castro brothers remain in power is consistent with the position of many Cuban-Americans who feel that Castro betrayed the Revolution when Cuba became a Communist state.

What Happened to Sloppy Joe's Bar?

Sloppy Joe's Bar is the establishment made famous in the film *Our Man in Havana*.

It was a popular establishment in the 1930s. Located on the corner of Zulueta and Ánimas Streets, its proprietor was José García, a Spanish immigrant who settled in Cuba in 1904. The bar's name was derived from its signature dish: a sandwich made from *ropa vieja*, which looked very much like an American Sloppy Joe.

José García left Cuba in 1907, going first to New Orleans and then to Miami. While in the U.S. he worked at bars and supper clubs. He returned to Havana in 1919 and went to work at the Greasy Spoon Café in central Havana. Less than a year later, after finding the ideal spot and with the savings he had from working in Miami, he opened his own place.

Sloppy Joe's Bar captured the ambiance of New Orleans and Miami, but with a Spanish-Cuban flair. It became a sensation in the 1920s, 1930s, and 1940s. Clark Gable, Spencer Tracy, and John Wayne were among the Americans who ate there. After *Our Man in Havana* was filmed, it became popular with Latin American visitors, including Mario Moreno, better known as Cantiflas, when he was a guest of his fellow comedian Leopoldo Fernández, better known as Tres Patines. Meyer Lansky and Lucky Luciano were among the mobsters who frequented the place. Frank Sinatra ordered food to take out. Errol Flynn was a regular when he was in Havana.

It was quite the spot for Cuban personalities of the time.

After the Revolution in 1959, Fidel Castro declared it a "bourgeois" indulgence. José García left Cuba after authorities seized his establishment and closed it. Forty-eight years later, as part of the renovations to abandoned properties in the area, the building was restored and refurbished.

It reopened in 2013, but the food is nothing special.

What Is the Story with Guantánmo Bay?

Guantánamo Bay Naval Base, also called GTMO, is located in Guantánamo Bay. The United States leased it as a naval and coaling station in the Cuban-American Treaty of 1903. It is the oldest U.S. Naval Base outside the U.S.

Cuba maintains that the U.S. unlawfully occupies the 45-square-mile territory. The Castro government has demanded the return of base, which it considers to be an occupation arising from the Spanish-American War of 1898.

The U.S. pays a lease fee that Cuba refuses to accept. In 2002, the naval base was converted into the Guantánamo Bay detention camp for individuals taken into U.S. custody in Iraq, Afghanistan, and other places as part of the War on Terror. These individuals have never been charged, nor have they been brought before a court. Cases of torture have been documented, and the denial of detainees' rights under the Geneva Convention has been condemned by nations around the world. Obama promised to close the detention camp, but this campaign promise has not been fulfilled.

What Is the Role of Religion in Changes in Cuba?

Pope Francis visited Cuba in September 2015. This is not the first time a pope has traveled to Cuba. Pope John Paul II visited the island nation in 1998 and declared: "Let Cuba open itself to the world and let the world open itself to Cuba." Pope Benedict XVI also visited Cuba in 2012.

185

Cuba is not Poland in 1989 where there was a fast transition from a dictatorship to a democracy. Pope Francis, however, set the seeds for the Catholic Church's role in helping Cuba evolve. The Obama administration, after all, availed itself of the pope's intervention for the reestablishment of diplomatic relations between the U.S. and Cuba. Havana Cardinal Jaime Lucas Ortega y Alamino also played an important role, meeting with Obama in the White House on an urgent visit to Washington, D.C., and he has intervened on behalf of the Ladies in White, a group that supports imprisoned dissidents.

On his visit, Pope Francis reaffirmed the Church's readiness to mediate Cuba's transition. He also affirmed the need for Cuba to integrate once more into the world community. And his third purpose was to give the Cuban people courage, reminding them that they are not forgotten and that their suffering is on the minds of their fellow human beings around the world.

Can I Interview Cubans?

"People still lowered their voices when they compained about the government," Catherine Watson wrote in the *Los Angeles Times* in May 2015, when reporting on changes in Cuba on the cusp of the U.S. and Cuba reestablishing diplomatic relations.

Yes, Cubans are more than happy to express their opinions—but almost always they do not want their names associated with their criticisms of the government. Most Cubans would welcome being taken out to a meal or for a drink, but remember not to put anyone on the spot. Bear in mind that Cubans want a validation that their lives matter; they want a connection to the outside world: You.

"Weren't there any good times after the Revolution?" Catherine Watson asked her host at one point. "When the Russians were here," her hostess, who, of course, is not named, replied. "There was enough food. There were clothes. Not good clothes, but clothes. And you couldn't travel anywhere. But the money the government gave was enough then—not enough to live in luxury, but enough to live."

On the street, Ms. Watson reported seeing one man, out of frustration, burst out: "To live like this for fifty-six years! Without electricity sometimes, without new clothes, without food, without getting or sending letters to people outside, without phoning outside, without belonging to any religion!"

The Cubans have a far different perspective on their country and their lives than a tourist might otherwise assume. Getting a new perspective on things is one of the pleasures of travel.

Why Did Fidel's Mother Slap Him?

Fidel Castro's mother, Lina Ruz de Castro, slapped him across the face when she was outraged that he appointed Argentine sociopath Che Guevara as head of the *Comisión Depuradora*, or revolutionary tribunal, in charge of deciding who was to stand before a firing squad.

She didn't slap him when Fidel Castro expropriated Las Manacas, the family's farm, an act she considered a betrayal. She loathed Che and believed Che was an evil, dangerous man; the old lady was the only one in the Castro family with a moral compass and the *cojones* to stand up to her Fidel Castro. She died in 1963.

186

24 ERNESTO "CHE" GUEVARA

Look good wearing a beret and smoking a Cuban cigar, and you're halfway to becoming an icon.

Just ask James Dean who looked so cool in blue jeans and a white T-shirt.

For Ernesto "Che" Guevara, how he photographed in his signature look, coupled with death at a young age, has made him a legend.

What becomes a legend most? Revisionism at the hands of apologist biographers, of course.

Young, charismatic, and photogenic, Che became the first celebrity revolutionary in Latin America after the invention of television. He has come to embody the ideal of youthful rebellion, one that college students around the world embrace.

On the surface, who can disagree with the goal of ending the human suffering caused by failures of the market system?

The truth about Che, however, is that he was a sociopath.

"A revolutionary must become a cold killing machine motivated by pure hate," he boasted.

187

This belief does not conform with our contemporary understanding of humanism, but it was how he conducted himself once the Revolution triumphed.

His ruthless actions against the Cubans were legendary; he delighted in supervising the executions at La Cabaña, where hundreds of men and women were shot by firing squads. And, as if anticipating the rise of terrorism in at the end of the twentieth century, he declared: "We will bring the war to the imperialist enemies' very home, to his places of work and recreation. We must never give him a minute of peace or tranquility. This is a total war to the death."

This sounds like al Qaeda whose kamikaze pilots committed mass murder in the U.S. on September 11, 2001, doesn't it?

But if Che is David against the Goliath of capitalism's failures, then he has been given a free ride. That he was portrayed with optimistic flair by the charming Mexican actor Gael García Bernal in *The Motorcycle Diaries*, released in 2004, only fuels the dreaminess of the Che the world wants to believe existed.

But the icon and the man are very different creatures.

"The cult of Ernesto Che Guevara is an episode in the moral callousness of our time. Che was a totalitarian," Paul Berman writes in *Slate*. "He achieved nothing but disaster. Many of the early leaders of the Cuban Revolution favored a democratic or democratic-socialist direction for the new Cuba. But Che was a mainstay of the hard-line pro-Soviet faction, and his faction won. Che presided over the Cuban Revolution's first firing squads. He founded Cuba's 'labor camp' system—the system that was eventually employed to incarcerate gays, dissidents, and AIDS victims."

In Cuba, among Cubans, the constant presentation of Che as a heroic figure is wearing. His image is everywhere, but the paint is chipping away and little effort is made to spruce up the murals. In recent years, swastikas have been etched into his eyes, a telling graffiti.

When this Editor asked a woman near the Plaza de la Revolución about what she thought of Che's image on the facade of the Ministry of the Interior, she replied, "I'm waiting for the day they take that monster's portrait down. When that happens, then you know Cuba is on the right path." Imagine if someone said that of the Lincoln Memorial in Washington, D.C.

Half a century of propaganda does not erase the truth that this man was mad. The most compelling evidence for insanity is found in his conduct during the Cuban Missile Crisis.

When the United States gave an ultimatum to the Soviet Union to remove nuclear missiles from Cuba, the world faced the possibility of a nuclear confrontation between Washington and Moscow.

During 13 days—October 16 through October 28, 1962—the world was on the verge of a full-scale nuclear war. Fidel Castro wrote a letter to Nikita Khrushchev in which he offered to sacrifice Cuba for the sake of socialism.

In other words, he was giving the Soviets permission to launch a nuclear attack against the U.S. from Cuba, knowing that Cuba would face nuclear annihilation.

For his part, Che welcomed nuclear war: "If the nuclear missiles had remained, we would have used them against the very heart of America, including New York City," Che said. "We will march the path of victory even if it costs millions of atomic victims. . . . We must keep our hatred alive and fan it to paroxysm."

Nikita Khrushchev believed Castro and Guevara were insane.

If Nikita Khrushchev thinks you're crazy, you probably are, at the very least, nuts. Khrushchev immediately cut Castro out of negotiations; Khrushchev and Kennedy negotiated an end to the crisis.

While Moscow and Washington were pulling back from the brink of nuclear war, the Soviets had to pretend to include Fidel and Che in the negotiations.

The Soviet embassy in Mexico City—the largest Soviet diplomatic presence in the Americas—asked for Mexican assistance. This came in the form of Mexico's ambassador to Cuba, Gilberto Bosques. He had served in Europe during World War II and was well versed in dealing with Nazis.

During these two weeks, Bosques conveyed messages from the Soviets to the Cubans and from the Americans to the Cubans. The purpose was to placate Fidel and Che while Khrushchev and Kennedy reached an agreement—without the Cubans.

Bosques, who had befriended Fidel Castro in Mexico before the Revolution, was able to mislead the Cubans into thinking they were part of the negotiations. They were not.

The remarkable, and largely unknown, role Bosques played during the Cuban Missile Crisis has led some, including historian Richard Grabman, to argue that Bosques may have prevented World War III through his manipulation of Fidel and Che. The deal that Moscow and Washington struck, as confirmed by Sergie Khrushchev, Nikita Khrushchev's son, was simple: The Soviets would pull their missiles out of Cuba and the U.S. would never invade the island nation.

When Khrushchev didn't launch a nuclear attack on Washington and New York, Che was enraged and felt betrayed. In other words, the world had averted a nuclear war in which millions would have perished, and this was an inferior outcome, as far as Che was concerned.

When Che learned the role Bosques played, he vowed to destroy Mexico. As for Khrushchev, he vowed to "retaliate" against the Soviet's "betrayal." Che flew to China to court Beijing; he wanted to play Beijing against Moscow.

But Mexican ambassador Bosques had one more message to relay to Fidel from Khrushchev: Che was toxic to Moscow. Fidel had to choose: Soviet subsidies, or Che.

Castro was only too happy to cut Che lose, sending him to Africa and then to Bolivia, where death awaited him.

In Jon Lee Anderson's biography, *Che Guevara: A Revolutionary Life*, there is almost nothing about Che's pleasure at overseeing the firing squads or of his being considered toxic by the Soviets. Anderson, an apologist for Che, is often regarded as an *anglosajón pendejo* in Latin America, meaning someone who has fallen under the spell of Che's myth.

Impressionable freshmen, dreamy-eyed, hang posters of Che on their dorm room walls, and Cubans wonder why, especially now that information from the Mexican ambassador to Cuba at the time, Gilberto Bosques, documents the Soviet concern over Che's madness.

JOSÉ MARTÍ

To understand the soul of Cuba it's necessary to know the heart of José Martí.

José Martí is in every Cuban's heart. There are schools, parks, airports, boulevards, and countless other things named after him. He, more than any other person who has ever lived, embodies what it means to be Cuban.

Born in 1853, he is hailed as the Apostle of Cuban Independence. José Martí traveled the world championing Cuban independence. He returned to Cuba from exile in 1895 to fight for Cuban independence. He died on the battlefield, but lives in the hearts of his countrymen and countrywomen.

José Martí was born on January 28, 1853. He was a poet and writer—and became a political revolutionary, for which he was exiled in 1871.

The story behind his exile foreshadows the history of Cuba in the twentieth century.

In 1868, Cuban nationalists clashed with Spanish loyalists in what became known as the Ten Years' War. Martí founded a newspaper, *La Patria Libre*, to advance the political idea of cutting all ties to Spain. Arrested, he was sentenced to six years hard labor. Afer serving six months, he was deported to Spain where he published *Political Imprisonment in Cuba*, a political manifesto.

While in Spain, he received a law degree from the Universidad de Zaragoza in 1875. The following year he left for Mexico. He championed Cuban independence throughout Mexico, speaking to Cuban nationalists living there. He spent considerable time in the Yucatán where he identified with the Maya struggle to resist Aztec (Mexican) domination.

By 1877, howver, Martí had grown disenchanted with Mexico. He left for Guatemala. He didn't leave alone; in Mexico he had met Carmen Zayas Bazán, whom he married and with whom he had one son, José. In Guatemala, he took a position as a college professor at the Universidad Nacional. He continued to write poetry in addition to teaching history, philosophy, and literature.

The Ten Years' War ended the following year. It included a general amnesty; Martí returned home to Cuba. The following year, however, he participated in the "Little War," an uprising against the Spanish king in Santiago de Cuba led by farmers and slaves.

Three years later, Martí found himself exiled in New York, where a considerable number of Cuban nationalists had settled. He supported himself as a columnist for *La Nación*, a newspaper published in Buenos Aires. His essays and literary criticism resulted in oneincluded a piece that became sensational: "Our America."

He called for nothing less that a unified Latin America, but with regional governments that reflected the diverse needs of its peoples and cultures. This idea solidified during his time in Mérida, Mexico, where he saw the need to accommodate the indigenous peoples and their culture within the context of a modern nation-state.

In 1892, he was named a delegate of the Cuban Revolutionary Party, which sought to sever all ties with Spain. His time in the United States, however, made him weary and fearful of the United States.

He feared the Americans would not be able to resist the temptation of meddling in Latin America. He planned for Cuban independence—but without the U.S. establishing control over the island.

It was now that Martí joined forces with two heroes of the Ten Years' War: Máximo Gómez and Antonio Maceo. With funds raised from Cubans living in the United States, Mexico, and Puerto Rico, he departed New York on January 31, 1895, to return to Cuba to participate in an independence war.

He arrived on April 11, 1895, ready for war. On May 19, he was shot dead during a battle in Dos Ríos. He was 42.

Cubans would continue to fight for independence for several more years. He is remembered as a national hero, the father of Cuba's independence.

One hundred years from now, not one statue to Fidel Castro will stand in Cuba, but José Martí will be everywhere.

Doing Business with Cuba

26 DOING BUSINESS IN CUBA, OR HOW TO CIRCUMVENT THE EMBARGO IF YOU MUST

Opening for Business

Raúl Castro has enacted reforms designed to emulate the Vietnam model: allow individuals to take ownership of their own economic well-being while preserving the government's monopoly on political control, ideology, and speech.

What you see in Cuba today is the opening of small-scale private enterprise under the watchful eye of officials who are nervous about how things will unfold. In essence, can people have economic freedom with no political liberties?

It's an interesting experiment. So, now, how can one do business in Cuba?

At present there are three areas in which to do business in Cuba: mass consumers, in partnership with the state, and as a purchasing agent.

Retail Consumers

"Can you tell me how to be a millionaire?" a Cuban in Old Havana asked this Editor when telling of his wish to open a coffee shop for tourists.

The proliferation of AirBNB places to stay and *paladares* to eat are the beginning of "creeping capitalism," which has the potential of transforming Cuba into a nation of shopkeepers. These businesses have, as their market, resident foreigners in Cuba, tourists, and Cubans who have access to hard currencies. The goods and services offered—from a meal to a haircut—are the most immediate form of entrepeneurship that people can see.

To this, one has to include artists. In centuries past, successful merchants became the patrons of the arts. Think of the Medicis of Italy who sponsored generations of artists. In Cuba, the situation is now reversed. Because artists sell their work for U.S. dollars and European euros, contemporary artists in Cuba have the capital to help friends and family open small businesses.

How do these businesses get off the ground?

Many Cuban entrepreneurs are using the savings they have accumulated over years of putting aside remittances they have received from family overseas. Others are relying on fellow Cubans who have savings—or access to hard currency, such as artists or employees in the tourism industry who receive tips from foreigners. The more common way, however, is for Cubans to receive money from relatives and investors outside Cuba. Remittances can take the form of money wired to Cuba or, more commonly, cash brought to Havana by a family member or investor.

195

Cubans who left during the 1980 Mariel Boat Lift are at the forefront of this new generation of Cuban entrepreneurs. It makes sense: these Cubans have lived under the current government; understand how the system works; how it can be manipulated or circumvented; and can master the cultural nuances to make it all work. Of all the Cubans living in exile, the Marielitos are the smoothest of operators.

In other words, artists and Mariel entrepreneurs are emerging as a post-Revolution élite, partnering with recently aspiring entrepreneurs.

Partnering with the Castros

At the other end of the economic spectrum lie corporate opportunities. The Cuban government participates in every business enterprise that takes place in Cuba. Whether it is the telephone company or a hotel operator, the Cuban government is a majority stakeholder in the business.

The resumption of diplomatic relations between the U.S. and Cuba has unsettled some of Cuba's allies. Venezuela, for instance, is alarmed that the Convenio Integral de Cooperación (Integral Convention on Cooperation) Caracas signed with Havana in 2012 will come to an end once the U.S. begins to dismantle restrictions imposed by the embargo.

Anticipating these changes, Cuba created a new agency, the Grupo Empresarial del Comercio, or the Business Commerce Group, known as GECOMEX, under the direction of Aurelio Mollineda. The name alone is enough to make Karl Marx die another death.

To learn about changes taking place, consider these resources:

Agencia Cubana de Noticias
Website: *www.ain.cu*

News about the U.S. Embargo
Website: *www.cubavsbloqueo.cu*

Official Website of the Cuban Government
Website: *www.cubagob.cu*

To contact specific government agencies, here are official contacts, keeping in mind never, ever to violate the U.S. embargo and to consult first with the Office of Foreign Assets Control (OFAC), Cuba Desk, at the Treasury Department for authorization.

Foreign Relations Ministry/Ministerio de Relaciones Exteriores
Bruno Eduardo Rodríguez Parrilla
Calle G #360, Vedado, Plaza de la Revolución
Tel: (53) 7 836-4500
E-mail: *cubaminrex@minrex.gov.cu*
Website: *www.cubaminrex.cu*

Economy and Planning Ministry/Ministerio de Economía y Planificación
Marino Alberto Murillo Jorge
20 de Mayo, between Territorial and Ayestarán, Plaza de la Revolución
Tel: (53) 7 881-9354
E-mail: *mep@ceniai.inf.cu*

Finance and Prices Ministry/Ministerio de Finanzas y Precios
Lina Olinda Pedraza Rodríguez
Obispo #211, on the corner of Cuba, Old Havana
Tel: (53) 7 867-1800, extension 4033 or 4034
E-mail: *yolanda.mederos@mfp.gov.cu*
Website: *www.mfp.cu*

Central Bank/Banco Central de Cuba
Ernesto Medina Villaveirán
Calle Cuba #402, between Lamparilla and Amargura, Old Havana
Tel: (53) 7 863-4061
E-mail: *webmaster@bc.gov.cu*
Website: *www.bc.gov.cu*

Agriculture Ministry/Ministerio de la Agricultura
Gustavo Rodríguez Rollero
Edificio Minag, on the corner of Carlos M. Céspedes, Nuevo Vedado, Plaza de la Revolución
Tel: (53) 7 884-5370
E-mail: *armando@minag.cu*
Website: *www.minag.cu*

Construction Ministry/Ministerio de la Construcción
René Mesa Villafaña
Carlos Manuel de Céspedes y Calle 35, Plaza de la Revolución
Tel: (53) 7 881-4745
E-mail: *sitio@mincons.cu*
Website: *www.mincons.cu*

Transportation Ministry/Ministerio del Transportation
César Ignacio Arocha Masid
Carlos Manuel de Céspedes, between Tulipán and Lombillo
Tel: (53) 7 885-5030
E-mail: mitrans@*mitrans.transet.cu*
Website: *www.transporte.cu*

Civil Aviation Ministry/Ministerio de Aeronáutica Civil

Ramón Martínez Echevarría
Calle 23 #64, Vedado
Tel: (53) 7 834-4949
E-mail: *iacc@avianet.cu*
Website: *www.iacc.gov.cu*

Tourism Ministry/Ministerio de Turismo

Manuel Marrero Cruz
Calle 3 #6, between Calle F and Calle G, Vedado, Plaza de la Revolución
Tel: (53) 7 836-3245
E-mail: *dircomunicacion@tur.cu*
Website: *www.cubatravel.cu*

National Commerce Ministry/Ministerio de Comercio Interior

Mary Blanca Ortega Barredo
Habana #258, between Empedrado and San Juan de Dios, Old Havana
Tel: (53) 7 867-0133 and 867-0071
E-mail: *Estadistica@cinet.cu*

Purchasing Agents

There's a big world of opportunities between working with a Spanish conglomerate like Sol Meliá operating a hotel in Havana in partnership with the Cuban state and backing a woman making breakfast for tourists from her kitchen on a side street in Old Havana.

If you're not interested in going into business with the Cuban state or are not in a position to partner with private Cuban citizens who open businesses, doesn't mean there are no other opportunities, primarily for third-party nationals.

Indeed, as a result of the economic embargo, Cuba has relied on a small army of individuals who have citizenships other than Cuban or American to act as purchasing agents. Ever wonder where the new towels in that hotel were purchased? Or who made it possible for a can of Coca-Cola to be on the restaurant's menu?

Purchasing agents, that's who.

This is how it has worked in the past. Cuba contracts individuals who have third-nation passports as purchasing agents. These agents fly to various countries, buy supplies, and ship them to Havana. The agents pay vendors and stores with checks drawn on U.S. dollar accounts from various banks in the region. These checks are paid through the international banking collection protocols, most of the time. In this way, Cuba can purchase what it needs, vendors are paid in U.S. dollars, and banks other than U.S. banks handle the transactions.

Here is an example. Cuba has contracted citizens of Venezuela to purchase supplies for the Cuban government. These agents have traveled to Mexico to purchase supplies at Mexican companies paying for these purchases with checks drawn on the Curacao branch of ING Bank. Mexican companies have deposited these checks into their bank accounts and, in a process that takes several weeks or even months, then waits for funds to clear.

This is how supplies worth millions of dollars of—curtains for hotels, soda crackers for the elderly, lighting fixtures for government offices, Coca-Cola for restaurants, auto supplies for vehicles, and so on—continue to make their way to Cuba.

The problem, however, is that Cuba is not part of the international banking system. When an agent hands over a check in payment that is drawn on the ING Bank in Curacao, how are funds deposited into that account?

It's done through an inefficient and cumbersome way. When a tourist arrives and exchanges U.S. dollars or European euros for Convertible Pesos, those dollars and euros make their way to the Banco Financiero Internacional. Cash is collected and, periodically, a diplomatic envoy is sent from Havana to Curacao to deposit the cash into Cuba's account. The system's very nature—collecting cash, notifying the bank in Curacao, arranging for a flight for the agent—means that it's difficult to balance the funds in the account with the purchases being made by scores of purchasing agents on assignments throughout the region.

So what happens when, for example, checks arrive at the ING Bank?

The banker in charge of this account has to contact Cuban officials to decide which check is paid first. If, for example, $300,000 in checks arrives but that account has only $250,000, which checks are paid? In a normal banking situation checks would be paid as they arrive. When funds run out, the other checks are returned as unpaid; those checks bounce.

With these accounts, however, the account executive holds the checks indefinitely until instructed to pay them—or until funds to cover the checks are deposited. As a result, a vendor accepting this kind of check may be in a situation where, months after depositing the check, the funds have not cleared. The check is neither paid nor is it returned as unpaid. It's the Twilight Zone of international banking, and the reason purchasing agents often have a difficult time; many vendors, over the years, have declined to accept these checks as payment.

Of course, the simple answer is that, if presented at the Banco Financiero Internacional in Havana for payment, the check would be honored. And, of course, there are specialized financial services that handle these checks on behalf of vendors selling to Cuban agents.

Partnering with Cuban Exiles

How to best navigate the changing landscape as the Castros' reign comes to a close? Many non-Cubans are partnering with Cuban exiles who are returning to Cuba.

Consider this description published in the *New Yorker* magazine. Jon Lee Anderson, in "Opening for Business," argues that Marielitos are positioning themselves to be entrepreneurs in the emerging Cuba. This is how the business climate is changing:

> [Hugo] Cancio is recognizably Cuban, but he is also a man of earnest American discipline. He meditates and does a hundred pushups each morning. His bedtime reading lately is Hillary Clinton's "Hard Choices" and a volume by Deepak Chopra. In 2012, he launched *OnCuba*, a

bimonthly magazine stocked with ads, profiles of artists and musicians, and articles on tourist destinations. In the past year, he has added a quarterly art magazine, aimed at collectors and investors, and a real-estate supplement. Cancio has ambitious plans to expand Fuego Enterprises. In 2010, after Raúl Castro announced sweeping reforms to open up the island's economy, allowing more Cubans to own their own businesses—known as *cuentapropismo*—and to buy and sell property, Cancio assembled a team to assess investment possibilities. He and his partners decided to focus on media and entertainment, and then move into real estate, tourism, and telecommunications. "Our goal was to position ourselves quickly, so when the market opened we would be among the first to be established," he said.

For now, Fuego is distinguished more by its potential than by its assets. "If you look at the financials of the company, it's a very speculative investment and not a lot to get excited about," Thomas Herzfeld, who manages the Herzfeld Caribbean Basin Fund, one of Fuego's largest investors, said. "But if you look at Hugo there's everything to get excited about. He's a leading expert on Cuba, he's well respected there, he cares about Cuba and its people."

If Cuban exiles have their way, Little Havana in Miami, Florida, is about to take over Big Havana in Havana, Cuba.

*See, "Opening for Business," by Jon Anderson, *New Yorker*,

Buying Property

Interested in speculating in real estate? That great property might be perfect for a Starbucks—soon enough, no?

Cuba now allows private individuals to purchase real estate. One has to be a Cuban citizen, however. The way around this restriction is to find a front person in whose name the deed will be held. This is so common that there is a name for a Cuban who agrees to accept a fee to be the nominal titleholder: *testaferros*.

The caveat, of course, is that under the law the *testaferro* is the legal owner, and should there be a disagreement, the speculator has no recourse.

This is a risk, but considering that Havana is in shambles, real estate properties cost less than the down payment for a property in the U.S. Recent purchases, for example, have ranged between $10,000 and $30,000 CUCs in central Havana. That does not mean that there aren't some beautiful properties for sale, especially since many Cubans see the privatization of real estate as an opportunity to sell their homes for hard currency and leave Cuba.

If you are interested in real estate, peruse the listings on this site for a better understanding of the real estate market.

Cuba Real Estate Listings
Site: *http://point2cuba.com*

200

Circumventing the Embargo

The Cuban economy limps along thanks to the efforts of a professional class of Cuban agents who violate the embargo. Cuba and the United States, to be honest, each exaggerates the effects of the U.S. embargo for political purposes. Washington claims it is a stranglehold on the Communist regime. Havana uses the embargo to justify the material deprivation the Cuban people suffer.

The truth is that the embargo is an encumbrance, but it is the *lack of money* that punishes the Cuban people. When the Russians were around, there was plenty of everything for everyone, the U.S. embargo notwithstanding. Remember that woman reminiscing to the *Los Angeles Times* about the good times when there was money flowing when the Soviets were in town?

Since the end of Soviet/Russian subsidies to Havana, Cubans have availed themselves of using Mexico as the primary source for what they need.

To understand how Cuba is finding what it needs, just order a soft drink. On a recent visit, the Coca-Cola can was bottled by "Embolletadora Peninsular," meaning it came from Cancún. The Sprint was from Venezuela.

When the U.S. announced in December 2014 that diplomatic relations were being restored, the Editor of this guide wanted to see how this news would impact how Cubans find provision. New America Media published this report on December 24, 2014.

For a Cuban Smuggler, It's Business as Usual

Havana–Cubana Airlines flight 154 departs Havana at 12:50 a.m., arriving in Cancún, Mexico, less than an hour later. It is one of a handful of flights that, every day, are used by agents of the Cuban government and self-styled "entrepreneurs" to smuggle consumer products onto the island that, due to the U.S. embargo and travel restrictions on most Cubans, would not otherwise be available.

Flight 154 is seldom on time, often departing more than an hour late. It makes no difference to Juan, a thirty-something Cuban who makes this flight multiple times each month.

"Anything they sell at Wal-Mart, Costco, or Comercial Mexicana I can get for anyone in Havana," he says.

What it takes to become a Cuban entrepreneur whose career it is to circumvent the U.S. economic embargo are three things: A visa from the Cuban government allowing you to travel to Mexico, knowing how bribes work at Havana's international airport for unfettered entry of consumer goods, and enough capital to cover the initial upfront money to travel to Mexico for a shopping spree.

If during the Cold War the United States operated an airlift to keep Berlin from collapsing, the commercial flights between Havana and Cancún offer a way of releasing pressure in Havana by establishing a mechanism that allows for the flow of consumer goods into Cuba, in turn allowing Cubans with dollars or euros to achieve a higher level of material comfort than would otherwise be possible.

When Flight 154 arrives in Cancún, the airport is almost deserted. Almost all the flights to Europe have departed. The first flights from the U.S., Canada and Mexico City have yet to arrive. Juan finds this pre-dawn arrival inconvenient; it will be hours before Wal-Mart, Sam's Club, Costco, Comercial Mexicana or Home Depot open their doors.

On occasion, he is met by Mexican friends or business associates who he emails when there is a request too difficult to find in just a few hours. He will often hang out for an hour or so with the Cubana Airlines crew, trading tips on where to get the best deal on this or that. Juan prefers the Wal-Mart on Avenida Coba, since they have a better selection of electronics and domestics. Although for cosmetics, sundries and foodstuff, he says the Mega Comercial Mexicana at the intersection of Tulum and Uxmal Avenues can't be beaten.

"I wouldn't be surprised if half the women in Havana weren't shampooing their hair with something from the Mega," he says.

Juan says that, when he is well organized, he can shop for everything on his list in a few hours. As a regular client at these stores, salespeople know him; they will set merchandise aside for him, and even pack it for cargo transport.

The prices he charges for the products back in Cuba reflect what he calls the "embargo tax," which is to say, he triples the price. A stainless steel Hamilton Beach 4-Slice Toaster Oven, that sells for just over $30 USD in Cancún, he sells for $100 USD in Havana. A Suave Professionals Shampoo + Conditioner that sells for $3 USD at Mega Comercial, he will sell for $10 USD in Havana.

"I have to pay between $100 and $200 USD in bribes at the airport in Havana, depending on how much I'm bringing in," Juan explains. "Plus the cost of the ticket—and this is how I make a living."

The news that the U.S. and Cuba were to resume diplomatic relations didn't bother him.

"It will be years before it affects me," he said with confidence. "The truth is that Wal-Mart could open a store in Havana tomorrow and it wouldn't make a difference. Why? Because the problem in Cuba is not that there isn't Coca-Cola, microwave ovens, or shampoo," he explains.

"The problem is that the Cuban people don't have money to buy things," he says. "I sell three microwave ovens and 10 toaster ovens a month—but that's because that's how few Cubans have the money to buy these things."

"The only customers I have are government officials—all of whom are corrupt so they have dollars—or Cubans who have access to dollars. And you can get dollars only one of two ways: you have family in Miami that sends you dollars or you work in the tourist industry where tourists give you dollars or euros as tips. That's it, that's the entire consumer economy."

"If the embargo ended tomorrow and Wal-Mart opened . . . it would be as empty as the Centro Comerical Palco or Galerias Paseo," he says, a reference to two shopping areas located in the heart of Havana, both of which remain largely empty of local customers. "Unless the embargo is going to mean that everyone in Cuba gets a paycheck in American dollars, I'm not going out of business anytime soon."

After a busy morning of shopping in Cancún, he is ready to head back to the airport. If he's lucky, there won't be a problem checking in all his luggage and cargo for the afternoon flight to Havana.

Juan prefers to arrive back in Havana before sunset. That allows him to clear customs—by which he means paying off his regular officials—and head home by evening. When Cubans have money to buy the products, they want instant gratification.

"I'm going to be up until 2 or 3 in the morning," he explains. "I have to stay up for people to pick up what they ordered."

As he's going over his list—as if he were a Cuban version of Santa Claus, he ticks off which items are packed where: toaster ovens; sundries and shampoos; two infant car seats; three Xbox 360 video game consoles, four pairs of Asics Gel-Kahana men's running shoes, in different sizes; plus three suitcases of children's, women's and men's clothing.

If there are no problems, after costs, he hopes to pocket $250 USD in profits. This is a princely sum, especially in a country where the average worker makes about $25 USD a month. "Some of my customers have to save for months to buy brand-name shampoo, or a pair of sneakers for their kids," Juan explains.

With that, the airline ticket agent hands him his boarding pass—and receipts for the luggage he checked in. A moment later, he smiles as he walks to the security checkpoint. Less than an hour after leaving Cancún, he will be back in Havana, where customers will be anxious to get their hands on everything he spent the entire morning securing.

—Reprinted from NewAmericaMedia.org

Advocacy Organizations

Would you like to advocate for changing the U.S. government's Cuba policies?

If you would, there are two organizations working to improve relations between the U.S. and Cuba. Here they are:

Latin American Working Group
To learn about the work of the Latin America Working Group (LAWG), which amplifies activists' voice in Washington, D.C., visit their website.

Website: *www.lawg.org*

Engage Cuba
To learn about the work of the bipartisan organization Engage Cuba, which was established in June 2015, visit their website.

Website: *www.CubaEngage.org*

Getting to Yes

Who knows what the future will bring?

Cuba might be able to make a peaceful transition from the current political economic model to another model. Then again, it might not.

The Castro family is hoping for a peaceful transition where they remain players. In fact, at present there is the systematic transfer of Cuban public assets to an organization known as the Grupo de Administración Empresarial, S.A., or GAESA. It is run by Raúl Castro's son-in-law, Brigadier General Luis Alberto Rodríguez Primo López-Callejas. This firm is part of the Revolutionary Armed Forces, or FAR. The military runs a parallel state within a state. GAESA is supervising the construction of the Zona Especial de Desarrollo Mariel.

It is clear that the Castro family—and the military—are positioning themselves to remain players in whatever happens in Cuba.

If there isn't a peaceful transition in Cuba from one economic model to the next, however, all bets are off.

But for now, work with GAESA, and you're in.

State Department Info for U.S. Citizens and Permanent Residents

GENERAL INFORMATION FOR U.S. CITIZENS AND PERMANENT RESIDENTS

This section contains information for U.S. citizens and permanent residents as compiled by the State Department.

U.S. Embassy in Havana

Address:
Calzado, between L and M Streets
Vedado District
Havana
Telephone: (53) 7 839-4100
Emergency After-Hours Telephone: (53) 7 831-4100, dial 1 to speak to the emergency operator

Political Assessment

Cuba is an authoritarian state that routinely employs repressive methods against internal dissent and monitors and responds to perceived threats to authority. These methods may include physical and electronic surveillance, as well as detention and interrogation of both Cuban citizens and foreign visitors. Human rights conditions in Cuba remain poor, as the Cuban government limits fundamental freedoms, including freedom of expression and peaceful assembly. U.S. citizens visiting Cuba should be aware that any on-island activities may be subject to surveillance, and their contact with Cuban citizens monitored closely.

Entry, Exit & Visa Requirements

The Cuban Assets Control Regulations are enforced by the Office of Foreign Assets Control (OFAC) of the U.S. Department of the Treasury and affect all U.S. citizens and permanent residents wherever they are located, all people and organizations physically located in the United States, and all branches and subsidiaries of U.S. organizations throughout the world. The regulations require that persons subject to U.S. jurisdiction be licensed in order to engage in any travel-related transactions pursuant to travel to, from, and within Cuba, or that the transactions in question be exempt from licensing requirements. Transactions related to travel for tourist activities are not licensable. This restriction includes travel to Cuba for tourist activities from or through a third country, such as Mexico or Canada. U.S. law enforcement authorities enforce these regulations at U.S. airports and pre-clearance facilities in third countries. Travelers who fail to comply with Department of the Treasury regulations may face civil penalties and criminal prosecution upon return to the United States.

All travelers to Cuba, including religious workers, should contact the Cuban Embassy in Washington to determine the appropriate type of visa required for their purpose of travel. Cuba requires visitors to have non-U.S. medical insurance, and sells a temporary policy to those who do not have it. Questions about this insurance requirement should be directed to the Cuban Embassy. Cuban authorities do not demand HIV tests of travelers to Cuba, with the exception of foreign students on scholarships. The Cuban authorities accept the results of HIV tests conducted by labs in the United States. Please verify this information with the Cuban Embassy before traveling.

Information about dual nationality or the prevention of international child abduction can be found here:

http://travel.state.gov/content/childabduction/english.html.

For the latest information on U.S. regulations governing travel to Cuba and to view the most accurate and updated travel restrictions information, please see the Department of the Treasury's OFAC website.

General and Specific Licenses for Travel

The U.S. Department of the Treasury's Office of Foreign Assets Control (OFAC) has issued general licenses within the 12 categories of authorized travel for many travel-related transactions to, from, or within Cuba that previously required a specific license (i.e., an application and a case-by-case determination). Travel-related transactions are permitted by general license for certain travel related to the following activities, subject to criteria and conditions in each general license: family visits; official business of the U.S. government, foreign governments, and certain intergovernmental organizations; journalistic activity; professional research and professional meetings; educational activities; religious activities; public performances, clinics, workshops, athletic and other competitions, and exhibitions; support for the Cuban people; humanitarian projects; activities of private foundations or research or educational institutes; exportation, importation, or transmission of information or information materials; and certain authorized export transactions. No further permission from OFAC is required to engage in transactions covered by a general license.

OFAC will consider requests for specific licenses on a case-by-case basis for travel that relates to one of these categories but does not fall within the scope of a general license. However, it is OFAC's policy not to grant specific licenses authorizing transactions for which the provisions of an outstanding general license are applicable. See 31 C.F.R. § 501.801(a). For further information on travel to Cuba under a general or a specific license, consult OFAC's Cuba Sanctions website.

Persons subject to U.S. jurisdiction are prohibited from doing business or investing in Cuba unless licensed by OFAC. An OFAC general license authorizes the exportation from the United States, and the re-exportation of 100 percent U.S.-origin items from third countries, to Cuba only in those cases where the exportation or re-exportation is licensed or otherwise authorized by the Commerce Department. The Commerce Department currently authorizes limited categories of items to be exported or re-exported to Cuba.

Persons subject to U.S. jurisdiction authorized to travel to Cuba may import into the United States as accompanied baggage merchandise acquired in Cuba with a value not to exceed $400 per person, including no more than $100 in alcohol and tobacco products.

Additional information may be obtained by visiting OFAC's website or by contacting:

Licensing Division
Office of Foreign Assets Control
U.S. Department of the Treasury
1500 Pennsylvania Avenue NW
Treasury Annex
Washington, DC 20220
Telephone (202) 622-2480; 1-800-540-6322; Fax (202) 622-1657
The OFAC's website for Cuba is:
http://www.treasury.gov/resource-center/sanctions/ programs/ pages/cuba.aspx

Cuban Requirements for Authorized Travelers

Should a traveler receive a license to travel or qualify under an existing general license, a valid passport is required for entry into Cuba. The Cuban government may also require that the traveler obtain a visa. The Cuban Interests Section in Washington issues visas. Attempts to enter or exit Cuba illegally, or to aid the irregular exit of Cuban nationals or other persons, are prohibited and punishable by stiff jail terms. Entering Cuban territory, territorial waters or airspace (generally within 12 nautical miles of the Cuban coast) without prior authorization from the Cuban government may result in arrest or other enforcement action by Cuban authorities. Immigration violators are subject to prison terms ranging from four years for illegal entry or exit to as many as 30 years for aggravated cases of alien smuggling. Visit the Cuban Embassy website for the most current visa information: *http://www.cubadiplomatica.cu/sicw/ EN/ConsularServices.aspx*

Civilian Aircraft Travel

The Cuban Air Force shot down two U.S.-registered civilian aircraft in international airspace in 1996. As a result of this action, the President of the United States and the Federal Aviation Administration (FAA) issued an "Emergency Cease and Desist Order and Statement of Policy," which allows for vigorous enforcement action against U.S.-registered aircraft that violate Cuban airspace. For additional information on restrictions on aircraft flying between the United States and Cuba, see the FAA's website on Cuba: *http://www.faa.gov/air_traffic/publications/ us_restrictions/#restrictCU*

Temporary Sojourn License

The U.S. Department of Commerce considers exports of aircraft or vessels on temporary sojourn to Cuba on a case-by-case basis. Temporary sojourn licenses are not available for pleasure boaters. Additional information is available at the Bureau of Industry and Security website:

http://www.bis.doc.gov/. Vessels of the United States, as defined in 33 CFR §107.200, may not enter Cuban territorial waters without advance permission from the U.S. Coast Guard. The U.S. Coast Guard provides permission information at (305) 415-6920.

Safety and Security

The security environment in Cuba is relatively stable and characterized by a strong military and police presence throughout the country. Demonstrations against the United States are less frequent and smaller than in past years. They are always approved and monitored by the Cuban government and have been peaceful in nature. The same cannot be said about state-organized demonstrations against domestic opposition groups, which can be violent. U.S. citizens should avoid all demonstrations.

Hijackings of vessels by those seeking to go to or depart from Cuba are no longer common. The United States government has publicly and repeatedly announced that any person who hijacks (or attempts to hijack) an aircraft or vessel (whether common carrier or other) will face the maximum penalties pursuant to U.S. law, regardless of nationality.

In recent years, the Cuban government has detained U.S. citizens it suspects of engaging in activities perceived to undermine state security. In 2011, it sentenced one such U.S. citizen to a lengthy prison sentence on arbitrary charges after a two-day trial that did not comport with due process. U.S. citizens traveling to Cuba should be aware that the Cuban government may detain anyone at any time for any purpose, and should not expect that Cuba's state security or judicial systems will carry out their responsibilities according to international norms.

Cuban territorial waters are extremely dangerous and difficult to navigate, even for experienced mariners. The potential for running aground is very high. Search-and-rescue capability in Cuba is limited and running aground will often lead to the complete destruction and loss of the vessel. U.S. boaters who enter Cuban waters have encountered problems that required repairs and/or salvage; costs for both are significantly higher than comparable services in the United States or elsewhere in the Caribbean. Cuban authorities typically hold boats as collateral payment. U.S.-registered or flagged vessels belonging to U.S. citizens have been permanently seized by Cuban authorities. Repairs take significantly longer in Cuba than they would in the United States due to lack of the most basic materials and to bureaucratic impediments. Boaters are often confined to their boats while repairs are made. Boaters can be detained while Cuban authorities investigate the circumstances of their entry to Cuba, especially if their travel documents are not in order or if they are suspected of illegal activities. Mariners and their passengers should not navigate close to Cuban territorial waters unless seeking a safe port due to emergencies. The ability of the U.S. Interests Section to assist mariners in distress is extremely limited due to Cuban restrictions on travel by U.S. personnel outside of Havana. Nevertheless, notifying the U.S. Interests Section is the most reliable way to obtain assistance.

The transfer of funds from the United States to Cuba to pay for boat repair and salvage is subject to restrictions relating to commercial transactions with the Government of Cuba. A Department of the Treasury license is required for such payments and applicants should be prepared to provide documentary evidence demonstrating the emergency nature of the repairs. U.S. credit or debit cards, personal checks, and travelers' checks cannot be used in Cuba so boaters should be prepared to pay for

210

all transactions in cash, keeping in mind that the Government of Cuba also does not allow the use of the U.S. dollar.

Up-to-date information on safety and security can also be obtained by calling 1-888-407-4747 toll-free in the U.S. and Canada, or for other callers, a regular toll line at 1-202-501-4444. These numbers are available from 8:00 a.m. to 8:00 p.m. Eastern Time, Monday through Friday (except U.S. federal holidays).

The Department of State urges U.S. citizens to take responsibility for their own personal security while traveling overseas.

To stay connected:

Enroll in the Smart Traveler Enrollment Program so we can keep you up to date with important safety and security announcements. Do so here: *https://step.state.gov/step/*.

Follow the Bureau of Consular Affairs on Twitter:

https://twitter.com/travelgov

and Facebook

https://www.facebook.com/travelgov?_rdr=p.

Bookmark the Bureau of Consular Affairs website, which contains the current Travel Warnings and Travel Alerts as well as the Worldwide Caution.

Follow the U.S. Embassy in Cuba on Twitter: *https://twitter.com/USAenCUBA*

In the event of an emergency, contact us at 1-888-407-4747 toll-free within the United States and Canada, or via a regular toll line, 1-202-501-4444, from other countries.

Take some time before traveling to consider your personal security and check for useful tips for traveling safely abroad. The website is here:

http://travel.state.gov/content/passports/english/ go/checklist.html

Crime

Official crime statistics are not published by the Cuban government, but reporting by U.S. citizens and other foreign travelers indicates that the majority of incidents are non-violent and theft-related – e.g., pick pocketing, purse snatching, or the taking of unattended or valuable items. There is anecdotal evidence that violent crime has increased in Cuba and is generally associated with assaults committed during a burglary or robbery. The U.S. government cannot confirm this information but rates the threat of crime in Cuba as medium. In the event of a confrontation, travelers should not resist, as perpetrators may be armed. Thefts generally occur in crowded areas such as markets, beaches, and other gathering points, including Old Town Havana and the Prado neighborhood. Travelers should exercise basic situational awareness at all times and are advised not to leave belongings unattended, nor carry purses and bags loosely over one shoulder.

Visitors should avoid wearing flashy jewelry or displaying large amounts of cash. When possible, visitors should carry a copy of their passport with them and leave the original at a secure location. U.S. visitors should also beware of Cuban "jineteros" (hustlers) who specialize in swindling tourists. While most jineteros speak English and go out of their way to appear friendly, e.g., by offering to serve as tour guides or to facilitate the purchase of cheap cigars, many are in fact professional criminals who may resort to violence in their efforts to acquire tourists' money and other valuables. When exchanging currency, use state-run offices to convert dollars and avoid independent/street vendors.

All travelers should ensure that valuables remain under their personal control at all times and are never put into checked baggage.

Victims of Crime

The loss or theft in Cuba of a U.S. passport should be reported immediately to the local police and to the U.S. Interests Section in Havana. If you are the victim of a crime while in Cuba, in addition to reporting to local police, please contact the U.S. Interests Section for assistance. The Interests Section staff can, for example, help you find appropriate medical care, contact family members or friends, and explain how funds may be transferred. Although the investigation and prosecution of the crime is solely the responsibility of local authorities, consular officers can help you understand the local criminal justice process and to find an attorney if needed.
The local equivalent to the "911" emergency line in Cuba is "106" for police and "105" for fire.

Please see our information for victims of crime, including possible victim compensation programs in the United States. See:
http://travel.state.gov/content/passports/english/ emergencies/victims.html

Local Laws & Special Circumstances

Criminal Penalties

While you are traveling in Cuba, you are subject to its laws. Foreign laws and legal systems can be vastly different from our own. Penalties for breaking the law can be more severe than in the United States for similar offenses. Persons violating Cuba's laws, even unknowingly, may be expelled, arrested, or imprisoned. Penalties for possession, use, or trafficking in illegal drugs in Cuba are severe, and convicted offenders can expect long jail sentences and heavy fines. Those accused of drug-related and other crimes face long legal proceedings and delayed due process. In some cases, the Cuban government has not permitted U.S. consular access to Cuban-American prisoners.

Criminal penalties are also harsh for persons, including foreigners and dual nationals, suspected of assisting Cuban migrants who attempt to leave Cuba illegally. Typical jail sentences for individuals charged with migrant smuggling range from 10 to 25 years.

Traffic laws in Cuba differ greatly from those in the United States. U.S. citizen drivers involved in traffic accidents that result in the death or injury of any party may be held criminally liable, regardless of fault. The U.S. Interests Section recommends extreme caution when driving in Cuba as hazardous road conditions, poor signage, and jaywalking pedestrians may result in accidents.

The Cuban government has strict laws prohibiting the importation of weapons. The Department of State warns all U.S. citizens against taking any type of firearm or ammunition into Cuba. Entering Cuba with a firearm or even a single round of ammunition is illegal, even if the weapon or ammunition is taken into Cuba unintentionally. The Cuban government strictly, enforces laws restricting the entry of firearms and ammunition at airports and seaports, and routinely x-rays all incoming luggage. U.S. citizens entering Cuba with a weapon or any quantity of ammunition, even accidentally, are subject to fines or possible imprisonment. We strongly advise travelers to thoroughly inspect all belongings prior to travel to Cuba to avoid the accidental import of ammunition or firearms.

There are also some activities that may be legal in the country you visit, but still illegal in the United States. For example, you can be prosecuted in the United States for engaging in sexual conduct with children or for using or disseminating child pornography in a foreign country regardless of the legality of these activities under that country's laws. See:

http://travel.state.gov/content/passports/english/ emergencies/arrest/criminalpenalties.html.

Bringing counterfeit and pirated goods into the United States may be illegal, and if you purchase them in a foreign country, you may be breaking local law as well.

While some countries will notify the nearest U.S. embassy or consulate if a U.S. citizen is detained or arrested in that country, the Cuban government may not, especially in the case of dual nationals. If you are arrested or detained in Cuba, you should promptly ask the authorities to notify the U.S. Interests Section so that it is aware of your circumstances and may offer appropriate assistance.

Special Circumstances

Cuba forbids photographing military or police installations or personnel, or harbor, rail, and airport facilities.

Dual Nationality

The Government of Cuba treats U.S. citizens born in Cuba, or those born in the United States to Cuban parents, as Cuban citizens and may subject them to a range of restrictions and obligations, including military service. The Cuban government requires U.S.-Cuban dual citizens (see the State Department's page on dual nationals: *http://travel.state.gov/content/travel/english/legal-considerations/us-citizenship-laws-policies/citizenship-and-dual-nationality/ dual-nationality.html*) to enter and depart Cuba using a Cuban passport. Using a Cuban passport for this purpose does not jeopardize one's U.S. citizenship; however, such persons must use their U.S. passports to enter and depart the United States.

Although the Cuban government lifted its exit permission requirement for most Cubans in January 2013, in some instances, dual nationals may be required to obtain exit permission from the Cuban government in order to return to the United States. There have been cases of dual nationals being forced by the Cuban government to surrender their U.S. passports. Despite these restrictions, dual nationals who fall ill may only be treated at hospitals for foreigners (except in emergencies). See the Consular Access section below for information on Cuba's denial of consular services to dual nationals who have been arrested, as well as the State Department's Office of Children's Issues website for information on how dual nationality may affect welfare inquiries and custody disputes. The website is here:

http://travel.state.gov/content/childabduction/english/about.html.

213

Dual nationals should be especially wary of any attempt by Cuban authorities to compel them to sign "repatriation" documents. The Government of Cuba views a declaration of repatriation as a legal statement on the part of the dual national that he or she intends to resettle permanently in Cuba.

Consular Access to Dual Nationals

U.S. citizens are encouraged to carry a copy of their U.S. passport with them at all times so that, if questioned by local officials, proof of identity and U.S. citizenship is readily available. The original should be kept in a secure location, preferably in a safe or locked suitcase.

Cuba does not consider itself obligated to allow U.S. consular officials to have access to detained Cuban-born U.S. citizens, whom the Cuban government views as Cuban citizens only. As such, Cuban authorities do not always notify the U.S. Interests Section of the arrest of dual nationals and may deny U.S. consular officers access to them. They may also withhold from U.S. authorities information concerning the welfare and treatment of dual nationals.

Currency Regulations

Since November 2004, the U.S. dollar has not been accepted for commercial transactions. U.S.-issued debit and credit cards also are not accepted in Cuba. The Cuban government requires the use of convertible Cuban pesos or non-convertible Cuban pesos ("moneda nacional") for all transactions. The official exchange rate for convertible Cuban pesos (CUC) is 1 USD = 1 CUC; however, a minimum 10 percent fee for exchanging U.S. dollars and other transaction fees make the effective exchange rate at hotels, airports, and currency exchange houses lower. The current exchange rate for CUC to non-convertible Cuban pesos (CUP) is 1 CUC = 24 CUP. In 2013, the Cuban government announced plans to consolidate its dual-currency system into a single system, but to date has not provided a timeline for when this change will occur.

Cuba-related Travel Transactions: Only persons whose travel falls into the categories mentioned above (under "Entry Requirements/Travel Transaction Limitations") may be authorized by the U.S. Department of the Treasury to spend money related to travel to, from, or within Cuba.

For more information, refer to OFAC's Cuba Sanctions website: *http://www.treasury.gov/resource-center/ sanctions/programs/pages/cuba.aspx.*

Licenses for Remittances

U.S. persons aged 18 or older may send remittances to a close relative in Cuba or to a Cuban national in a third country under certain circumstances. U.S. persons are also authorized to send emigration-related remittances to enable the payee to emigrate from Cuba to the United States, and remittances to religious organizations in Cuba in support of religious activities, under certain circumstances.

U.S. citizens and permanent residents are prohibited from using credit cards in Cuba. U.S. credit card companies do not accept vouchers from Cuba, and Cuban shops, hotels and other places of business do not accept U.S. credit cards. Neither personal checks nor travelers' checks drawn on U.S. banks are accepted in Cuba. Please see the website on Customs Information here:

http://travel.state.gov/content/passports/english/go/customs.html.

What May Be Brought Back From Cuba

If U.S. travelers return from Cuba with goods of Cuban origin, such goods, with the exception of informational materials, may be seized at U.S. Customs' discretion (see 31 CFR section 515.204). Cuban cigars and rum are routinely confiscated at U.S. ports of entry. Purchasing Cuban cigars and rum in a "duty-free" shop at the Havana Airport does not exempt them from seizure by U.S. Customs. There are no limits on the import or export of informational materials as set forth in 31 C.F.R. section 515.206. Blank tapes and CDs are not considered informational materials and may be seized. To be considered informational material, artwork must be classified under Chapter subheading 9701, 9702, or 9703 of the Harmonized Tariff Schedule of the United States (for example, original paintings, drawings, pastels, engravings, prints, and sculptures are exempt from import and export restrictions).

Fair Business Practices

Anyone authorized by the U.S. Department of the Treasury to provide travel services to, from, or within Cuba or services in connection with sending money to Cuba is prohibited from participating in the discriminatory practices of the Cuban government against individuals or particular classes of travelers. The assessment of consular fees by the Cuban government, which are applicable worldwide, is not considered to be a discriminatory practice; however, requiring the purchase of services not desired by the traveler is prohibited. Information provided to the U.S. Department of the Treasury regarding arbitrary fees, payments for unauthorized purposes, or other possible violations will be handled with confidentiality. Please see our *Customs Information*.

Women Traveler Information

If you are a woman traveling abroad, please review our travel tips for Women Travelers: *http://travel.state.gov/content/passports/english/go/Women.html.*

LGBT Rights

There are no legal restrictions on same-sex sexual relations or the organization of LGBT events in Cuba, but same-sex marriage is not legally recognized. For more detailed information about LGBT rights in Cuba you may review the State Department's annual Country Reports on Human Rights Practices. For further information on Lesbian, Gay, Bisexual and Transgender (LGBT) travel, please read the LGBT Travel Information page available here: *http://travel.state.gov/content/passports/english/go/lgbt.html.*

Accessibility

While in Cuba, individuals with disabilities may find accessibility and accommo-dation very different from in the United States. There are laws recommending that buildings, communications facilities, air

215

travel, and other transportation services accommodate persons with disabilities, but these facilities and services are rarely accessible to persons with disabilities in practice, and information for persons with disabilities is limited. Most roads and sidewalks throughout the country are poorly maintained.

Health & Hygiene

Health Care in Cuba

Medical care In Cuba typically does not meet U.S. standards. While medical professionals are generally competent, many health facilities face shortages of medical supplies and bed space. Many medications are unavailable, so travelers to Cuba should bring with them any prescribed medicine in its original container and in amounts commensurate with personal use. Travelers may also wish to consider bringing small additional amounts of prescribed medicines and over-the-counter remedies in the event that a return to the United States is delayed for unforeseen reasons. A copy of the prescription and a letter from the prescribing physician explaining the need for prescription drugs may facilitate their entry into the country.

Travelers to the Havana area should be aware that U.S. and other foreign visitors seeking medical care are generally referred to the "tourist" Cira Garcia Hospital located in the Miramar neighborhood of Havana. Medical consultations and treatment at Cira Garcia require payment in cash in Cuban convertible pesos (CUC) or by credit card issued by a non-U.S. bank (see section on Medical Insurance below).

Diarrhea

Diarrheal illness is common among travelers, even in those staying in luxury accommodations. Travelers can diminish diarrhea risk through scrupulous washing of hands and use of hand sanitizers, especially before food preparation and eating. The greatest risk of traveler's diarrhea is from contaminated food. Choose foods and beverages carefully to lower your risk (see the CDC Food & Water Safety website here: *http://wwwnc.cdc.gov/ travel/page/food-water-safety.*) Eat only food that is cooked and served hot; avoid food that has been sitting out on a buffet. Eat raw fruits and vegetables only if you have washed them in clean water or peeled them. Drink only beverages from factory-sealed containers, and avoid ice because it may have been made from unclean water.

Dengue

Dengue is a mosquito-borne illness that is becoming more frequent in tropical and equatorial climates around the world. Symptoms can include fever, rash, severe headache, joint pain, and muscle or bone pain. There are no specific treatments for Dengue and vaccines are still in the developmental phase. Preventing mosquito bites is the most important way to prevent these illnesses. Avoidance and prevention techniques include: reducing mosquito exposure by using repellents, covering exposed skin, treating clothing and tents with permethrin and sleeping in screened or air conditioned rooms.

216

You can also reduce exposure through mosquito control measures, including emptying water from outdoor containers and spraying to reduce mosquito populations. The *Aedes* mosquitos that carry this illness are primarily day biting and often live in homes and hotel rooms especially under beds, in bathrooms and closets. Travelers should carry and use CDC recommended insect repellents containing either 20% DEET, picaridin, oil of lemon eucalyptus or IR3535, which will help diminish bites from mosquitoes as well as ticks, fleas, chiggers, etc., some of which may also carry infectious diseases. For further information, please consult the Dengue Virus website which is: *http://www.cdc.gov/Dengue/*.

Cholera

In 2013, the Pan-American Health Organization (PAHO) issued an epidemiological alert noting the presence of cholera in Cuba and confirming that foreign travelers have contracted cholera during recent trips to Cuba. Eating or drinking fecally-contaminated food or water is the main risk factor. Unsterilized water, food from street vendors, raw fish dishes (e.g. ceviche) and inadequately-cooked shellfish are common sources of infection. Travelers are advised to follow public health recommendations, such as safe food and water precautions and frequent hand washing, to help prevent cholera infection. The U.S. Centers for Disease Control (CDC) and the World Health Organization both provide information about cholera to the travelling public.

Rabies

Risk exists in most parts of the country including urban areas of Havana. Rabies immunization is recommended for prolonged stays especially for young children and all travelers to rural areas where risk exists. Immunization is recommended for short term travelers who may have occupational exposure or are adventure travelers, hikers, cave explorers, and backpackers, especially at locations more than 24 hours' travel from a reliable source of post exposure treatment. Dog, mongoose, and bat bites or scratches should be taken seriously and post-exposure prophylaxis sought even in those already immunized.

You can find detailed information on vaccinations and other health precautions on the CDC website here: *http://wwwnc.cdc.gov/travel/*. For information about outbreaks of infectious diseases abroad, consult the World Health Organization (WHO) website available at:
 http://www.who.int/topics/ infectious_diseases/en/.
It contains additional health information for travelers, including detailed country-specific health information available at: *http://www.who.int/countries/en/*.

Travel & Transportation

Traffic Safety and Road Conditions

While in Cuba, U.S. citizens may encounter very poor and dangerous road conditions. The information below concerning Cuba is provided for general reference only, and may not be necessarily accurate in a particular location or circumstance.

Driving is done on the right-hand side of the road, as in the United States; speed limits are sometimes posted and generally respected in urban areas. Passengers in automobiles are generally required to wear seatbelts, and all motorcyclists are required to wear helmets.

Unconfirmed reports suggest that accidents involving motor vehicles are now the leading cause of death in Cuba. Many accidents involve motorists striking pedestrians or bicyclists. Drivers found responsible for accidents resulting in serious injury or death are subject to prison terms of up to ten years, and Cuban authorities may prohibit drivers of rental cars who are involved in accidents from leaving the country until all claims associated with an accident are settled. Witnesses to vehicular accidents may not be permitted to leave Cuba until an investigation into the accident has been completed.

Taxis are available in busy commercial and tourist areas; radio-dispatched taxis are generally clean and reliable. Travelers should be cautious in sharing information with taxi drivers or other strangers. In addition, travelers should not accept rides in unlicensed taxis, as they may be used by thieves to rob passengers. Buses designated for tourist travel, both between and within cities, generally meet international standards for both cleanliness and safety. Public buses used by Cubans, known as "guaguas," are crowded, unreliable, and havens for pickpockets. These public buses usually will not offer rides to foreign visitors.

Although popular with tourists, the three-wheeled, yellow-hooded "Co-Co" taxis are considered unsafe and should be avoided. "Co-Co" taxis are modified motorcycles that reach speeds of up to 40 mph, but have no seat belts or other safety features.

Drivers should exercise extreme care. Although the main arteries of Havana are generally well-maintained, secondary streets often are not. Many roads and city streets are unlit, making night driving dangerous, especially as some cars and most bicycles lack running lights or reflectors. Street signage tends to be insufficient and confusing. Many Cuban cars are old, in poor condition, and lack turn signals, reliable brakes, and other standard safety equipment.

The principal Cuban east-west highway is in good condition but lacks lighting and extends only part of the way from Havana to the eastern tip of the island. Road signage on highways may be lacking or confusing. Night driving should be strictly avoided outside urban areas. Secondary rural roads are narrow, and some are in such bad condition as to be impassable by cars. Due to the rarity of cars on rural roads, pedestrians, bicycles, horse-drawn carts, and farm equipment operators wander onto the roads without any regard to possible automobile traffic. Unfenced livestock constitute another serious road hazard.

Rental car agencies provide roadside assistance to their clients as a condition of the rental contract. Automobile renters are provided telephone numbers to call in case of emergency; agencies generally respond as needed with tow trucks and/or mechanics. A similar service is available to foreign residents of Cuba who insure cars with the National Insurance Company.

Anecdotal reports indicate the maintenance that rental car agencies provide to their fleets is inadequate and may cause an accident. Cuban authorities may prohibit drivers of rental cars who are involved in accidents from leaving the country, even if they are injured and require medical attention, until all claims associated with an accident are settled.

Travelers should not permit unauthorized persons to drive their rental vehicles. Please refer to our Road Safety page for more information here:

http://travel.state.gov/content/passports/english/ go/safety/road.html.

Aviation Safety Oversight

As there is no direct commercial air service to the United States by carriers registered in Cuba, the U.S. Federal Aviation Administration (FAA) has not assessed the government of Cuba's Civil Aviation Authority for compliance with International Civil Aviation Organization (ICAO) aviation safety standards. Further information may be found on the FAA's safety assessment page which is: *http://www.faa.gov/ about/initiatives/iasa/.*

The U.S. Interests Section permits travel by its employees and official visitors on Cuban air carriers, including the Cuban national airline, Cubana de Aviación (CUBANA), on a case by case basis.

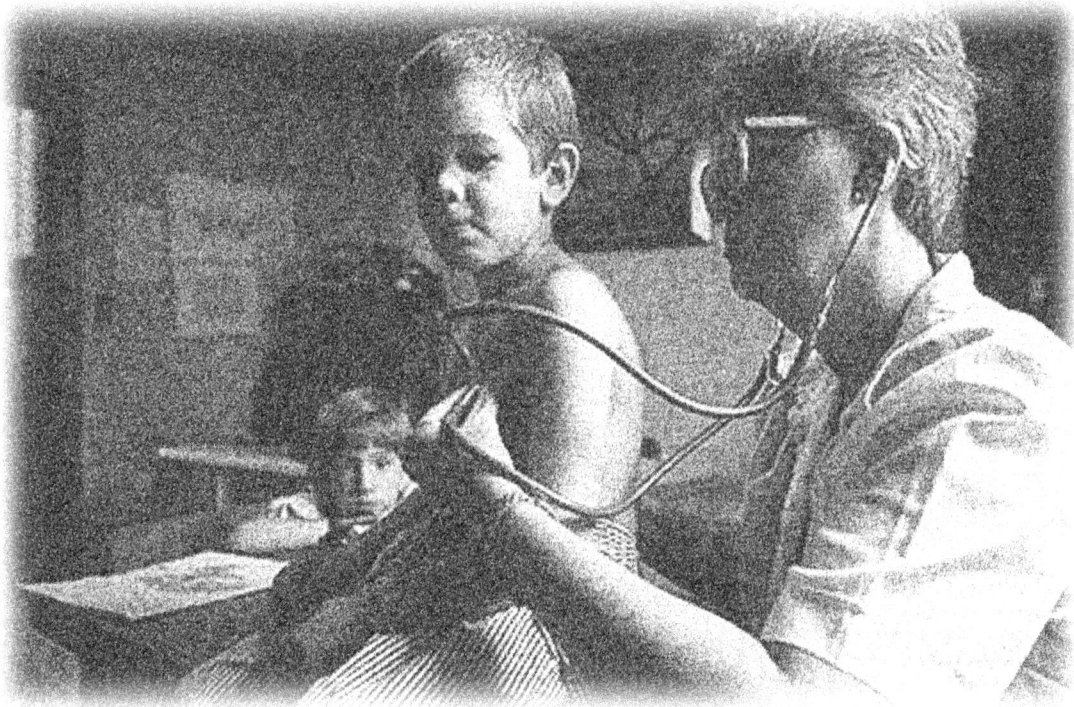

219

Beyond Havana

28 VARADERO

Varadero is Cuba's answer to Cancún and Cozumel: Beach resorts without the locals. Here are the top places to stay and eat.

Accommodations

Hotel Acuazul
Primera Avenida, between Calle 13 and Calle 14

Hotel Los Delfines
Avenida de la Playa and Calle 39

BelleVue Palma Real
Calle 64

Hotel Meliá Marina Varadero
Punta Hicaco, Autopista del Sur

Sun Beach by Excellence Style Hotels
Calle 17, between Calle 1 and Calle 3

Royalton Hicacos Varadero Resort & Spa
Carretera de las Morlas, Kilometro 15, Punta Hicacos

Paradisus Varadero Resort & Spa
Punta Francés

Gran Caribe Villa Tortuga
Calle 8, by Avenida Kawama

Hotel Club Kawama
Calle 1, Reparto Kawama

Blau Varadero Hotel Cuba
Carretera de las Morlas, Kilometro 15

Starfish Cuatro Palms
Avenida 1, between 60 and 64

Islazul Mar del Sur
Avenida 3 and Calle 30

Hotel Casa Granda
Heredia #201, between Calle San Pedro and Calle San Félix

Sol Sirena Coral Resort
Avenida Las Américas and Calle K

Sol Palmeras
Carretera de las Morlas, Kilometro 12

Mercure Playa de Oro
Carretera de las Morlas, Kilometro 12.5

Iberostar Varadero
Carretera de las Morals, Kilometro 17.5

Hotel Villa Cuba
Avenida Las Américas, Kilometro 3

Club Tropical
Avenida 1, between Avenida 21 and Avenida 22

Meliá Las Américas
Playa Las Américas

Hotel Barceló Solymar Arenas Blancas
Calle 64, between Avenida 1 and Autopista

Hotel Club Puntarena
Avenida Kawama and Final

Hotel Roc Arenas Doradas
Autopista Varadero, Kilometro 17

Blue Marina Varadero Resort
Autopista Sur at Punta Hicacos

Hotel Roc Barlovento
Avenida 1, between Avenida 10 and Avenida 12

Hotel Aguas Azules
Carretera de las Morlas, Kilometro 14

AirBNB Options

The following accommodations are recommended. The price listed is the average rate, in U.S. dollars.

Casa Olivia, Calle
7 #7, between D and E, Reparto La Playa: $25 USD

Villa Magaly & Richard
Calle 127 #20811, between 208 and 210: $30 USD

Hostal Costa Azul
Calle 127 #20817, by 208: $31 USD

Hostal el Villareño
Calle 44 #208, between Avenida 2 and Avenida 3: $36 USD

Hostal Villa Mar Room 1
Calle 127 #20809, between 208 and 210: $37 USD

Hostal Villa Mar Room 2
Calle 127 #20809, between 208 and 210: $37 USD

Casa Amarilis
Calle B #33, Reparto La Playa: $40 USD

Casa Belisa
Avenida 2 #2003, between 20 and 21: $40 USD

Casa Papos House
Calle 55 #114, between 1 and 2: $40 USD

Varadero 7.3
Double Room, Intersection of Avenida 1 and 17: $56 USD

Restaurants & *Paladares*

Waco's Club
Avenida 3 #212, between 58 and 59

Don Alex
Calle 31 #106, between Avenida 1 and Avenida 3

La Gruta
Interior of Parque Josone

Paladar Nonna Tina
Calle 38 #5, between Avenida 1 and Playa

Varadero 60
Corner of Calle 60 and Avenida 3

La Rampa
Calle 43, between Avenida 1 and Playa

La Vaca Rosada
Calle 21 #102, between Avenida 1 and Avenida 2

Paladar Pequeño Suárez
At Calle 18 and Avenida 3

Beatles Bar
Calle 59, between Avenida 1 and Avenida 2

Los Amigos
La Curva #1, steps from Puente de Varadero

Xanadu
DuPont Mansion, Varadero Golf Course

Salsa Suárez Restaurant & Bar
Calle 31 #103, between Avenida 1 and Avenida 3

Restaurante La Arcada
Meliá Las Américas

Kiki's
Avenida Kawana at Calle 5

Calle 62
Calle 62, between Avenida 1 and Avenida 2

Julia's at Calle 54
Calle 54, between Avenida 1 and Playa

Barbacoa
Calle 64, on the corner of Avenida 1

El Mojito
Vía Rápida #509-A, Santa Marta District

La Casa del Chef
Avenida 1 and Calle 12

La Casona del Arte
Calle 47 #6, between Avenida 1 and Playa

La Bodeguita del MedioR
Calle 40, between Avenida 1 and Avenida 2

Restaurante Terraza
Calle 43 #206, off Avenida 1

El Caney
Avenida Playa, between Calle 42 and Calle 43

Cielo Mar
Corner of Calle 57 and Playa

Places of Interest

Varadero Beach
This is a beach resort, so it's not surprising that most people spend as much time at the beach as possible.

Saturno Caves
Nature tour to nearby caves and caverns.

Casa del Ron (House of Rum)
An excellent selection of Cuban rums.

Coral Beach
The best place for snorkeling in Varadero.

Parque Josone

A popular park for strolling in city center.

Delfinario

Off Carretera Las Morlas, worth a quick trip, although seeing dolphins in captivity raises concerns for some visitors.

Ambrosio Cavern

A fascinating cave, especially if you are interested in bats.

Varadero Street Market

In town, worth an hour's stroll just to see what's left of the personal possessions seized by the Revolution and now being sold at this urban flea market.

Iglesia Santa Elvira

A charming church on Avenida 1 at Calle 47.

FerTour

Fernando offers a terrific guided tour that accommodates requests and offers insights into this part of Cuba. For information, call (53) 5 271-6015.

I Love Cuba Photo Tour

This comes in second when it comes to tours. Contact Yosel at (53) 5 293-2057 for rates and times.

Cuba With Us

The third recommended tour is run by this family-owned business. Karel is a thoughtful and authoritative guide. For information, call (53) 5 264-8431.

29 SANTIAGO DE CUBA

Santiago de Cuba is Cuba's second largest city—and a delight to visit.

Accommodations

Hotel Casa Granda
Heredia #201, between Calle San Pedro and Calle San Félix

Hotel San Basilio
Calle San Basilio #403

Gran Hotel Escuela
Enramadas on the corner of San Félix

Meliá Santiago de Cuba
Calle M and Avenida de las Américas

Villa Gaviota Santiago de Cuba
Avenida Manduley #502

Islazul Hotel Libertad
Calle Aguilera and Plaza de Marte

Hotel Versalles
Alturas de Versalles, Kilometer 1–2, Reparto Versalles

Isazul Hotel Las Américas
Avenida de las Américas and General Cebreco

Islazul Hotel San Juan
Carretera de Siboney, Kilometer 1.5, Reparto Santa Bárbara

Islazul Costa Morena
Carretera de Baconao, Kilometer 32, Sigua

AirBNB Options

The following accommodations are recommended. The price listed is the average rate, in U.S. dollars.

Lazulita Stana, Calle Aguilera: $18 USD

Julio & Delly, Heredia: $20 USD

Guest Apartment, Mayía Rodríguez: $23 USD

Apartamento Céntrico, Donato Mármol #3, between Paseo de Martí and Narciso: $24 USD

La Casita Roja Adis & Alberto, Bartolomé Masó: $24 USD

Casa Don Carlos, Heredia #416, between Clarín and Reloj: $25 USD

Casa "Las Mezillas," Escario: $25 USD

Amanecer Cubano, Santa Rita #465, between Reloj and Calvario: $28 USD

La Casona de Alina, Calle Félix Pena #453, between San Francisco and San Gerónimo: $28 USD

Casa Colonial, Heredia: $30 USD

Casa Colonial 1893, Room 1, Sánchez Hechavarría, San Gerónimo: $30 USD

Casa Colonial 1893, Room 3, Sánchez Hechavarría, San Gerónimo: $30 USD

Santiago 3.2, Calle Diego Palacios, Santa Rita: $32 USD

Casa de Alquiler Nelson y Deysi, José A. Saco # 513, between Mayia Rodríguez and Donato Mármol: $33 USD

Hostal Girasol, Santa Rita #409, Diego Palacios: $33 USD

Roy's Terrace Inn, Diego Palacios (Santa Rita) #177: $35 USD

El Santiaquito, Avenida Céspedes #614, between Calle K and Calle L, Reparto Sueño: $55 USD

Restaurants & *Paladares*

Restaurante Setos Cuba
Avenida Manduley #154

Restaurante Aurora
General Portuondo # E, between Calle General Moncada and Calle Calvario

Restaurante Primos Twice
Calvario# 262, between Calle Habana & Calle Trinidad

El Palenquito
Avenida de Rio #28, between Calle 6 and Carretera del Caney

Rumba Café
San Félix #455-A

230

Compay Gallo
San Germán #503, on the corner of Carniceria

Restaurante El Cayo
Cayo Granma

El Holandés
Heredia #251, on the corner of Hartman

Restaurant Salón Tropical
Fernández Marcane # 310, between Calle 10 and Calle 8

Chocolatería Fraternidad
Plaza de Marte, on the corner of Calle Aguilera

El Madrileño
Avenida 8 and Calle 3-5, Reparto Vista Alegre

St. Pauli
Enarmadas #605, between Calle Barnada and Calle Plácido

Restaurant San Francisco
Calle San Francisco, between Calvario and Carnicería

El Morro
Carretera del Morro Km 8.5, Bahía de Santiago

El Barracón
Avenida Victoriano Garzón, between Paseo de Martí and Calle 1, Reparto Sueño

El Alazán
San Félix #909, between San Carlos and Santa Rosa

Paladar Terraza
Calle Aguilera #602, between Calle Barnada and Calle Paraíso

Bendita Farandula
Calle Barnada #513

Casa Micaela
Corona, between Enrramadas y Aguilera

Fonda Matamoro
Calle Calvario, between Calle Aguilera and Calle Reloj

Terrazas la Caridad
Avenida Del Rio #3, Rajayoga

La Fortaleza
Calle 3, between Avendida Manduley and Calle 8

Las Gallagas Paladar
San Basilio #305

Hotel Casa Granda Restaurant
Heredia #201, between Calle San Pedro and Calle San Félix

Restaurant Sabor Cubano
San Basilio #156

Places of Interest

San Pedro de la Roca del Morro Castle
Breathtaking panoramic views of Santiago de Cuba.

La Gran Piedra
To appreciate the mountains and views of Cuba, this is the spot.

Casa de las Tradiciones
This bar, located at Calle General Lacret #651, is renowned for the musicians and bands that play here, and this town is known as the musical soul of Cuba.

Casa de La Trova
In keeping with the musical tradition of this great city, this place is great to have a drink while enjoying wonderful music—in city center.

Iris Jazz Club
The best place for jazz, and conveniently located at the intersection of Paraíso and Aguilera streets.

Céspedes Park
Located in city center, this park is an ideal place to people watch. Vendors also sell all manner of Revolution tchotchkes, just in case you need more Che bandannas.

Cementerio Santa Ifigenia
An afternoon stroll through this historic and well-kept cemetery is an enjoyable activity.

Moncada Barracks

These are the barracks Fidel Castro attacked, launching the Revolution. Well worth a visit.

Diego Velázquez Museum

Located on Félix Peña #612, this museum offers a wonderful view into what Cuba—and New Spain—was like when the Spanish kings ruled over most of the New World.

Casa Velázquez

Across from the Cathedral, this museum offers insights into a bygone world.

Cathedral of Our Lady of the Assumption

Before or after a visit to the Casa Velázquez, a stroll through this gracious cathedral is a must.

Plaza de la Revolución

Socialist Realism at its most egalitarian.

Hotel Casa Grande Terrace Bar

This hotel has a great roof-terrace, and the bar is a great way to spend an afternoon, enjoying the view and a couple of drinks.

Parque de Baconao

There is a great botanical garden in this park—and some absurd dinosaur statues, but it's a pleasant day trip.

Patio de los Abuelos

A modest place on Calle Pérez Carbo, off Plaza de Marte, would-be Social Club players gather to play music as if this were a Cuban version of the *Lawrence Welk Show*.

Cayo Granma

An ideal half-day morning trip, it's a pleasant tour, and there is exceptional seafood on the key.

30 CIENFUEGOS

Deep in the heart of Cuba, Cienfuegos is a small treasure that captivates visitors in search of the Cuba of yesteryear.

Accommodations

Casa Particular Gladys
Avenida 52 #4314-E, between Avenida 43 and Avenida 45, second floor

Cubanacán Boutique La Unión
Calle 31, corner of Avenida 54

Jagua Hotel
Avenida 37 #1, corner of Punta Gorda

Club Amigo Faro Luna
Carretera Pasacaballo Kilometro 18

Punta La Cueva
Carretera de Rancho Luna, Kilometro 3.5 and Circunvalación

Hotel Rancho Luna
Carretera de Rancho Luna, Kilometro 18

Islazul Pasacaballo Hotel
Carretera de Rancho Luna Kilometro 22

AirBNB Options

The following accommodations are recommended. The price listed is the average rate, in U.S. dollars.

Mirian Hostal, Calle 4 Noreste #5101, between Avenida 51 and Avenida 53: $20 USD
Hostal D + D, Calle 62 #4513, by Avenida 45: $21 USD
Hostal Marcellino, Cary & Orli, Calle 4 Noroeste #4919: $23 USD

Casa Anay & Efraín, Avenida 60 #4728, corner of Avenida 47: $25 USD
Hostal Casa Verde, Avenida 58 # 3709, between Avenida 37 and Avenida 39: $25 USD
Hostal "La Lolita," Avenida 52 #3711, between Avenida 37 and Avenida 39: $29 USD
Casa Odalis, Calle 45, Noroeste: $30 USD
Hostal "La Verde," Avenida 18 #5705, between Avenida 57 and Avenida 59: $30 USD
Hostal San José, Calle 39, corner of Calle 18, Noroeste: $34 USD
Casa Vista al Mar, Calle 37 #210, between Calle 2 and Calle 4: $34 USD
Casa Familia Leo, Calle 41 #4408, Calle 44 and Calle 46: $45 USD

Restaurants & *Paladares*

Paladar Ache
Avenida 38 #4106, between Avenida 41 and Avenida 43

D'Carmelina
Calle 59 #402, between Calle 3 and Calle6

El Tranvía
Calle 37 #4002, between Calle 40 and Calle 42

Casa Prado
Calle 37 #4626

Florida Blanca 18
Avenida 38 #3720

Finca del Mar
Calle 35, between Avenida 4 and Avenida 6

Villa Lagarto
Calle 35 #45, between Avenida 0 and Litoral

Doña Nora
Calle 37 #4219

Te Quedarás
Avenida 54 #3509, between 35 and 37

De París
Calle 31 #5212, between 52 and 54

Las Mámparas
Calle 37 #4004, between Avenida 40 and Avenida 42

Restaurante Bahía
Avenida 40 #3713, between Calle 37 and Calle 39

Grill Punta Gorda
Calle 37 #2001, between Avenida 20 and Avenida 22

Café Telégrafo
Avenida 56, between Calle 33 and Calle 35

El Pescador
Castillo de Jagua

Places of Interest

Plaza José Martí
This is the perfect place to soak up the ambiance of Cienfuegos, especially at dusk and evening. There are vendors selling tchochkes and shops selling cigars. It's a great place to people watch.

Teatro Terry
Still in use, this historic theater in city center is a must.

El Nicho Cascades
These waterfalls are nature's marvel and well worth a day trip with your group.

Delfinario de Cienfuegos
Located off the Carretera a Pasacaballo, this facility allows visitors to swim with dolphins.

Guanaroca Lagoon
This sanctuary is a great nature reserve. Plan ahead and make a day trip of it.

Punta Gorda
This is a quiet, reserved place where a stroll will take you back in time.

Palacio del Valle
Wonderfully maintained, this grand structure, often called the Cuban Taj Mahal, has a rooftop bar that's an ideal place for a drink in the evening.

236

Jagua Castle

Fortifications that protected the Spanish from pirate attacks dominate the Caribbean, and this castle is among the most impressive.

Jardín Botánico Soledad de Cienfuegos

The nature theme is reinforced by this botanical garden/arboretum. It has a solid collection of flora that delights visitors.

Rancho Luna Beach

This beach, not ranch, is a good place to swim in the Caribbean. It's best to pack your lunch before you head out. Locals don't understand the difference between a Cuban peso, a Convertible Peso, a U.S. dollar, and a European euro, and paying for anything is a hassle.

Cemeterio La Reina

Located on Calle 7, this cemetery is the city's oldest and worth a visit.

Cemeterio Tomás Aceo

Another pantheon filled with wonderful mausoleoms and tombs. It offers an insight into the wealth of this city in centuries past.

Jardines de la Uneac

The best spot for Afro-Cuban music—as well as salsa and son—and conveniently located off Parque José Martí.

Catedral de la Purísima Concepción

Located on the Plaza de Armas, this cathedral is representative of the style that dominated European colonial possessions throughout the Caribbean.

Club Benny More

Located on Avenida 54, this club has very good music—but be mindful that it's a popular place for working girls to find clients.

31 TRINIDAD

~~~~~~

Trinidad, one of the more charming cities in the Caribbean, is well worth a visit. Following are recommended places to stay and dine, and sights not to miss.

Accommodations

Iberostar Grand Hotel Trinidad
Calle José Martí #262

Hotel La Ronda
Martí #238 (formerly the Hotel Isalzul La Ronda)

Villa Guajimico
Carretera 42

Brisas Trinidad del Mar
Península Ancón

Hotel Los Helechos
Topes de Collantes, Sancti Spiritus

Hotel Ancón
Carretera María Aguilar, Playa Ancón

Horizontes Finca María Dolores
Carretera de Cienfuegos, Kilometro 1 ½

Hotel Las Cuevas
Finca Santa Ana, Sancti Spiritus

Hospedaje Guasima
Calle Julio Mella #275

Hostal Dr. Amaro y Dra. Yamira
Manuel Solano (Callejón del Pinpollo) #7-A, between Francisco Javier Zerquera and Patricio Lumumba, Sancti Spiritus

AirBNB Options

The following accommodations are recommended. The price listed is the average rate, in U.S. dollars.

Novoa House
Valdespino #65-B: $21 USD

Hostal Betty & Saavedra
, Calle Gutiérrez: $22 USD

Authentic Cuba
, Calle Colón: $24 USD

Hostal Borrell Iznaga

, Calle Borrell: $25 USD
Casa Santo Domingo
, Calle Santo Domingo: $29 USD

Casa Ana
, Franciso Cadahía: $29 USD

Casa Mario & Damaris
, Camilo Cienfuegos: $30 USD

Casa Colonial
, Calle Gloria: $40 USD

TRI-17.1
, José Martí: $49 USD

Mi Casa es Tu Casa
, Miguel Cazada: $68 USD

Restaurants & *Paladares*

Restaurante San José
Maceo #382, between Calle Colón and Calle Smith

Zelatto
Calle Fernando Hernández #34

Paladar Estella
Simón Bolívar #557

El Dorado
Piro Guinart (Boca) #226, between Antonio Maceo and Gustavo Izquierdo

Café Don Pepe
Piro Guniart, across from the Museo de Lucha Contra Bandidos

Restaurante Museo 1514
Simón Bolívar #515 between Juan Manuel Márquez and Fernando Hernández Echerri

Paladar Davimart
Anastasio Cárdenas #518, between Simón Bolívar and Fidel Claro

Taberna La Botija
Amargura #71-B, on the corner of Boca

Paladar La Marinera
Jovellanos #178, between Iglesia and Perla, Casilda

Restaurante Taberna Ochun Yemaya
Piro Guinart #151-B, between Frank País y José Martí

Sol Ananda
Real #45

Quince Catorze
Calle Simón Bolívar # 515

Wakey Wakey & Shakey Shakey
Jesús Menéndez #205

Cubita Restaurant Bar Santander
Maceo #471

Restaurante La Coruña
José Martí #430

Villalba
Calle Simón Bolívar #442

Hostal El Rin Tintín
Calle Simón Bolívar #553

Sabor a Mi
Cristo #62, between San José and Boca

Paladar Sol y Son
Simón Bolívar #283, between Frank País and José Martí

Paladar Clara
Rubén Martínez Villena #93

Places of Interest

Plaza Mayor
Town mMain square

Casa de la Música
Off the Plaza Mayor, Casco Histórico

Disco Ayala
Las Cuevas, at the top of the hill

Iglesia Parroquial de la Santísima Trinidad
Off the Plaza Mayor

Salto del Caburni
Topes de Collantes

Trinidad Architecture Museum
Off the Plaza Mayor

Casa de la Trova
Fernando H. Echerri #29

Valle de los Ingenios
San Isidro, Trinidad

Yudit Vidal Faife
Desengaño #294, between José Martí and Frank País

Museo de Historia Municipal
Calle Simón Bolívar (just off the Plaza Mayor)

Bar Floridita Trinidad
Calle General Lino Pérez #313

Palenque de los Congos Reales
Corner of Echerri and Avenida Jesús Menéndez

Lake Embalse Hanabanilla
Between Trinidad and Santa Clara

Museo Romántico
Calle Cristo #52

Museo de Arquitectura Colonial
Plaza Mayor, adjacent to Rispalda #83

Convento de San Francisco de Asis
Trinida, Cuba

Casa Muñoz Horse Trek
José Martí #401, between Fidel Claro (Angarilla) and Santiago Escobar (Olvido)
Tel: (53) 4 199-3673 (International)
0 41 993673 (From Havana)
E-mail: *trinidadjulio@yahoo.com*

Ancón Beach
Peninsula Ancon
Accessible at these hotels: Brisas, Ancón, and Club Amigo

CAMAGUEY

Camaguey is a city of artists and a colonial treasure. Enjoy!

Accommodations

Hostal Sonia
Felipe Torres #25, between Maxilimiano Ramos and San Ramón

Islazul Gran Hotel
Maceo #67, between General Gómez and Ignacio Agramonte

Islazul Hotel Colón
República #472

Hotel Islazul Isla de Cuba
San Estevan #453, on the corner of Popular

Islazul Hotel Camaguey
Carretera Central Este, Kilometro 4.5

Islazul Hotel Plaza
Calle Van Horne #1, between República y Avellaneda

Hotel Puerto Principe
Avenida de los Mártires #60

AirBNB Options

The following accommodations are recommended. The price listed is the average rate, in U.S. dollars.

Casa Manolo, Santa Rita 18 (El Solitario), between República y Santa Rosa: $21 USD
Casa Eduardo "Tinajón," Ignacio Sánchez # 419-A, between República and Joaquín de Agueros: $23 USD
Las Marías, Casa Las Marías # 257 Calle Avellaneda, between San Esteban and Correa: $28 USD

Michel Residence
Bembeta #571, between Orca and San Ramón: $29 USD

Casa Ana, San Ramón
#319, between Línea and San José: $30 USD

Casa Lourdes
Goyo Benítez #4, between Hermanos Aguero and San Ramón: $30 USD

Lunamar House
San Pablo #103, between Martí and Luaces: $30 USD

One Bedroom Apartment
Apodaca #14, between General Gómez and Martí: $30 USD

Hostal Doña Elisa
Joaquín de Agüero #120, between Andrés Sánchez and Tomás: $31 USD

Mayra's House
Calle Guatemala #5, between Perú and Chile: $39 USD

Casa Caridad
Calle San Esteban #310-A, between San Fernando (Bartolomé Masó) and Pobres: $41 USD

CAM 1.2
Calle San Esteban #310-A, between San Fernando (Bartolomé Masó) and Pobres: $42 USD

Restaurants & *Paladares*

La Caribeña
Javier de la Vega #22, between Cornelio Porro and Braulio Peña Garrido

Restaurant Rocola Club
Avenida Carlos J. Finlay #462

Restaurante 1800
Plaza San Juan de Dios #113

El Paso Restaurant
Calle Hermanos Aguero #261, on Plaza de Carmen

Mesón del Principe
Calle Astilleros #7, between San Ramón and Lugareño

Café Ciudad
Corner of José Martí and Cisneros

Restaurante Italiano Santa Teresa
Avenida de la Victoria #12, by Alturas del Casino

Casa Austria
Calle Lugareño, between San Rafael and San Clemente

Paladar la Terraza
Santa Rosa #8

CubaVa
Julio Sanguily #320

Casa Italia
Calle San Ramón #11

El Edén
Calle Villa Lola #8-A at Avenida Monaco Sur

La Campana de Toledo
Plaza San Juan de Dios

La Isabela
Ignacio Agramonte, near Plaza de los Trabajadores and Casa Natal Ignacio Agramonte

Bodegón Don Cayetano
Calle Republica #79

Places of Interest

Plaza del Carmen
Town Main Square

Galería Marta Jiménez
General Gómez #274-B, between Lugareno and Masvidal

Plaza Juan de Dios
Plaza San Juan de Dios

Church of San Juan de Dios
Plaza San Juan de Dios

Shark Dive Center
Brisas Santa Lucia, Avenida Turística

Church of Nuestra Señora de la Merced
Plaza de los Trabajadores

Casa Natal del Mayor (Ignacio Agramonte)
Ignacio Agramonte #459

Centro Storico
Calle República

Catedral de Nuestra Señora de la Candelaria
Parque Agramonte

Teatro Principal
Padre Valencia #64

Church of La Soledad
República and Maceo Streets

Museo Provincial General Ignacio Agramonte
Avenida de los Mártires #2

Casino Campestre
On Carretera Central

Coco Beach
Coco Beach Recreation Park

Rancho King Tourist Farmz
On highway between Camaguey City and Santa Lucia Beach

Time to Say
Good-bye to Havana

FIDEL'S FINAL DAY

In February 2008, Cuban officials invited this guide's Editor to visit Cuba.

Fidel Castro had resigned for health reasons and his brother, Raúl, was taking over. Following is an account of what it was like to be Havana during Fidel's final day in office. This report was published by Pacific News Service in San Francisco, California, on February 29, 2008.

It is reprinted here because so many readers have asked what it was like to be in Havana when Fidel relinquished power to his brother, Raúl.

Fidel's Final Day

Havana, Cuba—On Jan. 8, 1959, Fidel Castro triumphantly arrived in Havana to the adulation of the joyful multitudes that lined the streets of the Cuban capital, welcoming the man who had liberated them from the hated dictatorship.

Fidel entered the swank Hilton Hotel, where Ernesto "Che" Guevara had taken over the mezzanine and second floor as the Revolution's headquarters. The Hilton's management also welcomed Fidel: the presidential suite on the 22nd floor was placed at his disposal. Euphoria was in evidence, and electricity was in the air as thousands of Cubans amassed across the street in Quijote Park (where the Coppelia ice cream parlor, made famous in the film *Strawberry and Chocolate*, is located), shouting "Viva Fidel!"

By time afternoon arrived, the first declarations were being made, as a government was being formed and officials throughout the government issued public declarations pledging their allegiance to the Revolution: Fidel Castro's first day in power thus began.

Fast-forward 49 years to Saturday, Feb. 23, 2008, the last full day of Fidel Castro's government.

The Hilton, with its stylish 1950s design, was, soon after Fidel checked out of the presidential suite, expropriated and rechristened the "Habana Libre." Photographs of Conrad Hilton's opening reception, two years before the revolution, still grace the mezzanine level, but, like an impoverished dowager dressed in a decades-old, threadbare gown, the hotel has the painful appearance of decades of neglect. The lights are turned low to hide the dirt, cracks and coats of cheap paint; the furnishings, haphazardly assembled from different rooms, are strewn about the lobby; doormen in coats with frayed sleeves man the doors. It is like walking into the bedroom of an elderly relative who lives alone, and has long been sick. It smells of mold and disinfectant in the humid air.

This reporter wanted to be there, at that hotel on the mezzanine level looking down on the lobby, to witness the last day of Fidel's rule as Cuba's leader.

The waitress at the bar was blissfully unaware of the historic meaning of the lobby where she served tourists drinks—rum and generic cola (no Coca-Cola available), beers and *mojitos*. "How interesting," she said, when informed that Fidel's administration had begun here, rolling her eyes. "Lord, give me patience."

The *mojito* she delivered had to be sent back; parsley had been substituted for mint—which is not abundant.

Tourists from Korea, Venezuela, Germany and Canada lingered about, under the watchful eyes of hotel security. Defeated workers mixed drinks, their sad expressions betraying the weariness of living in a perpetual revolution, and as dusk arrived, the sounds of birds in Quijote Park competed with the belching sounds the diesel buses made as they passed down the streets, could be heard.

It was clear that the hotel management had no plans to commemorate this historic day.

Outside the hotel, the same indifference prevailed. People walked by, with bored expressions, or in a hurry. Buses filled to overcapacity rolled by, blank expressions on the faces of the passengers, who avoided eye contact with each other. Tourists, dressed inappropriately, as if they were at the beach, consulted guidebooks to get their bearings. Police officers pretended to patrol the streets, but just marked time, hanging in small groups, talking. Only the children, like children the world over, smiled and played with each other.

The greatest excitement centered on the movie theater across the street, where *Rush Hour 3*, starring Jackie Chan and Chris Tucker, had finally arrived in Havana. "It's a stupid movie, but it's better than nothing," a black teenager said, standing arm in arm with his girlfriend. The line snaked down the sidewalk, and not one person was prepared to concede that Fidel's final day in office portended any change.

A few blocks away, the former American Embassy, now the U.S. Interests Section, was visible. An older gentleman, moonlighting as an unofficial taxi driver, expressed frustration as he drove there. "My wife and sister are sick, and I need to get 'convertibles' [hard currency pesos] to pay for their medicines. And I'm not well myself, driving all day, breathing this diesel exhaust."

When asked what it would take to fix things, the reply comes: "No way, this place is over. Havana is like Pompeii—future archaeologists are going to dig it all up and wonder what disaster struck here! But we know what calamity destroyed this place: Fidel."

Workers were busy raising Cuban flags on a field of flagpoles raised in front of the U.S. Interest Section—the Bush administration had ordered an LCD display running across the midsection of the office tower with headlines from the outside world, similar to the displays found in Times Square in New York. The Cubans retaliated by raising flagpoles designed to block the stream of uncensored headlines.

Across the street, along the Malecón, the broad seaside wall that hugs the city, young people sat in groups, listening to rap music in Spanish, drinking bootleg rum from open bottles, and talking softly. An old man, who claimed to have done heroic things during the revolution, was selling bags of popcorn for a peso, or four cents at the rate of exchange from pesos for Cubans and "convertible pesos" for imported consumer groups. "I have to sell 25 bags of popcorn to buy one beer," he said. "At my age, I'm doing this. The only consolation I have is the knowledge that when I die, I'm going straight to heaven—being in Cuba has been purgatory enough!"

A teenage couple looked out onto the Straits of Florida, the sea as calm as glass. "We make believe we're in the U.S, and we tell stories of what we would do," the boy said. "Wouldn't it be wonderful to go to a store and just buy anything?" the girl rhetorically asked. "I've seen pictures of shopping malls in Italian magazines. I know what the rest of the world has."

The peanut vendor looked on, amused. "Youth, they don't know we once had everything, too. The Manzana de Gómez was a beautiful shopping center, the envy of Latin America. There was once a real country here, but that was before there was Fidel."

Dusk had arrived, and the city was darkening. Many streets are without streetlights, and an eerie darkness consumes the capital. It was a quiet 15-minute stroll back to the lobby of the Habana Libre. Two fat tourists looked at the photographs on the mezzanine level, while a security guard stood in front of the bank of elevators, lest a Cuban dare attempt to accompany a foreigner into a hotel room.

Prostitution rules where Fidel first governed.

This was Fidel's final day in power, and there was a lingering sadness at the denouement of how it unfolded. Where once there was adulation and hope, now there was exhaustion and indifference.

This time the following day, Fidel's reign would be history, and no one gave a damn.

— *Reprinted from PacificNewsService.org*

34 WHY THE RAPPROCHEMENT?

For Raúl Castro, two funerals and a handshake.

When Barack Obama announced on December 17, 2014, that the U.S. and Cuba would reestablish diplomatic relations after more than half a century, the unanswered questions were: Why now? What changed?

It was clear that Obama had wanted to improve relations with Cuba—that was one of his campaign promises—but reality presented obstacles. Cuba demanded the U.S. return Guantánamo, and the U.S. insisted that opposition parties be legalized in Cuba.

This standoff did not prove an obstacle to moving forward—Guantánamo will remain occupied by the U.S. and no opposition parties are permitted in Cuba—but embassies have reopened.

To believe the *New York Times*, the road to reconciliation included a suicidal Jew imprisoned in Havana and a Cuban prisoner in California who wanted to get his wife pregnant through artificial insemination.* Perhaps one man trying to end his life and another trying to engender a new one played a role, but there was more to it than that.

We know what Barack Obama wanted. But what changed Raúl Castro's mind?

I have never had the opportunity to speak with Raúl Castro, but I decided to meet with two Cuban officials with knowledge of the rapprochement between Washington, D.C., and Havana. I had dinner with one at La Guarida restaurant and drinks with the other at the Capri Hotel. Their accounts are almost identical and speak to the fleeting nature of our lives.

Two Funerals and a Handshake

The answer to Raúl Castro's abrupt change of heart, surprisingly, lies in events that took place in 2013: *two funerals and a handshake.*

But first, a historical recap is in order. The Cuban Revolution has had, at its core, the goal of asserting Cuba's national sovereignty. Cuba was, for 400 years, a colony of Spain. Then it was a possession of the U.S. after the Spanish-American War ended in 1898. Fidel Castro's 1959 Revolution sought to sever Cuba's dependence on the U.S. and assert Cuban self-determination.

That goal has been frustrated. First, the U.S. refused to surrender Guantánamo to Cuba. Second, within a few years after coming to power, Cuba became a client state of another master: Moscow.

When the Soviet Union dissolved in December 1991, Cuba struggled to reinvent itself. The "Special Period," as it was called, required many sacrifices of all the Cuban people. Cubans, in fact, continue to endure material deprivation as a result of the end of Soviet subsidies.

Fidel Castro, out of desperation, looked to Venezuela's Hugo Chávez to save his faltering revolution. In 2001 Cuba and Venezuela entered into an economic agreement under which Venezuela supplied Cuba with 53,000 barrels of oil per day. Castro received an economic lifeline. Chávez cemented his ideological ties as a socialist before the world community.

252

Hopes of a prosperous future for Cuba, however, ended when Chávez died of cancer on March 3, 2013.

"Chávez's death affected everyone's thinking," a Cuban official said over dinner. "It meant that we were at the end of having economic help to keep going. With Chávez dead and the Soviet Union gone, only China was there, but Beijing demanded we follow their reforms."

In the months that followed Chávez's death, Raúl Castro, a Latin Hamlet, vacillated, thinking and rethinking his options: continue the path to perdition, adopt a Wild West capitalism like Beijing, or make peace with the United States.

That Obama had made it clear he was open to improving relations with Havana weighed heavily on Raúl Castro's mind.

"What Raúl wondered was if Obama was sincere," the Cuban official said.

This hesitation continued into the fall of 2013.

Then, Nelson Mandela died exactly nine months after Chávez: December 5.

World leaders assembled for a state funeral—one at which both Castro and Obama were present.

"Raúl was shaken by Mandela's death," another Cuban official said, over drinks at the Capri Hotel.

The flight from Havana to Johannesburg takes more than 15 hours.

An official familiar with Raúl Castro's flight to Nelson Mandela's memorial service said that the Cuban leader kept talking about Mandela's legacy. Raúl Castro marveled at how loved Mandela was and how his people held him in such high esteem.

This reflective sentiment set the tone for the Cuban delegation: somber and restrained.

"Would the world mourn Fidel and Raúl Castro as much as it mourned Nelson Mandela?" an official said everyone in the Cuban delegation kept thinking. (Fidel Castro was too ill to travel to South Africa; his public outings are limited.)

"Then, it happened," the Cuban official said at the Garida. "Obama came over and shook Raúl's hand [at the state funeral]."

The official marveled at the memory: "It was stunning. Obama was walking with an umbrella, and he neared the stand where Raúl was sitting next to [Brazilian president] Dilma Rousseff. He bounced up the steps and reached out to shake Raúl's hand and greet Dilma with a kiss. Raúl was shocked—and so were we."

For more than half a century, leaders hosting American presidents and Fidel Castro went out of their way to coordinate events so the sitting American president would never run into either Fidel or Raúl. This made for interesting diplomatic maneuvers, most notably when Ronald Reagan was on a visit to Mexico and, because of scheduling delays, almost ran into Fidel Castro.

In Johannesburg, however, Obama deliberately sought out the Cuban leader.

"On the flight back, that's all Raúl could talk about. 'It's time,' he said over and over again," the official reported.

The Cuban plane had not landed in Havana before overtures to make peace with the U.S. and reestablish diplomatic relations accelerated.

One year later, in December 2014, Obama announced at the White House that Cuba and the U.S. would reestablish diplomatic relations. Seven months after that, embassies in both capitals reopened after 54 years.

This is a first step, but the Cuban Revolution has paid a price in its efforts to assert that nation's sovereignty. The next step is for reconciliation within the Cuban family as the United States and Cuba move to a common future.

Rock star Bono performed at Nelson Mandela's memorial. And for Cuba and the United States, lyrics from one of U2's hits, resonate: Both have held the hands of the devil, but neither has found what they've been looking for.

*See "A Secretive Path to Raising U.S. Flag in Cuba," by Julie Hirschfeld Davis and Peter Baker, *New York Times*, August 13, 2015.

The Road from Perdition

January 2009: As he begins his first term, Barack Obama orders his staff to prepare a broad reassessment of U.S.–Cuba relations.

December 2009: Alan Gross is arrested in Havana and is accused of unlawfully bringing satellite and communications equipment to Cuba and espionage.

February 2013: Senator Patrick Leahy meets with Raúl Castro over the imprisonment of Alan Gross; Leahy meets Adriana Pérez, wife of Gerardo Hernández, a Cuban convicted of espionage and imprisoned in the U.S. Ms. Pérez asks Leahy's help in becoming pregnant by her husband. (Mr. Hernández is one of the "Cuban Five," a group of Cubans convicted in the U.S. of espionage.)

March 2013: Hugo Chávez dies of cancer, ending the last economic lifeline that had been thrown to Havana in the wake of the catastrophic failure of economic reforms implemented following the Special Period.

April 2013: In the wake of Chávez's death and the impending cutoff of Venezuelan subsidies to Cuba, Raúl Castro agrees to enter into discussions to reestablish diplomatic relations with the U.S. in secret negotiations.

July 2013: Negotiations between Cuba and the U.S. begin in Ottawa, Canada. Benjamin J. Rhodes and Ricardo Zúñiga negotiate for the Obama administration.

September 2013: Beijing demands economic reforms, along China's model, for a commitment of financial assistance to Havana to replace the uncertainty Chávez's death created; Raúl rejects this idea, signaling reconciliation with the U.S. as the only viable alternative left for Cuba.

December 2013: Nelson Mandela dies and at his state funeral Barack Obama walks over to shake hands with Raúl Castro, a stunning encounter that convinces Raúl Castro of American sincerity.

January 2014: Raúl Castro, reflecting on the worldwide outpouring of affection for Mandela, voices melancholy about how the death of his brother and himself would be greeted by the world; negotiations for reestablishing relations accelerate.

March 2014: At the suggestion of the U.S., Pope Francis intervenes, asking both Obama and Castro to move past historic animosities and reach a broad reconciliation.

April 2014: Adriana Pérez becomes pregnant through artificial insemination. U.S. Attorney General Eric Holder agrees to commute the sentences of the three remaining Cubans convicted of espionage, known as "The Five"; Gerardo Hernández, Ms. Pérez's husband, is included. This sets the stage for a prisoner exchange with Alan Gross.

July 2014: Alan Gross, unaware of negotiations to reestablish diplomatic relations, despairs and suggests to his lawyer that he is contemplating suicide.

September 2014: The U.S. presents the deal with Cuba to Pope Francis for his approval.

December 2014: Barack Obama announces the U.S. and Cuba will reestablish diplomatic relations. Alan Gross is released and returns to the U.S.; Gerardo Hernández, Antonio Guerrero, and Ramón Labañino are released from prison and return to Cuba. Officially, this is not a prisoner exchange; Rolando Sarraff Trujillo, a Cuban who worked for the CIA, is also released in exchange for the remaining Cuban Five; Gross is technically released on humanitarian grounds.

April 2015: Obama certifies that Cuba is no longer a state sponsor of terrorism.

May 2015: Cuba opens a bank account in the U.S. to handle official business.

July 2015: The U.S. and Cuba reopen embassies in each other's capitals.

August 2015: An exodus of Cubans fleeing Cuba accelerates; political crackdowns continue, with Cuban authorities targeting the Ladies in White.

September 2015: Pope Francis arrives in Havana on a visit. American Roberta S. Jacobson and Cuban Josefina Vidal begin the arduous task of subsequent negotiations on pending issues.

October 2015: Cubans begin to understand that, not unlike Puerto Rico, they have never been fully sovereign. They were first a Spanish colony, then a U.S. possession. Their nominal "independence" was characterized by economic domination by corporate America; the U.S. military occupied Guantánamo. The Revolution transformed Cuba into a client state of Moscow, and then a nation dependent on massive subsidies from Caracas. As Cuba begins to reconcile with the U.S., the lingering question is whether Cubans will be able, for the first time in their history, to be fully sovereign, or will become dependent on the U.S. once more.

Current Negotiations

In September 2015, the U.S. and Cuba began negotiations to continue the process of normalizing relations. Josefina Vidal, one of the most powerful women in Cuba, leads the Cuban delegation. Roberta S. Jacobson, Assistant Secretary of State for the Western hemisphere, heads the U.S. team.

While progress on simple things, such as allowing airlines to fly to each other's nations, immigration agreements, or regularizing postal services, are straight-forward, there are other issues that may take years, if not the death of both Fidel and Raúl Castro, to be resolved.

What Cuba Wants:
1. End of the U.S. embargo
2. End of the U.S. occupation of Guantánamo
3. Compensation for the economic damages inflicted by the embargo

What the U.S. Wants:

1. Reestablishment of the human rights of the Cuban people, including the legalization of political parties and free elections
2. Negotiations on compensation for claims against Cuba by U.S. citizens and corporations whose assets were nationalized by Cuba
3. Continued occupation of Guantánamo

Bear in mind that everything about these demands is complex. The U.S., for instance, wants Cuba to respect human rights—but it reserves the right to deny those same human rights in the only place in Cuba where the U.S. exercises jurisdiction, the Guantánamo Naval Base. Cuba, for its part, is not interested in discussing compensation for assets seized from U.S. citizens and corporations, although it entered into such an agreement with Spain to settle Spanish claims against Cuba.

THE FUTURE OF CUBA

Your presence in Cuba is part of Cuba's future.

Of the billions of people on this planet, fewer than 15 million are Cuban.

Cubans are few indeed. But they are a family that has been torn asunder by the Cuban Revolution. The divisions in the Cuban family, both as a nation and as blood relations, will remain until Cubans come to peace with the past and are able to build a future together. These divisions are more than political or ideological; they divide entire families. Fidel and Raúl Castro, for example, are estranged from their sister, Juanita, who lives in exile in Miami. Fidel and Raúl Castro's nephew, Mario Díaz-Balart, is a member of the U.S. House of Representatives who votes to tighten the embargo aginast Cuba.

Imagine if your nephew was a member of Congress and spent his time introducing legislation to make your life more difficult. Fidel's own mother, Lina Ruz, as pointed out, slapped him across the face. Alina Fernández, one of Fidel's daughters, fled Cuba using a fake passport and wearing a wig. She denounces her father on her radio show broadcast from Miami. Imagine if your kid had a radio show where you were denounced for being a murderous tyrant. This family is something out of a Greek tragedy.

The reestablishment of diplomatic relations between the U.S. and Cuba is the first step in Cuba's post-Castro future. Fidel and Raúl may be alive, but they are the past, not the future.

What does the future hold?

Reconciliation; history shows the way. There came a time in France, after all, when people began to admit that the use of Antoine Louis's invention — at the suggestion of Dr. Joseph-Ignace Guillotine — had been extreme. That's when everyone knew the Reign of Terror had run its course. There will come a time when Cubans begin to discuss honestly the evil unleashed by Fidel Castro — firing squads, seizing his fellow countrymen's livelihoods, and the forced exile of millions of his countrymen. When this happens, everyone will know that this present reign of terror will have concluded.

But it is up to the Cuban people, among themselves, to make peace with the Cuban Revolution. Those in Cuba who were born and have lived under this regime must come to peace with the truth that they have endured decades of needless material deprivation, unable to fulfill their dreams and aspirations. Those in exile must come to peace with the truth that their lives were interrupted, uprooted, and they were forced to flee their homeland, making lives for themselves in foreign countries, learning foreign customs and languages.

Cubans everywhere must come to peace with what could have been, the nostalgia for what was, and acceptance of the fate that has befallen their nation.

How will we know when they are moving ahead purposefully?

When Cubans begin to speak of coming together and speak honestly about what happened. It could take the form of a Truth Commission as other nations, like South Africa, have established. It could be more subtle, such as small changes in Cuba that reflect an acceptance of all that was lost in the frenzy of revolutionary zeal. In the same way, for example, that Germany marks the injustices committed against its Jewish citizens and the way the United States honors those killed on September 11, one concrete step would be to acknowledge that, amid all the festive tourists wandering throughout Old Havana, there is one site where thousands of Cubans were executed by firing squad in a capricious and unjust manner.

When there is a plaque listing all the men and women executed at La Cabaña, then you will know that, like the French who woke up from the nightmare of the Reign of Terror and came to their senses, the Cubans are putting the past behind him.

And in the spirit of helping the family of Cubans move away from a failed past, here is a list of those executed by firing squad whose surnames begin with the letter *A*. The entire list numbers more than 1,000 people who have been executed at this one location since January 1959.

When there is a tribute to memorialize these men and women, that will be evidence that Cubans no longer live in fear.

In Memoriam (Opening fragment)

Abreu González, Emilio
Abreu Villau, Enrique
Acosta Valdés, Benjamín
Acosta, Mateo
Aguiar Alonso, Abelardo
Aguila, Pedro
Aquino Limonta, Rafael
Aguirre, Juan
Aguirre Moya, German
Aguín, Roberto
Alayón, Pelayo
Alejo Fernández, Amador
Alemán Díaz, Alfredo
Alemán, Ariel
Álfaro Sierra, José Luis
Álfaro, Pedro
Alfonso Ibañez, Wilfredo
Almeida, Humberto
Almeida, Álfaro
Alonso Riquelmo, Mariano
Alonso Roche, Rodolfo
Álvarez Aballí, Dr. Juan Carlos
Álvarez de la Rosa, Carlos

Álvarez Álvarez, Roberto
Álvarez Bernal, Cruz
Álvarez Bocanegra, Amado
Álvarez Margolles, Manuel
Álvarez, Mario
Álvarez, Rafael Angel
Álvarez, Mario A.
Alvariña, Bienvenido
Alvaro, José L.
Amador Cruzata, Radamés
Amador Navarro, Ramón
Anaya, Secundino
Antunes, Héctor
Arias, Armando
Armengol, Arístides
Armentero Aruca, Segio
Armento Domínguez, Juan
Arroyo Maldonado, José
Arteaga, José María
Arteaga, María
Aspurus, Lázaro
Ávila, Ruperto

LEAVING CUBA

As you prepare to leave, keep in mind these words from one of José Martí's most famous poems . . .

Cultivo Una Rosa Blanca

Cultivo una rosa blanca
en junio como enero
para el amigo sincero
que me da su mano franca.
Y para el cruel que me arranca
el corazón con que vivo,
cardo ni ortiga cultivo;
cultivo la rosa blanca.

I cultivate a white rose
In July as in January
For the sincere friend
Who gives me his hand frankly
And for the cruel person who tears
Out the heart with which I live,
I cultivate neither nettles nor thorns:
I cultivate a white rose.

Appendix I – Suggested Reading

Would you like to learn more about Cuba?

Here is a list of suggested books to help bolster your knowledge and understanding of Cuba—and her history, people, and future. Please note that the description of each book is provided by the publisher.

Waiting for Snow in Havana: Confessions of a Cuban Boy
by Carlos Eire

"Have mercy on me, Lord, I am Cuban." In 1962, Carlos Eire was one of 14,000 children airlifted out of Havana—exiled from his family, his country, and his own childhood by Fidel Castro's revolution. This stunning memoir is a vibrant and evocative look at Latin America from a child's unforgettable experience.

Waiting for Snow in Havana is both an exorcism and an ode to a paradise lost. For the Cuba of Carlos's youth—with its lizards and turquoise seas and sun-drenched siestas—becomes an island of condemnation once a cigar-smoking guerrilla named Fidel Castro ousts President Batista on January 1, 1959. Suddenly the music in the streets sounds like gunfire. Christmas is made illegal, political dissent leads to imprisonment, and too many of Carlos's friends are leaving Cuba for a place as far away and unthinkable as the United States. Carlos will end up there, too, and fulfill his mother's dreams by becoming a modern American man—even if his soul remains in the country he left behind.

Narrated with the urgency of a confession, *Waiting for Snow in Havana* is a eulogy for a native land and a loving testament to the collective spirit of Cubans everywhere.

Havana: The Making of Cuban Culture
by Antoni Kapcia

This is the first sweeping account of Havana and its cultural history in English. The author introduces us to a marginal city with roots in the sixteenth century, taking us through the periods when it was a sugar boomtown, pulled between empires, a decadent metropolis, a site of both cultural revolution and relative stagnation during the development of the Revolution to its revival in the 1990s. Cosmopolitan playground and nationalist vanguard, Havana has developed its own original style while at the same time both reflecting and directing the complicated politics of the whole of Cuba. This book offers a concise guide to one of the most intriguing cities of the twenty-first century.

The Man Who Invented Fidel: Castro, Cuba, and Herbert L. Matthews of the New York Times
by Anthony DePalma

In 1957, Herbert L.Matthews of the *New York Times*, then considered one of the premiere foreign correspondents of his time, tracked down Fidel Castro in Cuba's Sierra Maestra mountains and returned with what was considered the scoop of the century. His heroic portrayal of Castro, who was then believed dead, had a powerful effect on American perceptions of Cuba, both in and out of the government, and profoundly influenced the fall of the Batista regime. When Castro emerged as a Soviet-backed dictator, Matthews became a scapegoat; his paper turned on him, his career foundered, and he was accused of betraying his country.

In this fascinating book, *New York Times* reporter DePalma investigates the Matthews case to reveal how it contains the story not just of one newspaperman but of an age, not just how Castro came to power but how America determines who its enemies are. He re-creates the atmosphere of revolutionary Cuba and Cold War America, and clarifies the facts of Castro's ascension and political evolution from the many myths that have sprung up around them. Through a dramatic, ironic, in ways tragic story, *The Man Who Invented Fidel* offers provocative insights into Cuban politics, the Cuban-American relationship, and the many difficult balancing acts of responsible journalism.

The Real Fidel Castro Paperback
by Leycester Coltman

The Real Fidel Castro is a first-hand account, and an authoritative biography, that provides a clear and dispassionate analysis of Castro, without the political rhetoric that typically accompanies any discussion of the man. The book describes the key events that shaped Castro's life from his political activism as a student, his years as a communist revolutionary and guerrilla fighter alongside Che Guevera, to his decades in power surviving the Cold War, assassination attempts, the missile crisis, and the collapse of the Soviet Union.

As British Ambassador to Cuba in the early nineties, a time when Cuba's economy contracted by a third, and many outside observers were anticipating the collapse of the Cuban government, Sir Leycester Coltman had privileged access to Castro, with regular contact and frequent discussions. These conversations at a critical juncture in Cuba's history provide a unique insight into the thoughts, personality, and motivations of the Cuban leader.

This Is Cuba: An Outlaw Culture Survives Paperback
by Ben Corbett

Beyond the throngs of tourists streaming through Central Havana's broad Prado Avenue, and outside the yoke of Castro's 43-year-old Revolutionary program, there exists a parallel Cuba - a separate evolution of a people struggling to survive. With personal stories that depict a people torn between following the directives of their government and finding a way to better their lot, journalist Ben Corbett gives us the daily life of many considered outlaws by Castro's regime.

But are they outlaws or rather ingenious survivors of what many Cubans consider to be a forty-year mistake, a tangle of contradictions that has resulted in a strange hybrid of American-style capitalism and a homegrown black market economy? At a time when Cuba walks precariously on the ledge between socialism and capitalism, *This Is Cuba* gets to the heart of this so-called outlaw culture, taking readers into the living rooms, rooftops, parks, and city streets to hear stories of frustration, hope, and survival.

Havana Nocturne: How the Mob Owned Cuba and Then Lost It to the Revolution
by T. J. English

To underworld kingpins Meyer Lansky and Charles "Lucky' Luciano, Cuba was the greatest hope for the future of American organized crime in the post-Prohibition years. In the 1950s, the Mob—with the corrupt, repressive government of brutal Cuban dictator Fulgencio Batista in its pocket—owned Havana's biggest luxury hotels and casinos, launching an unprecedented tourism boom complete with the most lavish entertainment, top-drawer celebrities, gorgeous women, and gambling galore.

But Mob dreams collided with those of Fidel Castro, Che Guevara, and others who would lead an uprising of the country's disenfranchised against Batista's hated government and its foreign partners—an epic cultural battle that bestselling author T. J. English captures here in all its sexy, decadent, ugly glory.

Bacardi and the Long Fight for Cuba: The Biography of a Cause
by Tom Gjelten

In this widely hailed book, NPR correspondent Tom Gjelten fuses the story of the Bacardi family and their famous rum business with Cuba's tumultuous experience over the last 150 years to produce a deeply entertaining historical narrative. The company Facundo Bacardi launched in Cuba in 1862 brought worldwide fame to the island, and in the decades that followed his Bacardi descendants participated in every aspect of Cuban life.

With his intimate account of their struggles and adventures across five generations, Gjelten brings to life the larger story of Cuba's fight for freedom, its tortured relationship with America, the rise of Fidel Castro, and the violent division of the Cuban nation.

Dreaming in Cuban Paperback

by Cristina García

"Remarkable . . . An intricate weaving of dramatic events with the supernatural and the cosmic … Evocative and lush . . . A rich and haunting narrative, an excellent new voice in contemporary fiction." *San Francisco Chronicle*.

Here is the dreamy and bittersweet story of a family divided by politics and geography by the Cuban revolution. It is the family story of Celia del Pino, and her husband, daughter and grandchildren, from the mid-1930s to 1980. Celia's story mirrors the magical realism of Cuba itself, a country of beauty and poverty, idealism and corruption. *Dreaming in Cuban* presents a unique vision and a haunting lamentation for a past that might have been.

Havana: Autobiography of a City

by Alfredo José Estrada

Havana: Autobiography of a City takes readers from the Plaza de Armas, the tree-lined square where Havana was founded by conquistadors in 1519, to the Malecón, the elegant boulevard along the shore where Fidel Castro rode a Russian tank in triumph. Estrada portrays the adventurers and dreamers who left their mark on Havana, including José Martí, martyr for Cuban independence; and Ernest Hemingway, the most American of writers who became an unabashed Habanero. The book is a deeply personal account of a love affair with a city, as well as an entertaining portrait of a place not easily forgotten.

Cuba Confidential: Love and Vengeance in Miami and Havana

by Ann Louise Bardach

From America's number one Cuba reporter, PEN award–winning investigative journalist Ann Louise Bardach, comes the big book on Cuba we've all been waiting for. An incisive and spirited portrait of the twentieth century's wiliest political survivor and his fiefdom, *Cuba Confidential* is the gripping story of the shattered families and warring personalities that lie at the heart of the forty-three-year standoff between Miami and Havana. Famous to many Americans for her cover stories and media appearances, Ann Louise Bardach has been covering Cuba for a decade. She's talked to the crooks, spooks and politicians who have made history, and to their hired assassins and confidants.

Based on exclusive interviews with Fidel Castro, his sister Juanita, his former brother-in-law Rafael Díaz-Balart, the family of Elián González, the friends and family of the legendary American fugitive Robert Vesco, the intrepid terrorist Luis Posada Carriles, and the inner circles of Jeb Bush and the late exile leader Jorge Mas Canosa, *Cuba Confidential* exposes the hardball take-no-prisoners tactics of the Cuban exile leadership, and its manipulation and exploitation by ten American presidents.

Bardach homes in on Fidel Castro and his cronies, taking us closer than we've ever been—and on the militant exiles who have devoted their lives, with CIA connivance, to trying to eliminate him. From Calle Ocho to Juan Miguel González's kitchen table in Cárdenas, from Guantánamo Bay to Union City to Washington, D.C., Ann Louise Bardach serves up an unforgettable portrait of Cuba and its exiles.

Cuba Diaries: An American Housewife in Havana
by Isadora Tattlin

Isadora Tattlin was accustomed to relocating often for her husband's work. But when he accepted a post in Cuba in the early 1990s, she resolved to keep a detailed diary of her time there, recording her daily experiences as a wife, mother, and foreigner in a land of contraband. The result is a striking, rare glimpse into a tiny country of enormous splendor and squalor. Though the Tattlins are provided with a well-staffed Havana mansion, the store shelves are bare.

On the streets, beggars plead for soap, not coins. A vet with few real medical supplies operates on a carved mahogany coffee table in a Louis XIV–style drawing room. The people adore festivity, but Christmas trees are banned. And when Isadora hosts a dinner party whose guest list includes Fidel Castro himself, she observes the ultimate contradiction at the very heart of Cuba. Vividly capturing Cuba's simultaneously appalling and enchanting essence, *Cuba Diaries* casts an irresistible spell and lifts the enigma of an island that is trapped in time, but not in spirit.

The Other Side of Paradise: Life in the New Cuba
by Julia Cooke

Change looms in Havana, Cuba's capital, a city electric with uncertainty yet cloaked in cliché, 90 miles from U.S. shores and off-limits to most Americans. Journalist Julia Cooke, who lived there at intervals over a period of five years, discovered a dynamic scene: baby-faced anarchists with Mohawks gelled with laundry soap, whiskey-drinking children of the elite, Santería trainees, pregnant prostitutes, university graduates planning to leave for the first country that will give them a visa.

This last generation of Cubans raised under Fidel Castro animate life in a waning era of political stagnation as the rest of the world beckons: waiting out storms at rummy hurricane parties and attending raucous drag cabarets, planning ascendant music careers and black-market business ventures, trying to reconcile the undefined future with the urgent today. Eye-opening and politically prescient, *The Other Side of Paradise* offers a deep new understanding of a place that has so confounded and intrigued us.

The Cuba Reader: History, Culture, Politics (The Latin America Readers)

by Aviva Chomsky (Editor), Barry Carr (Editor), Pamela Maria Smorkaloff (Editor)

Cuba is often perceived in starkly black and white terms—either as the site of one of Latin America's most successful revolutions or as the bastion of the world's last communist regime. *The Cuba Reader* multiplies perspectives on the nation many times over, presenting more than one hundred selections about Cuba's history, culture, and politics.

Beginning with the first written account of the island, penned by Christopher Columbus in 1492, the selections assembled here track Cuban history from the colonial period through the ascendancy of Fidel Castro to the present.

The Cuba Reader combines songs, paintings, photographs, poems, short stories, speeches, cartoons, government reports and proclamations, and pieces by historians, journalists, and others. Most of these are by Cubans, and many appear for the first time in English. The writings and speeches of José Martí, Fernando Ortiz, Fidel Castro, Alejo Carpentier, Che Guevera, and Reinaldo Arenas appear alongside the testimonies of slaves, prostitutes, doctors, travelers, and activists. Some selections examine health, education, Catholicism, and santería; others celebrate Cuba's vibrant dance, music, film, and literary cultures. The pieces are grouped into chronological sections. Each section and individual selection is preceded by a brief introduction by the editors.

The volume presents a number of pieces about twentieth-century Cuba, including the events leading up to and following Castro's January 1959 announcement of revolution. It provides a look at Cuba in relation to the rest of the world: the effect of its revolution on Latin America and the Caribbean, its alliance with the Soviet Union from the 1960s until the collapse of the Soviet bloc in 1989, and its tumultuous relationship with the United States. *The Cuba Reader* also describes life in the *período especial* following the cutoff of Soviet aid and the tightening of the U.S. embargo.

For students, travelers, and all those who want to know more about the island nation just ninety miles south of Florida, *The Cuba Reader* is an invaluable introduction.

Havana Revisited: An Architectural Heritage

by Cathryn Griffith

Interpreting the present in light of the past, eleven renowned architects, historians, scholars, preservationists, and urban planners in Cuba and the United States provide a rigorous examination of Havana old and new that provokes exploration of the ways we look at all cities. These authoritative policy makers and thinkers raise issues of how the most important city in Spanish colonial America developed and changed over several centuries and the extent to which it is being restored and preserved today.

More than 350 illustrations juxtapose historical colored postcard images of Havana with recent digital color photographs of the same views. The imagery, based on years of exhaustive research and investigation, draws from Cathryn Griffith's collection of more than 600 postcards of Havana from

1900 to 1930, over 3,000 photographs made there during multiple trips since April 2003, and extensive interviews with experts in Havana and the United States.

The Havana Guide: Modern Architecture 1925–1965
by Eduardo Luis Rodríguez

While Havana's colonial mansions have recently received worldwide attention, the immense wealth of modern architecture in Cuba has long been neglected. The first half of the twentieth century was a culturally rich era for Cuba, a time in which the architects of the Modern Movement sought to define an identity for this Caribbean nation. However, within a few years after the revolution of 1959, design ideology became allied with the mass-production aesthetic promoted by the Soviets, and many Cuban architects fled to seek creative and political freedom abroad.

The Havana Guide is the first to recognize the enormous importance of Cuba's modern architecture. It features over 200 structures, including hotels, churches, theaters, social clubs, and private residences. Street maps for all neighborhoods as well as archival and contemporary photographs supplement the texts. Also included is a history of modern architecture in Cuba. This is an essential source book of modern architecture for travelers and architects alike.

Havana: History and Architecture of a Romantic City
by Maria Luisa Lobo Montalvo

Havana, the legendary capital of Cuba, bears the traces of every stage of the island's rich history, from its indigenous traditions to the introduction of European culture in the late fifteenth century to the development of the unique amalgam of these influences that is unmistakably Cuban.

In this exquisite volume, author María Luisa Lobo Montalvo presents the architecture and history of Havana—part of which has been declared a UNESCO World Heritage Site—in an accessible and engaging text and specially commissioned color photographs. Among the structures featured are the famed great forts such as Castillo del Morro and Castillo de la Punta, the city's oldest extant structures; an array of houses, from all periods of Havana's history and in all styles, simultaneously offering architectural and cultural history; and the great churches, including the Church of La Merced and the great baroque Havana Cathedral, and institutional structures, such as the magnificent Palace of the Captains General, showing the public face of Havana at its most resplendent.

Havana Deco
by Alejandro G. Alonso, Pedro Contreras, Martino Fagiuoli

An unparalleled tour of the Art Deco-style architecture, interiors, decoration, and art objects of Havana, this colorful book shows the work of Cuban artists, open to the winds of change and to outside influences, who filtered the movement born in Paris through the dazzling beauty of Caribbean nature and made the art their own.

Exteriors and interior spaces, the graphic artists who spearheaded Art Deco's popularity, monumental sculpture, and the contributions of painters are explored here in rich detail. 300 color photographs.

Adios, Havana: A Memoir
by Andrew J. Rodríguez

Havana . . . lilting rumbas, café con leche, sultry sea breezes. Sparkling white beaches by day, scintillating nightclubs after dark. This sophisticated, international capital was the crown jewel of an island paradise-until the idealism that fed the Cuban Revolution yielded a nightmare of soul-crushing dictatorship. Adios, Havana is a true account of romance and peril, adventure and patriotism. Fueled by love-love of family, of country, and of each other-a young couple must face the most wrenching of choices: remain in the country they cherish, lose the wealth and position their families strove for generations to attain, and watch their children grow up impoverished under a terrifying regime; or risk escaping with no money or possessions and leave behind all they have ever known to begin a new life in a strange land.

A legacy to future generations, this memoir is intended to remind readers of the fragility of freedom . . . to describe the disintegration of a prosperous civilized society and offer counsel on how to prevent a similar catastrophe from happening in America . . . and to show how and why penniless refugees flourish in the land of the free-why anyone who resists oppression would be driven to tell his beloved homeland, Adios.

The Pride of Havana: A History of Cuban Baseball
by Roberto González Echevarría

From the first amateur leagues of the 1860s to the exploits of Livan and Orlando "El Duque" Hernández, here is the definitive history of baseball in Cuba. Roberto Gon-zález Echevarría expertly traces the arc of the game, intertwining its heroes and their stories with the politics, music, dance, and literature of the Cuban people. What emerges is more than a story of balls and strikes, but a richly detailed history of Cuba told from the unique cultural perch of the baseball diamond.

Filling a void created by Cuba's rejection of bullfighting and Spanish hegemony, baseball quickly became a crucial stitch in the complex social fabric of the island. By the early 1940s Cuba had become major conduit in spreading the game throughout Latin America, and a proving ground for some of the greatest talent in all of baseball, where white major leaguers and Negro League players from the U.S. all competed on the same fields with the cream of Latin talent. Indeed, readers will be introduced to several black ballplayers of Afro-Cuban descent who played in the Major Leagues before Jackie Robinson broke the color barrier once and for all.

Often dramatic, and always culturally resonant, González Echevarría's narrative expertly lays open the paradox of fierce Cuban independence from the U.S. with Cuba's love for our national pastime. It shows how Fidel Castro cannily associated himself with the sport for patriotic p.r.—and reveals that his supposed baseball talent is purely mythical. Based on extensive primary research and a wealth of interviews, the colorful, often dramatic anecdotes and stories in this distinguished book comprise the most comprehensive history of Cuban baseball yet published and ultimately adds a vital lost chapter to the history of baseball in the U.S.

The Duke of Havana: Baseball, Cuba, and the Search for the American Dream
by Steve Fainaru, Ray Sánchez

In 1998, a mysterious right-handed pitcher emerged from the ashes of the Cold War and helped lead the New York Yankees to a World Championship. His origins and even his age were uncertain. His name was Orlando El Duque Hernández. He was a fallen hero of Fidel Castro's socialist revolution.

The chronicle of El Duque's triumph is at once a window into the slow death of Cuban socialism and one of the most remarkable sports stories of all time. Once hailed as a paragon of Castro's revolution, the finest pitcher in modern Cuban history was banned from baseball for life for allegedly plotting to defect. Instead of accepting his punishment, he fearlessly fought back, defying the Communist party authorities, vowing to pitch again, and ultimately fleeing his country in the bowels of a thirty-foot fishing boat.

Here, for the first time and in astonishing detail, the secrets behind El Duque's persecution and escape are revealed. Moving from the crumbling streets of post Cold War Havana to the polarized world of exile Miami, from the deadly Florida Straits to the hallowed grounds of Yankee Stadium, it is a story of cloak-and-dagger adventure, audacious secret plots, the pull of big money, and the historic collision of ideologies.

Present throughout are the larger-than-life characters who converged at this bizarre intersection of baseball and politics: El Duque himself, Fidel Castro, the Miami sports agent Joe Cubas, the late John Cardinal O'Connor along with scouts, smugglers, and the Cuban ballplayers who gave up their lives as tools of socialism to test the free market and chase their major-league dreams. Reported in the United States and Cuba by two award-winning journalists who became part of the story they were covering, The Duke of Havana is a riveting saga of sports, politics, liberation, and greed.

Eating Cuban: 120 Authentic Recipes from the Streets of Havana to American Shores
by Beverly Cox, Martin Jacobs

To "eat Cuban" is to savor a deliciously complex culinary culture. Spanish, Native American, African, Chinese, and French traditions have all contributed to Cuban cooking, producing a distinctive Caribbean cuisine as richly chorded as the island's music. Beverly Cox and Martin Jacobs's itinerary takes them from the barrio, *paladars* (private restaurants), and chic nightspots of Havana to the eateries of Florida's emigré communities. From their journeys, they've gathered more than 120 recipes that comprehensively document Cuban cooking's diversity, from the black bean soup found on any Cuban table, to the empanadas sold by Havana's street vendors, to the grilled sandwiches that are a mainstay of Miami's Calle Ocho, to the innovative dishes devised by chefs at top Cuban restaurants.

Gorgeously illustrated with Jacobs's photographs—many shot on the authors' travels through Cuba—*Eating Cuban* highlights Cuban food's historical roots, the classic Creole dishes that evolved from these disparate cultural influences, current trends in Cuban cooking, street foods and on-the-go snacks, and quintessential Cuban beverages from café Cubano to the mojito. A valuable resource list helps American cooks locate the required ingredients, and a restaurant directory points the way to the very best in Cuban cuisine—in Cuba and the U.S.

Havana Salsa: Stories and Recipes
by Viviana Carballo

With more than seventy mouthwatering recipes throughout, *Havana Salsa* is the vibrant memoir of Viviana Carballo and her extraordinary childhood growing up in Cuba. A collection of stories about her large, extended family—an eccentric group who conducted their lives against the extraordinary backdrop of Havana—Carballo recalls the 1940s and 1950s when Havana was a nonstop party, and food and music defined the culture, until Fidel Castro took power in 1959, and she was forced to leave her beloved country.

With each delightful family memory, Carballo showcases the food of her culture and a delectable recipe, beginning with her childhood in the forties (calabaza fritters, sweet plantain tortillas, and oxtail stew), through the sensual fifties (roast shoulder of lamb, Cuban bouillabaisse), and then the first eighteen months of Castro's revolution (mango pie, tamal en cazuela, and papas con chorizo). *Havana Salsa* tells the history of Carballo's Havana as only she can—through the intimate and unifying experience of food, family, and friends.

Habanos: The Story of the Havana Cigar
by Nancy Stout

Throughout the history of the cigar, the *habano* has been unequivocally considered the pinnacle of smoking pleasure. This unparalleled quality of the Havana cigar has bound the idea of Cuba with its most coveted export, and has held the imaginations of *aficionados* around the world for 500 years. By way of explaining the enduring phenomenon known as the *habano*, author and photographer Nancy Stout journeys deep into the history and culture of a nation, beginning in the beautiful and often enigmatic capital of Havana, then striking out to one of the great plantations of the *Vuelta Abajo*, where the tobacco's delicate leaves grow under protective canopies, and to an agricultural collective in the *Vuelta Arriba*, where *tobaco del sol* thrives under Cuba's brilliant sun.

Along the way she introduces us to the doctrinaire *jefe* of the Antonio Briones Montoto collective farm; a master grower whose family has been cultivating tobacco for more than 150 years; and a legendary cigar roller who gives a transfixing lesson in the art of rolling the perfect cigar. The pursuit of the story of the Havana cigar extends into time as well as space. Included is a thorough history of Cuban tobacco cultivation, beginning with Columbus's first voyage to the West Indies and chronicling Cuba's legacy of exploration, conquest, and struggle for economic and political independence.

The Havana Cigar: Cuba's Finest
by Charles Del Todesco

It appears the cigar has arrived. Long relegated to boardroom or back room card table, the cigar has emerged into broad daylight, attaining mass appeal while holding on to its macho mystique. And amid the available (or not so available) assortment of cigars, the Havana stands head and shoulders above the rest. Grown on patches of land at the western tip of Cuba, cured, and rolled following centuries-old traditions, for decades illegal in the United States, it has a flavor—and a cachet—all its own.

After two years in Cuba researching the production of the cigar, Charles Del Todesco has pulled together a remarkable two-part testament to this legendary status symbol. In part one he reviews the hollowed history of cigars in Cuba, then describes in detail the processes involved in creating them. The color photographs that accompany his cogent text reveal the beauty of the land and the hands and faces of the craftsmen and women behind each new Havana.

Part two is an invaluable cigar reference, featuring a catalogue raisonne that provides a handsome portfolio of all Havana cigars currently available, shown actual size. An ideal introduction for the cigar neophyte as well as a superb guide for the experienced smoker, The Havana Cigar is, like its subject, without peer.

Che's Chevrolet, Fidel's Oldsmobile: On the Road in Cuba
by Richard Schweid

Vintage U.S.-made cars on the streets of Havana provide a common representation of Cuba. Journalist Richard Schweid, who traveled throughout the island to research the story of motor vehicles in Cuba today and yesterday, gets behind the wheel and behind the stereotype in this colorful chronicle of cars, buses, and trucks. In his captivating, sometimes gritty, voice, Schweid blends previously untapped historical sources with his personal experiences, spinning a car-centered history of life on the island over the past century. Packard, Studebaker, Edsel, De Soto: cars long extinct in the United States can be seen at work every day on Cuba's streets.

Havana and Santiago de Cuba today are home to some 60,000 North American cars, all dating back to at least 1959, the year the Cuban Revolution prevailed. Though hardly a new part has arrived in Cuba since 1960, the cars are still on the road, held together with mechanical ingenuity and willpower. Visiting car mechanics, tracking down records in dusty archives, and talking with car-crazy Cubans of all types, Schweid juxtaposes historic moments (Fidel Castro riding to the Bay of Pigs in an Oldsmobile) with the quotidian (a weary mother's two-cent bus ride home after a long day) and composes a rich, engaging picture of the Cuban people and their history.

The narrative is complemented by fifty-two historic black-and-white photographs and eight color photographs by contemporary Cuban photographer Adalberto Roque

Havana Dreams: A Story of a Cuban Family
by Wendy Gimbel

A fascinating, powerfully evocative story of four generations of Cuban women, through whose lives the author illuminates a vivid picture—both personal and historical—of Cuba in our century. "When I want to read a culture," writes Wendy Gimbel in her prologue, "I listen to stories about families, sensing in their contours the substance of larger mysteries." And certainly in the Revuelta family she has found a source of both mystery and revelation.

At its center is Naty: born in 1925, educated in the United States, a socialite during the Batista era, who after marriage to a prominent doctor and the birth of a daughter became intoxicated with Castro and his revolution (here, published for the first time, are the letters they exchanged while he was in jail).

Though her husband and daughter immigrated to the United States after Castro's victory, Naty remained in Cuba to raise her second child, Castro's unacknowledged daughter, only to be ultimately confronted by his dismissive, withering judgment: "Naty missed the train." Her two daughters, one of whom settles well into life in America, while the other never recovers from her father's intransigent repudiation of her; her granddaughter, who Naty desperately believes will return to Cuba when—not if—Castro is removed from the island; and her mother, an unregenerate reactionary: these are the lives that complete this extraordinary story. Each of the women is irrevocably marked with a part of the island's terrible and poignant tale, and Wendy Gimbel has created a rich and intense narrative of their lives and times.

Havana Dreams leaves us with an indelible impression of familial obligation and illicit love; of the heady but doomed romanticism of revolution; and of the profound consequences of Cuba's contemporary history for the ordinary and most intimate lives of its people.

Queens of Havana: The Amazing Adventures of Anacaona, Cuba's Legendary All-Girl Dance Band
by Alicia Castro, Ingrid Kummels

The 1930s saw Havana undergoing a seismic cultural renaissance. At night in the *aires libres* (open air cafes), tourists and foreign investors rubbed shoulders with the likes of Ernest Hemingway as they sipped cocktails, cavorted with Cuban beauties, and listened to suggestive melodies from Havana's unmatched musical community. It was rare for women to attend, and unheard of for them to perform. But when greengrocer Matias Castro, father of thirteen, goes bankrupt, his eldest daughter has the idea of starting an all-girl band with her sisters, an outrageous idea in macho Cuba, but a surefire money maker.

Every evening, as the rum began to flow, Anacaona took to the stage to let rip, jazz, mambo, rumba, and cha-cha their infectious rhythms, cheeky lyrics, and sheer sex appeal conquer their audiences' hearts. In this evocative memoir, saxophonist Alicia Castro, now in her eighties, looks back on the Havana of yesterday and the dazzling career of the dance band, from concerts in Paris and New York, to appearances with Dizzy Gillespie, Celia Cruz, Duke Ellington, and Cab Calloway. Spirited and conversational, *Queens of Havana* is a touching piece of hidden history guaranteed to set your heart racing and get your toes tapping!

Tropicana Nights: The Life and Times of the Legendary Cuban Nightclub
by Rosa Lowinger, Ofelia Fox

It was to Havana what the Moulin Rouge was to Paris or the Blue Note to New York. The brightest jewel in 1950s Cuban nightlife, Tropicana was a "paradise under the stars" where you could gamble, hear the finest mambo and jazz musicians, and ogle the extravagantly risqué floorshows. Nat "King" Cole played Tropicana; so did Josephine Baker. Americans-celebrities and suburbanites both-were drawn to its kinetic sensuality and tropical setting. And Tropicana remained a uniquely Cuban institution; unlike most Havana nightclubs, it operated free from the American mob's control. Journalist Rosa Lowinger and Ofelia Fox, widow of Tropicana's last owner, vividly portray the cultural richness and roiling social problems of pre-Revolutionary Cuba and take the reader on an intimate insider's tour of one of the world's most glamorous venues at its most brilliant moment.

Telex from Cuba
by Rachel Kushner

From the National Book Award Finalist and *New York Times* bestselling author of *The Flamethrowers*, an astonishingly wise, ambitious, and riveting novel set in the American community in Cuba during the years leading up to Castro's revolution—a place that was a paradise for a time and for a few. The first novel to tell the story of the Americans who were driven out in 1958, this is a masterful debut with a unique and necessary lens into US-Cuba relations. Young Everly Lederer and K.C. Stites come of age in Oriente Province, where the Americans tend their own fiefdom—three hundred thousand acres of United Fruit Company sugarcane that surround their gated enclave. If the rural tropics are a child's dream world, Everly and K.C. nevertheless have keen eyes for the indulgences and betrayals of the grown-ups around them—the mordant drinking and illicit loves, the race hierarchies and violence.

In Havana, a thousand kilometers and a world away from the American colony, a cabaret dancer meets a French agitator named Christian de La Mazière, whose seductive demeanor can't mask his

272

shameful past. Together they become enmeshed in the brewing political underground. When Fidel and Raúl Castro lead a revolt from the mountains above the cane plantation, torching the sugar and kidnapping a boat full of "yanqui" revelers, K.C. and Everly begin to discover the brutality that keeps the colony humming. Though their parents remain blissfully untouched by the forces of history, the children hear the whispers of what is to come.

The Man Who Loved Dogs
by Leonardo Padura

A gripping novel about the assassination of Leon Trotsky in Mexico City in 1940

In *The Man Who Loved Dogs*, Leonardo Padura brings a noir sensibility to one of the most fascinating and complex political narratives of the past hundred years: the assassination of Leon Trotsky by Ramón Mercader. The story revolves around Iván Cárdenas Maturell, who in his youth was the great hope of modern Cuban literature--until he dared to write a story that was deemed counterrevolutionary. When we meet him years later in Havana, Iván is a loser: a humbled and defeated man with a quiet, unremarkable life who earns his modest living as a proofreader at a veterinary magazine. One afternoon, he meets a mysterious foreigner in the company of two Russian wolfhounds. This is "the man who loved dogs," and as the pair grow closer, Iván begins to understand that his new friend is hiding a terrible secret. Moving seamlessly between Iván's life in Cuba, Ramón's early years in Spain and France, and Trotsky's long years of exile, *The Man Who Loved Dogs* is Padura's most ambitious and brilliantly executed novel yet. This is a story about political ideals tested and characters broken, a multilayered epic that effortlessly weaves together three different plot threads-- Trotsky in exile, Ramón in pursuit, Iván in frustrated stasis--to bring emotional truth to historical fact. A novel whose reach is matched only by its astonishing successes on the page, *The Man Who Loved Dogs* lays bare the human cost

The Sugar King of Havana: The Rise and Fall of Julio Lobo, Cuba's Last Tycoon
by John Paul Rathbone

The son of a Cuban exile recounts the remarkable and contradictory life of famed sugar baron Julio Lobo, the richest man in prerevolutionary Cuba and the last of the island's *haute bourgeoisie*.

Fifty years after the Cuban revolution, the legendary wealth of the sugar magnate Julio Lobo remains emblematic of a certain way of life that came to an abrupt end when Fidel Castro marched into Havana. Known in his day as the King of Sugar, Lobo was for decades the most powerful force in the world sugar market, controlling vast swathes of the island's sugar interests. Born in 1898, the year of Cuba's independence, Lobo's extraordinary life mirrors, in almost lurid technicolor, the many rises and final fall of the troubled Cuban republic.

The details of Lobo's life are fit for Hollywood. He twice cornered the international sugar market and had the largest collection of Napoleonica outside of France, including the emperor's back teeth and death mask. He once faced a firing squad only to be pardoned at the last moment, and later survived a gangland shooting. He courted movie stars from Bette Davis to Joan Fontaine and filled the swimming pool at his sprawling estate with perfume when Esther Williams came to visit. As Rathbone observes, such are the legends of which revolutions are made, and later justified.

But Lobo was also a progressive and a philanthropist, and his genius was so widely acknowledged that Che Guevara personally offered him the position of minister of sugar in the Communist regime. When Lobo declined-knowing that their worldviews could never be compatible-his properties were nationalized, most of his fortune vanished overnight, he left the island, never to return to his beloved Cuba.

Financial Times journalist John Paul Rathbone has been fascinated by this intoxicating, whirligig, and contradictory prerevolutionary period his entire life. His mother was also a member of Havana's storied haute bourgeoisie and a friend of Lobo's daughters. Woven into Lobo's tale is her family's experience of republic, revolution, and exile, as well as the author's own struggle to come to grips with Cuba's, and his family's, turbulent history. Prodigiously researched and imaginatively written, *The Sugar King of Havana* is a captivating portrait of the glittering end of an era, but also of a more hopeful Cuban past, one that might even provide a window into the island's future.

Paradiso
by José Lima

In the wake of his father's premature death, José Cemi comes of age in a turn of the century Cuba described in the Washington Post as "an island paradise where magic and philosophy twist the lives of the old Cuban bourgeoisie into extravagant wonderful shapes."

Dancing with Cuba
by Alma Guillermoprieto

In 1970 a young dancer named Alma Guillermoprieto left New York to take a job teaching at Cuba's National School of Dance. For six months, she worked in mirrorless studios (it was considered more revolutionary); her poorly trained but ardent students worked without them but dreamt of greatness. Yet in the midst of chronic shortages and revolutionary upheaval, Guillermoprieto found in Cuba a people whose sense of purpose touched her forever. In this electrifying memoir, Guillermoprieto— now an award-winning journalist and arguably one of our finest writers on Latin America—resurrects a time when dancers and revolutionaries seemed to occupy the same historical stage and even a floor exercise could be a profoundly political act. Exuberant and elegiac, tender and unsparing, *Dancing with Cuba* is a triumph of memory and feeling.

Cobra and Maitreya: Two Novels
by Severo Sarduy

The late Severo Sarduy was one of the most outrageous and baroque of the Latin American Boom writers of the sixties and seventies, and here bound back to back are his two finest creations. *Cobra* (1972) recounts the tale of a transvestite named Cobra, star of the Lyrical Theater of the Dolls, whose obsession is to transform his/her body. She is assisted in her metamorphosis by the Madam and Pup, Cobra's dwarfish double. They too change shape, through the violent ceremonies of a motorcycle gang, into a sect of Tibetan lamas seeking to revive Tantric Buddhism.

Maitreya (1978) continues the theme of metamorphosis, this time in the person of Luis Leng, a humble Cuban-Chinese cook, who becomes a reincarnation of Buddha. Through Leng, Sarduy traces the metamorphosis of two hitherto incomparable societies, Tibet at the moment of the Chinese invasion, and Cuba at the moment of revolution. Transgressing genres and genders, reveling in literal and figurative transvestism, these two novels are among the most daring achievements of postmodern Latin American fiction.

Explosion in a Cathedral
by Alejo Carpentier

A swashbuckling tale set in the Caribbean world at the time of the French revolution, Explosion in a Cathedral focuses on Victor Hugues, a historical figure who led the naval assault to take back the island of Guadeloupe from the English at the beginning of the nineteenth century. In Carpentier's telling, this piratical figure walks into the lives of the wealthy orphans Esteban and Sofia and casts them abruptly into the midst of the immense changes sweeping the world outside their Havana mansion.

Three Trapped Tigers
by Guillermo Cabrera Infante

Three Trapped Tigers is one of the most playful books to reach the U.S. from Cuba. Filled with puns, wordplay, lists upon lists, and Sternean typography—such as the section entitled "Some Revelations," which consists of several blank pages -- this novel has been praised as a more modern, sexier, funnier, Cuban Ulysses. Centering on the recollections of a man separated from both his country and his youth, Cabrera Infante creates an enchanting vision of life and the many colorful characters found in steamy Havana's pre-Castro cabaret society.

Che Guevara: A Revolutionary Life
by Jon Lee Anderson

Acclaimed around the world and a national best-seller, this is the definitive work on Che Guevara, the dashing rebel whose epic dream was to end poverty and injustice in Latin America and the developing world through armed revolution. Jon Lee Anderson's biography traces Che's extraordinary life, from his comfortable Argentine upbringing to the battlefields of the Cuban revolution, from the halls of power in Castro's government to his failed campaign in the Congo and assassination in the Bolivian jungle. Anderson has had unprecedented access to the personal archives maintained by Guevara's widow and carefully guarded Cuban government documents. He has conducted extensive interviews with Che's comrades—some of whom speak here for the first time—and with the CIA men and Bolivian officers who hunted him down. Anderson broke the story of where Guevara's body was buried, which led to the exhumation and state burial of the bones. Many of the details of Che's life have long been cloaked in secrecy and intrigue. Meticulously researched and full of exclusive information, Che Guevara illuminates as never before this mythic figure that embodied the high-water mark of revolutionary communism as a force in history.

APPENDIX II – THE LETTERS EXCHANGED BETWEEN BARACK OBAMA AND RAÚL CASTRO

These are the letters that Barack Obama and Raúl Castro sent each other.

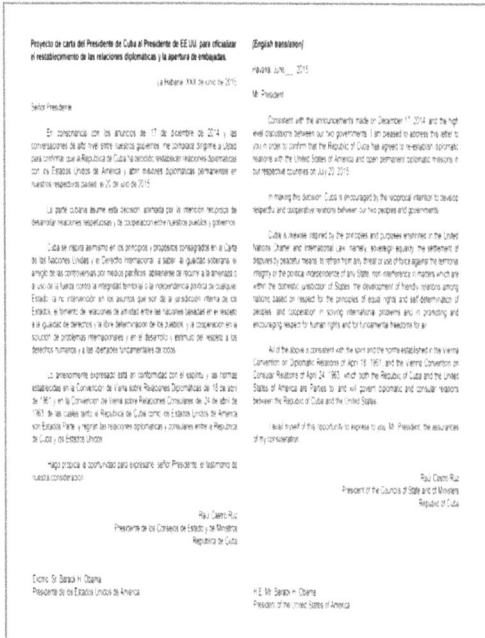

Havana June 2015

Mr. President:

Consistent with the announcement made on December 17, 2014, and the high level discussions between our two governments, I am pleased to address this letter to you in order to confirm that the Republic of Cuba has agreed to re-establish diplomatic relations with the United States of America and open permanent diplomatic missions in our respective countries on July 20, 2015.

In making this decision, Cuba is encouraged by the reciprocal intention to develop respectful and cooperative relations between our two peoples and governments.

Cuba is likewise inspired by the principles and purposes enshrined in the United Nations Charter and International Law, namely, sovereign equality, the settlement of disputes by peaceful means, to refrain from any threat or use of force against the territorial integrity or the political independence of any State, non-interference in matters which are within the domestic jurisdiction of States, the development of friendly relations among nations based on respect for the principles of equal rights and self-determination of peoples, and cooperation in solving international problems and in promoting and encouraging respect for human rights and for fundamental freedoms for all.

All of the above is consistent with the spirit and the norms established in the Vienna Convention on Diplomatic Relations of April 18, 1961, and the Vienna Convention on Consular Relations of April 24, 1963, which both the Republic of Cuba and the United States of America are Parties to, and will govern diplomatic and consular relations between the Republic of Cuba and the United States.

I avail myself of this opportunity to express to you, Mr. President, the assurances of my consideration.

Raúl Castro Ruz
President of the Councils of State and of Ministers
Republic of Cuba

THE WHITE HOUSE
WASHINGTON
June 30, 2015

His Excellency
Raul Castro Ruz
President of the Council of State
  and the Council of Ministers
  of the Republic of Cuba

Havana

Dear Mr. President:

I am pleased to confirm, following high-level discussions between our two governments and in accordance with international law and practice, that the United States of America and the Republic of Cuba have decided to re-establish diplomatic relations and permanent diplomatic missions in our respective countries on July 20, 2015. This is an important step forward in the process of normalizing relations between our two countries and peoples that we initiated last December.

In making this decision, the United States is encouraged by the reciprocal intention to develop respectful and cooperative relations between our two peoples and governments consistent with the Purposes and Principles enshrined in the Charter of the United Nations, including those related to sovereign equality of States, settlement of international disputes by peaceful means, respect for the territorial integrity and political independence of States, respect for equal rights and self-determination of peoples, non-interference in the internal affairs of States, and promotion and encouragement of respect for human rights and fundamental freedoms for all.

The United States and Cuba are each parties to the Vienna Convention on Diplomatic Relations, signed at Vienna on April 18, 1961, and the Vienna Convention on Consular Relations, signed at Vienna on April 24, 1963. I am pleased to confirm the understanding of the United States that these agreements will apply to diplomatic and consular relations between our two countries.

Sincerely,

(signed, Barack Obama)

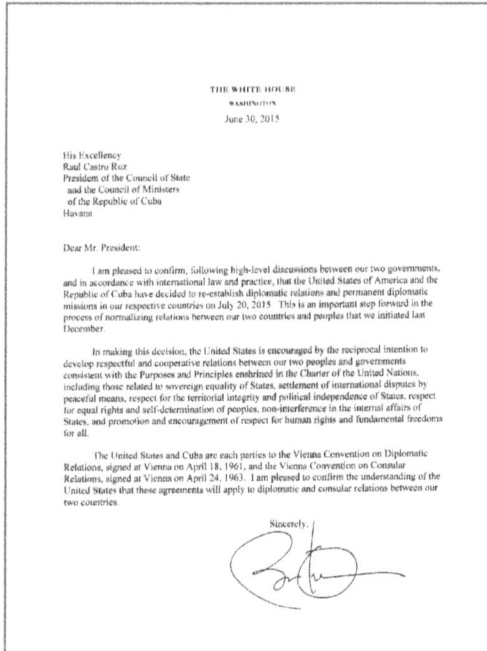

278

About the Editor

The Editor has been covering Cuba for two decades and is a leading analyst of developments on the island.

He can be contacted at: *CubaComoNunca@gmail.com*

www.ingramcontent.com/pod-product-compliance
Lightning Source LLC
Chambersburg PA
CBHW080455110426
42742CB00017B/2897